Observations

At the Speed of Life

ED DOHERTY

NEWMAN SPRINGS PUBLISHING
320 Broad Street
Red Bank, NJ 07701

First originally published by Newman Springs Publishing 2023

ISBN 979-8-89061-288-5 (Paperback)
ISBN 979-8-89061-289-2 (Digital)

Printed in the United States of America

To Betty and Joe.

CONTENTS

CHAPTER 1: LEADING OFF

Third-Class Unskilled

In many cases when we learn some-thing at work or in our personal life, what is learned is not what we expected to learn but instead, some-thing else that surprises us.

If I was ever young and impres-sionable, this is a story about that time. It was a taste of a different kind of life and created both an appreci-ation of those who work with their hands for a living, as well as some not-so-admirable feelings about how some employees abuse the system.

Looking back, even though I had been working for several years by the time this story takes place, it was surely my first "big-boy" job.

The fact that it took place in the middle of Vietnam War made the lessons even more impactful to me at nineteen years old, when between my freshman and sophomore year in college, I worked at the General Dynamics Shipyard in Quincy, or the Fore River Shipyard as it was known in the neighborhood. It was walking distance from my house.

At one time, it was the largest employer on the South Shore of Massachusetts, with three shifts and more than ten thousand employees. It absolutely boomed during World War II. It has been closed for many years now.

I was a pipefitter, third-class unskilled. Great title, eh?

Yeah, everyone knows that when you add "third class" or "unskilled to a job title, it really helps self-esteem. Put both of them in the same title, and you are really making your point.

At the shipyard, your hard hat was color coded to your job. Pipefitters wore baby-blue hats that showed off all the dirt at the bot-tom of the hull. Other trades had green, red, dark blue, and so forth. You could tell someone's occupation by the color of their hard hat.

That summer, I mostly installed liquid level indicators in soon-to-become fuel and water tanks that were five stories high inside the ship, the soon-to-become USS *Dixon*. I also unexpectedly learned a lot about productivity, a little about patriotism, and some things about greed or laziness that have stuck with me.

There have been a lot of outstanding contributions made by labor unions and their leaders in the history of our country. They have made a major impact to the development of our workforce and work practices, but the leaders of the AFL/CIO union I belonged to that summer had no part in contributing to anything, other than lining the pockets of its members, short-term.

But that union did contribute to my education. It taught me how to stop working because I needed a pipe. As a pipefitter, I wasn't allowed to *carry* pipes, I was only allowed to *fit* pipes. If I needed a pipe, I needed a "chaser" to carry it for me. Yes, even from one end of the ship to the other. Even from the dock to the deck. If I was seen walking and chewing gum, I mean walking and carrying a pipe, I could be written up and incur the wrath of the other members of the pipefitter gang I was assigned to (*gang* is the shipyard technical term for team).

It could take days to get a pipe from a warehouse to a ship through the archaic ordering system. This rule, among many, significantly drove up the cost of operating that shipyard and cost the US Navy, and taxpayers, a ton of money.

And in the significant knowledge category, the union rules, and my mentors, also taught me that if I was in the restroom, which was called the sh-thouse in the local language, I didn't have to leave.

You read that right. Once you were in there, you didn't have to come out. Our dock had one forty-stall open-air-but-covered-and-walled, always-packed-to-the-gills restroom, or actually, it was a rest area. It was where I, and many others, slept most days. I could stay in there for hours or until the smell chased me out. Can you imagine a home away from home like that?

The contract specified that you couldn't regulate how long you-know-what should take. To stay productive, upon entry, I gathered all the Boston and New York newspapers lying around and read them cover to cover. I even did a crossword puzzle or three. Even at nineteen, I was into time management and multitasking.

I also learned that a 160-pound kid like me, a college soccer player in peak shape, who could fit through a 15"×24" hatch in the deck that his 275-pound supervisor couldn't fit through, was basically unsupervised.

In fact, in the very lowest bowels of the ship at the bottom of those five-story fuel and water tanks, reached only by a very long and very scary five-story ladder welded to the bulkhead, there were stacks of flattened cardboard boxes assembled by men who I assume had large supervisors. That cardboard was used for sleeping during the shift, with less of an odor.

And finally, I also learned about Pete's. One of the mechanics who was taking me under his wing and teaching me how not to be productive and how to avoid getting caught doing nothing, one time, brought me to Pete's Grille, founded in 1958.

Here was the deal: at 11:29 a.m., a minute before the thirty-minute lunch period started, 250 workers drifted from the ships and warehouses and docks and gathered in lines at the time card shed inside the South Street Gate.

When the whistle blew, everyone punched out at 11:30 a.m. and ran—yes, ran—across the street to Pete's to get a seat. When you entered Pete's, every single seat was preset with a ham sandwich and an open quart of Budweiser next to it. All 250 of them.

They might have varied the cold cuts daily, but the one time I joined in, I was lucky it was ham and cheese. At Pete's, it was free to get in, and you paid $2 to get out and were back in the time card shack at 11:59 a.m.to punch back in (except for a few guys who paid other guys to clock them back in but stayed at Pete's until the end of their shift).

No IDs were necessary. With the shipyard dirt all over me, including my face, I looked of age. Since guys my age were in Vietnam wishing they could have a beer and a ham sandwich in a place like Pete's, no one was going to hassle me.

All this took place when the boats we were "working" on were needed a half a world away.

- Did I mention that drug use was rampant on my ship?
- Did I mention that one time it took me three weeks to weld pipes into a guardrail around one of the engines? A four-hour job at most.
- Did I mention that I had no training on how to use a welder?

As a nineteen-year-old, I can tell you that, given what I was watching daily, I wasn't sure how the boats floated.

Not too many years later, General Dynamics decided to abandon the Quincy Yard since their costs were so much higher than the shipyards they were bidding against (go figure), and thousands of high-paying jobs were lost.

Just before the final death knell, there was some buzz about the workers buying the shipyard to keep it alive. A friend of mine, who also previously worked there, laughed at that and said simply, "The people who are trying to buy it are the same greedy pigs that are causing it to close. If they had worked harder or had been more honest, it would still be open."

I'm sharing this story because the one thing we all have in common with those shipyard workers is this: we control the future of our organizations—whether they grow or shrink, whether they succeed or fail, whether they last for years or close.

Those greedy pigs who were milking the clock, sleeping during their shift, and having lunch and more at Pete's should have known at the time that they were killing their organization one Bud at a time. But apparently, they didn't give a sh-t. They were all about themselves, every day and every way. What you do when no one is looking does make a difference.

That summer, I learned one of the most important lessons a nineteen-year-old can learn: Character is doing the right thing when nobody's looking. There are too many people who think that the only thing that's right is to get by, and the only thing that's wrong is to get caught.

A Little Red Towel

One of the hardest things to do is to pretend that you love what you are doing. We've all tried it from time to time, pretending, that is. It could be a particular part of our role, or it could be our entire role.

Convincing others that you love what you are doing when you don't is virtually impossible. Conversely, when you are passionate and enthusiastic about what you are doing, you can't hide it either, no matter what you do.

I once had a friend who caught my attention with his enthusiasm, couldn't hide his passion for what he did, and helped teach me what enthusiasm is really all about.

At the end of a Red Sox-Yankees game at Fenway Park many years ago, I met the best usher in Boston, Bill Maskell.

Bill was an experienced usher who worked a full shift at the Garden and at Fenway. In his section at Fenway, the grandstand split by the aisle between sections 17 and 18. Just up from the Red Sox on deck circle, everyone who attended even one game in that area knew Bill loved his job. He couldn't hide it, and the fans couldn't miss it. He winked at the girls, could be comically gruff with big strong men, and gentle as a butterfly with little kids. He had something to say or a special smile for everyone he met. Tall and thin, he was unabashedly enthusiastic and talked nonstop to everyone who came his way.

In fact, he greeted almost every fan by name at every game. How did he do that? He knew the names of a lot of the season ticket holders, and (I think) he made up names for the rest—but he greeted everyone, and it was obvious to all that he had a spirit and passion for being at the ballpark and helping people.

Ushers don't make a ton of money; most work the job part-time, but because Bill was full-time, his jacket may have been a little bit frayed at the sleeve, and the small towel he used to wipe off seats for an occasional tip might have been faded, but he loved his job, and everyone knew it.

For a couple of years, I worked close enough to Fenway to hear the national anthem from my restaurant's dining room. I had a standing invitation from Bill to sit in row 32, seat 2 on the aisle between sections 17 and 18, in one of a pair of seats in his section that a season ticket holder never used (something only an usher would know).

He would join me from the fourth inning to the ninth inning, when he was (technically?) off duty, and he'd have some popcorn and a Coke. We talked about the Red Sox, life, and more. Mostly Bill would talk, and I would listen; he had a lot to say, and I had a lot to learn. We sat in those two seats on the aisle, together for six innings, for more than one hundred games over two seasons. By the time we met, he had been ushering for almost five decades with the same spirit and enthusiasm, so I wasn't exaggerating when I called him the best usher in the park. He was not only the most knowledgeable and the friendliest, it was apparent he was also the usher who loved his job more than anyone else.

Bill was almost fifty years older than me when we met, and I'm not sure how much of whatever wisdom I possess was a gift from him, but I know that I try to do my job (most days) with the same enthusiasm that I saw in that best usher at Fenway Park all those years ago.

During my family's last holiday season in Massachusetts, before we relocated to California, we decided to invite Bill to join us at our house on Christmas Eve. We had realized he didn't have anywhere to go during holidays and hadn't had anywhere to go for a long while. He had been a widower for years and had a daughter who lived somewhere out west but rarely visited. Naturally, we wanted to get him a present or two to thank him for his friendship and those wonderful nights of wisdom in row 32.

But what do you get an eighty-year-old usher in addition to maybe some aftershave you could smell all the way to the bleachers? After some discussion, we got him a little red towel he could use to dust the seats in his section, something he would use every day.

After a great dinner, expertly prepared by my wife, he slowly opened the wrapped package that contained the little red towel and held it up for everyone to see. It may have been the first Christmas gift he'd unwrapped in years. He instantly knew what it was and why, and you'd have thought we'd given him gold, frankincense, and myrrh. Of all the presents I have given to friends and family over the years, that little red towel, at that moment, may have been the most appreciated. His eyes teared up as he looked at the towel, and mine just teared up writing this sentence. I think we also gave him that aftershave as well.

We moved away that spring but came back to visit, and I saw Bill almost every year, sometimes making it to Fenway, sometimes to the Garden. The last time I saw him was when he was ninety-one years old. I went to a Red Sox game and couldn't find him in front of section 18 and thought the worst, but his replacement directed me to the concourse under the right field stands.

The Red Sox had found him a sitting job, because of his poor health, guarding the exit turnstile over in a corner, under section 2 or 3 past the ambulance gate. We were glad to see each other, and he asked about my family. We chatted about that year's team and the seasons we sat together on the aisle between sections 17 and 18. I could tell he wasn't doing well. He could tell I could tell.

We made the kind of eye contact people make who are never going to see each other again and know it. I thanked him for being a friend and for all the wisdom I gained from him over the years, and he thanked me for the little red towel that he held up, just like he did on that Christmas Eve twelve years before. He had such a tight grip on it, you couldn't have pulled it from his hands with a pickup truck.

The next year, when I hit Fenway for my annual trip back East, I learned that Bill was making people smile at that big ballpark in the sky. Although I don't know for sure, my guess is that the little red towel went with him.

Two Fifty-Year-Old Cocktail Napkins

On August 24, many years ago, my future wife and I had our first date, and every year we celebrate the event that changed the world, or at least our world.

We were just kids and, of course, had no idea what life had in store for us. I knew within a couple of weeks that she was the girl of my dreams. I think it took her a little longer to categorize me in a similar fashion.

I've never been one to kiss and tell, and in this first-date story, there is no kiss involved.

However, the details of that date are more or less etched in stone, or at least the highlights are.

Act 1

Bill was my big brother in the fraternity, and he went to work at the university bookstore after graduation. A year later, a new girl at the information desk—my future wife—started there as well. About a year after that, I also went to work in the bookstore, creating logoed and graphic T-shirts when logoed and graphic T-shirts first became a thing.

The day my first check was supposed to be there, I walked up to this person behind the information desk—my future wife—and asked if the checks had come in. She curtly replied no.

Well then.

I went back to work, and sometime later—I really don't remember how long I waited—I went back to the information desk, looking for "information" about my check. When I asked again, I got a fast answer like, "I'll let you know when they are here," which I translated as "Don't be a pest," or "Don't bother me again or else."

Not a good start to the relationship. Eventually I got my check.

Fast-forward many months later, and after I left the job at the bookstore—I don't remember exactly how long—my big brother decided to play matchmaker. He shared with me that, apparently, my future wife's current boyfriend didn't exactly have her on the pedestal he felt she deserved, and he thought I might be a better match.

He seized an opportunity to connect us when my future wife, who, at the time, had a brother coaching soccer at a local high school, wanted to get him a book on soccer coaching. Bill offered my expertise to her since I was a soccer player. I went to the bookstore and helped her pick out a book for him. Pretty simple. Not sure when or how what happened next happened, but shortly after helping her pick out a great book, I made the big move and called her for a date.

She said no, meaning that Act 1 ended unsuccessfully.

Act 2

I remember what I said, and so does she when she said she wouldn't/couldn't go out with me. I said, "Let me pick myself up off the floor." She always remembered that line.

With that kind of charm, the next time I asked her out on what would become our first date, she gave me a definite maybe.

Here's the story of that eventful evening.

The brand-new UMass Campus Center building had a beautiful lounge on the top floor with great vistas of the campus and low lighting, if you know what I mean. So I asked her to have a drink with me up there when she got off work. (Note to reader: the rest of this story sounds made up, even to us, but it really happened this way.)

She indicated she couldn't do that since she wasn't yet twenty-one, and they were pretty strict on campus at the time. You'd have to have a really perfect fake ID to get served there.

Little did she know that one of the waitresses who worked there was in an English class with me. So like the big man on campus that I pretended to be, I said, "I can get you served." Well, of course that clinched the date. This was about 4:00 p.m., and I had about an hour to make the necessary arrangements.

I scrambled to the Top of the Campus Bar, found my classmate, and asked her to serve my future wife, who I was going to bring up in about an hour. She refused. Uh-oh. When I asked why, she indicated she'd be fired if she got caught. I told her I would find her another job. After some negotiation, she said, "Put it in writing." So I did.

On a cocktail napkin, I wrote, "I will find you another job if you get fired for serving my date."

She looked at it and then said, "What if I get fined?"

"Of course," I replied, "I will pay your fine." And I promptly put that on a second napkin.

With things in hand, I met my future wife at the door to the bookstore when she got off work, rode the elevator up to the tenth floor with her, went to the prearranged table in my classmate's section, and we both ordered an alcoholic beverage. My future wife had to be impressed, right? Right. She was. Act 2: a success. Now for act 3.

Act 3

At the time, I was working as houseboy at Kappa Gamma Sorority (more fun than the bookstore). In exchange for helping the cook, cleaning the kitchen, setting the dining room, and serving a formal dinner in a white waiter coat five nights a week, houseboy compensation was that we got to eat free. Not only that, but we were also allowed stay in the house an hour after we were done cleaning up, and play ping-pong or hang around.

We were also useful for the sisters as last-minute platonic dates if someone needed an escort to something, so we were asked out about as much as we asked out. Lisa, who was the kitchen steward at KKG, was worthy of the crush I had on her, and we went out on one date to the Delaney House in Holyoke, about ten miles from campus.

It was an old mansion set way back off the road at the end of a winding trail through the woods. We sat in front of a fireplace in a candlelit room. It was awesome.

It was exactly the type of place I wanted to take this beautiful woman who was illegally drinking with me at the Top of the Campus Bar that night.

I had borrowed a fraternity brother's Volkswagen Beetle, and after drinks, we set off for Holyoke as dusk turned to night. I turned right off US 5 and drove up the six-hundred-yard two-lane winding road to the Delaney House, and—nothing. No restaurant, no lights, no nothing. Looks like someone is going to think I am a creep. We were in a very small VW bug in the middle of nowhere, surrounded by darkness, and both of us are nervous but for different reasons.

My future wife started polishing the door as she moved further and further away from me as I stammered my confusion and mumbled apologies to her. She couldn't get out, probably wanted to, and I don't think she believed a word I was saying.

I quickly turned the car around, and we left. As we got closer to campus, both hungry, I pulled into McDonald's on Route 9 in Hadley, where we enjoyed some fries and burgers on our first date. (Years later, not two or three but ten or fifteen, we ran across a story about the Delaney House burning down in a fire, and she finally believed me.)

I wish I still had the cocktail napkins from that night, but I still have her on the same pedestal. We still go to McDonald's on the anniversary of our first date. I'm still a big spender.

CHAPTER 2: SURPRISE, SURPRISE

Cleanup on Aisle 12

"Cleanup on aisle 12." That phrase made you instantly visualize your supermarket and a kid with a mop pushing around a splatter of pizza sauce on a linoleum floor, didn't it?

This story isn't really about supermarket cleanups, but it seemed like a great title that might grab your attention.

I wanted to share a dream that can only be fulfilled in a supermarket, plus some observations about human behavior and some unanswered questions I have about food shopping.

How and why did I become knowledgeable and philosophical about grocery stores?

First (but using a phrase I really don't like), out of an abundance of caution, I was the designated shopper for our family for a spell.

Additionally, I made the momentous decision to seek out the wisdom of a nutritionist. I haven't eaten sprouts yet, and I'm not a vegetarian, but I do put some strange stuff in my basket.

Anyway, as a result of these two forces, I found myself gaining superior and valuable knowledge of the local supermarket scene. What is superior and valuable knowledge? Coffee is in aisle 4, and whole wheat English muffins are in aisle 9. Is that impressive enough for you, or would you like to know where buffalo sauce (aisle 7) and garbanzo beans (aisle 10) are as well? I can keep going if you are a skeptic?

In spite of how much I have learned, there are some things that still baffle me and plenty of things about this world where displays in the middle of the aisle are a thing.

Part 1: Supermarket Questions

Some of the things about the supermarket world I wonder about include the following:

Lobster tank: Are those real lobsters at the seafood shop? How come I've never seen anyone buy one? In New England, if you buy a lobster at a supermarket instead of a seafood market, are you also the type of person to buy sushi at a 7-Eleven? Speaking of food safety.

Produce area: Why is the produce department the first zone you see when you enter most stores? And where in the cart is the best place to put the produce? In the toddler seat if you don't have a toddler? If you put it in the big basket, won't it get crushed by the other things? Speaking of the produce area, it seems to be the only part of the store where you can wander in any direction you want, and most people do.

Hamburger fat percentage: Do we really need hamburgers that are 10 percent, 15 percent, 20 percent, and 25 percent fat to choose from? Could you, in a blind test, really taste the difference? Can we just vote on two fat levels and call it a day? How do you recognize a cow that is 25 percent fat? Just asking.

Bananas: What is the difference between regular bananas and organic bananas? Plastic content? In fact, isn't everything in the produce department "organic"? If not, what is it, inorganic?

Hummus: Who is eating all that hummus? There are mountains of hummus at every store. The variety is spectacular. What the heck is hummus anyway? Is there a hummus plant or tree? So confusing. When I was a kid, there wasn't any hummus, was there? Who invented it?

Snow emergencies: Going to a grocery store right before a storm is real entertainment. I love the adrenaline, the drama, the worn-out staff, the lack of carriages available because they are all over the parking lot, the joy of waiting in a long line with people who have to have hummus to wait out the storm. So exciting, but it also begs the question: How do bread and milk help you weather a storm?

Juice: When it comes to orange juice, I have always wondered if they take pulp out of the juice with pulp to make a pulp-free juice, or do they add pulp to the juice without it?

Cashews: Why are cashews never on sale? Have you noticed that "whole cashews" are 50 percent more than "cashew pieces"? Don't they taste the same? Whoever broke them made expensive mistakes. But even if you buy whole cashews, after they are in your mouth, aren't they just pieces?

Coffee: Why is Dunkin' coffee never on sale? Why are Keurig pods so expensive? And speaking of coffee flavors, what is the fascination with French vanilla? Is there Spanish vanilla and Canadian vanilla?

Cold cuts: What is the recommended thickness for sliced cold cuts at the deli? Why does everyone have a preference? And to make it worse, they hold up the slice to ask you if it is okay, like you could see the difference between two millimeters and three millimeters from a distance. What would happen if you asked for a pound of ham and directed them, "Don't slice it"? How would they do that? What would that kid in the deli do? Call the manager on you?

Befuddled: What do you do, for example, when you were assigned to get a twelve-ounce bottle of something with no added salt or sugar, and you are not really familiar with the product, and they only have eight-ounce bottles with added sugar or sixteen-ounce bottles with added salt? Do you call home or take a chance? I see guys facing this dilemma all the time. I think sometimes my wife does it to me on purpose.

Grapes: Why are green grapes more per pound than other grapes? Are they elite? Did they escape from the chardonnay bounty hunters?

Magazines: Do people still buy magazines from the checkout line, or are those simply props? They might be supermarket decor. Where do you fall on the Meghan Markle controversy? How about J.Lo and Ben? What about aliens?

Yogurt: Forget hummus, who is eating all that yogurt, and how do you decide which one to buy? And when did the Greeks get into the yogurt business? I just realized I don't even know where yogurt comes from. It looks dairy-ish, but there could be a yogurt tree or a yogurt plant. (Told you this was about my ignorance.)

Energy drinks: Is there a human energy crisis? In looking at the number of energy drinks with bizarre symbols on the cans, there must be a boatload of lazy-ass people looking for artificial jump starts. And the stuff is everywhere, even surrounding the magazine decor at the registers. Are people eating hummus and yogurt with energy drinks and organic bananas?

Ice cream: How much melting takes place with ice cream between the store and home? Sometimes I bring in an insulated bag for the checkout bagger to put the frozen stuff in to solve this problem. Of course, they use it for coffee and cashews instead.

Apples: What did I say about hamburger fat levels? Ditto for apples. So many varieties, so complicated. Who invented all those varieties of apples and why? By the way, we all miss Johnny Appleseed's birthday on September 26 every year.

Sustainability: I wonder how long it takes for a rotisserie chicken to dry out, and do they reuse them the next day? Is that the base for their chicken salad in deli?

Part 2: Shopping Carts

My supermarket cart dream is simple.

Some would call it an impossible dream that I get that single cart where all four wheels spin nicely. Can you imagine your glee if you got a cart where all the wheels work right? I think I have personally experienced this twice: once in 2011 and again in 2017.

I also dream that one day, I will be able to pry the first cart I try out of the cart it is wedged into. My regular embarrassment at the supermarket is when I feel weak because the damn thing is stuck. Every time. Nothing is better for the ego than to struggle with carts when there is an audience or line of folks behind you.

But I've done more than dream in the store and wondered about hummus. I have also studied human behavior and may have developed a new interview question: What do you do with a shopping cart after you have loaded your car?

I have realized that whether you are a regular shopper, or you only occasionally venture out to drive a supermarket shopping cart, your personality comes out behind the basket, just like it does on the road.

So I have identified at least three types of shoppers when it comes to returning carts after putting groceries into your vehicle. Which one are you?

The sensitive and courteous type: This is the shopper who may have worked in a service job or is just aware of the tough job of wrangling the carts together and back to the store, or they are just nice people. They are respectful of others and always return their carts to the designated area. And you know what? You can tell they feel good about themselves for doing so. Salt of the earth.

The above-the-fray-and-busier-than-you type: This is the shopper who leaves the cart anywhere they darn well please in the parking lot, even if it blocks another space, because after all, they are busier than the rest of us and have to get going. They are above moving the cart to the corral or back to the store. They just don't have the time for that.

The situational returner type: This is the shopper who *would* have returned the cart to the store or to the corral but feels that it is too far, and the supermarket should have more spaces to return carts, or if the weather were better, they would return it to the store or cart corral. But situationally, they are going to nest it "right here." And right here could be a flower bed, a handicapped parking space, or a sidewalk.

One of the powerful parts of being an author—and I use that term loosely—is that people sometimes remember what you wrote, and although this is not designed to be inspiring or, for that matter, particularly helpful, I can almost guarantee the next time you are pushing a cart with only three good wheels, you'll think of me. And the next time you can't separate two carts, you'll think of me. You might even think of me when you have hummus or try to open one of those flimsy produce bags.

In case I forget, thanks for thinking of me.

Additionally, I hope the next time you debate whether or not to return the cart to its proper location in the parking lot, you think of me and do the right thing. Unless it is raining?

Black-and-White Linoleum

The two five-year-old boys ran alongside the tall barbed wire fence that separated the treeless asphalt pavement from the train tracks beside the housing project in Boston. They didn't know, and didn't care, that the tracks went straight to New York City and beyond.

The two kids ran everywhere as best friends. From the dumpster to the back door of one building and between two buildings—front step to front step. Although there were many kids in the projects, these two were inseparable on the asphalt range they called home.

In those days, you just went outside to see who was available to play, or you knocked on someone's door and asked if so-and-so could come out to play (really, not making that up).

At that time, five-year-old kids, and maybe some even younger, were old enough to hang together without adult supervision or even older-kid supervision. Both of these friends were fast runners, both were friendly, and both shared a bottle cap collection that was the envy of the neighborhood.

Who knows why, but when they weren't running, they picked up bottle caps from the gutter or the playground and counted them. They were working toward one hundred caps when this story takes place.

Both boys were named Jimmy, and both preferred being with each other, even occasionally venturing out of the neighborhood together on the Hyde Park-Roslindale line and running the five blocks to the corner store for some licorice or hard candy.

One day, one of the boys invited the other boy to his apartment to play with the new metal dump truck he'd received for his birthday. The venue? His kitchen floor. The offer was enthusiastically accepted, and both headed off.

Leading the way, one five-year-old ran into his apartment and headed right to the kitchen floor where he had parked his truck earlier in the day, loaded with wooden blocks just waiting to be dumped on the floor.

The other kid entered the apartment, but when he shut the door behind him, he was greeted with surprised stares from the three adults sitting around the living room, and he froze, his eyes flicking from one adult to the next, trying to figure out if they were grinning or grimacing, until he heard his name called from the kitchen and quickly and quietly moved toward the sound.

Once both of them were on the floor, the visiting Jimmy said to the Jimmy busy with the dump truck, "Why did they look at me that way?"

The truck driver simply said, "You're the first white boy to come into our apartment."

With a puzzled look on his face, the other Jimmy replied, "What's that? What's a white boy?"

The perceptive among you have already guessed that I was the second boy named Jimmy asking the questions, and this story is about the moment I learned I was white. When I was a kid, my nickname was Jimmy (i.e., Edward James Doherty), to distinguish me from my dad, Eddie.

It really didn't occur to me at 10 years old that the symbolism of two boys, one black and one white, sharing a truck on a black-and-white linoleum floor was a metaphor for something, but it does now.

I've often wondered what happened to my first best friend, because we moved away, and since there wasn't any social media to bind us, we didn't keep in touch. My family was in the housing project, probably like Jimmy's family, because my dad was a returning Korean War veteran, and housing former soldiers and their families was a big part of what public housing was for in those days.

The two kids in this story had no concept of color when they were six but learned whatever they learned about color from adults as they grew up. Somewhere along the way, probably not as a five-year-old but well before I had the chance to form other opinions, I associated racism with a lack of intelligence. That's what I thought growing up, and I like to think it guided, and guides, my behavior.

I am not perfect, just ask my wife and son and maybe a former boss or two. And I probably don't meet a lot of the definitions of woke that float around out there, but there are a few things I do know.

Five-year-olds are clueless; regardless of color, their adult attitudes are shaped by others and learned by them, not born with them. I was instructed to avoid New York Yankee fans, but very few other prejudices were passed on to me.

Attitudes are perpetuated, generation to generation. It only takes an attitude change from one generation to change the entire future. As children, we don't see the things that come to divide us. Perhaps we see people around us more clearly, not influenced by society's prejudices. Perhaps seeing each other through the eyes of a five-year-old might make this world a better place.

The Golden Rule of treating others as you would like to be treated was a pretty good philosophy at its inception and is probably even more important and valid as a code of behavior today. Everyone is important to someone, and everyone deserves to be treated fairly.

Sometimes when I see a bottle cap on the ground, I think of those two kids running along the barbed wire fence beside the train tracks, and I remember.

Five-year-olds. Bottle caps. Black-and-white linoleum floor. White boy. Golden Rule. Yankee fans. Grinning or grimacing. Some lessons do last a lifetime.

Sh-t Happens

Downtown Boston was not always the vibrant, polished, commercial, financial, and retail center it is today. In fact, when I graduated from college, it was fairly rundown with lots of boarded-up storefronts, petty crime, vagabonds, and despair.

Into that environment, my employer, a fast-food franchise owner, decided to open a new store in what is now called Downtown Crossing, but back then, it was simply a location across from the Old South Meeting House on Washington Street.

Surrounded by those boarded-up storefronts mentioned earlier, and next to a 125-year-old jewelry store, on the ground floor of a mostly empty eight-story building, I was the opening manager for one of a handful of urban franchises in the country.

An aspect of working there that didn't include a manual was handling the lowlifes that regularly visited the location. What's a lowlife, you ask? The two cornerstones of lowlife society for retail spaces were the pickpockets and till-tappers.

A pickpocket is someone who jostles you and walks away with your wallet, whether it was in your purse or your pocket. They work best in crowds, and the crowded lines of a fast-food downtown restaurant were very attractive to them.

It sounds silly when I say this now, but when any of the management team recognized a pickpocket in the waiting line, working the crowd, so to speak, one of them would shout, literally shout, "There is a pickpocket in the store, please protect your wallet." The lowlife would leave. To this day, if I am walking in a downtown location, any city, I move my wallet to a front pocket—much harder to get.

A till-tapper is someone who has studied the location of the button that opens the register and, when no one is looking, hits the button to open the cash drawer and then grabs the $20 bills and runs. They are always on the right side of the cash drawer. Yeah, really.

Less frequent but no less exciting: If we saw till-tapping happening, we would slam the cash drawer on the perpetrator's fingers; they would usually wriggle out and run. This happened while I was standing behind the counter.

So it was this rough-and-tumble urban world that I walked into one morning when one of the crew members stopped me before I could get too far inside and asked me to come with him to the men's room.

I opened the door and quickly shut it again. Someone had used the sink, instead of the toilet, to do their business, and I'm not talking a liquid deposit but a more substantial type of body waste. Additionally, the individual got creative and smeared this particular brown substance all over the walls, mirrors, and partitions. They must have been saving up for this art installation.

I briefly looked at the employees who were on the clock and quickly realized there was no one I could send in there. I knew that I had to do it myself, so I asked the kid who was with me to grab some bleach from the back and another kid to hook up the hose we used to clean the alley behind the store.

With the door open just enough to fit the hose through, I started spraying water and splashing bleach until all the "artwork" was dissolved down the floor drain, about thirty minutes worth of spraying and splashing. I'm sure I held my nose when I could.

I finished up with a mop and bucket and went to resume normal duties. To this day, that day was one of the best I've ever had on any job as a leader. Everyone was upbeat, volunteering to stay or help or get something for me.

- The attitudes and performance were fantastic. When I went to pour a coffee for myself after the rush, I was shooed away with the message, "We'll bring your coffee to you. Go relax."

- I've always been glad that I did it, and not just because the next four times it happened, there was a line of crew members who willingly took on the challenge.
- I was glad I did it because it was an early time where my personal belief in the importance of leading by example was tested, and I passed.

Leading by example is easier said than done sometimes, but nothing impacts your credibility or followers more. I consider myself a cliché creator, and one of my originals that was tested in this situation was, never ask anyone to do anything you haven't done, won't do, or can't do.

That phrase is probably not something found in management books, because it isn't really a management concept; it is more of a personal motto. And of course, I've asked people with expertise beyond my own to do things; that's not what I'm talking about. I will hire an electrician or defer to a technical expert with the best of them. I'm talking about those tasks or responsibilities where leaders and followers are involved.

If you think about it, leadership by example may be exactly how *you* rate whoever is leading you, because if you were to confess your personal, private opinion about that person or that leadership team, it generally starts with your assessment of how well they lead by example or their level of hypocrisy. Raise your hand if you like working for a hypocrite?

Sh-t happens. Leading by example might be the best leadership style of them all. The more artwork, the more important the example.

The good feeling from that day lasted a long time, and word on the street, literally on the street, was that the store I managed was a good place to work. During a time period when many restaurants struggled to get enough staff, that location did not.

In fact, during the annual inspection by the franchisor, the location exceeded standards significantly and was selected the national store of the year.

Free Coffee Is Contagious

As one of my personal habits to minimize stress, feel good about myself, and maintain a positive perspective, I try to make it a point to generally let other cars in when I am driving.

In 1959, a coffee maker was an optional extra in Volkswagen car.

That might mean flashing my lights to signal to another driver, or it might mean slowing down so that a car entering the highway can merge easier, or it could mean letting a truck change lanes in front of me, because it must be hard to change lanes in a tractor trailer.

Now don't get me wrong; I can deliver an artistically appropriate gesture to someone who has earned it. After all, I am from Massachusetts.

I had something happen to me in a Dunkin' Donuts drive-through that started me thinking about a way we could all make the world a better place, one coffee at a time. Deep, I know, but occasionally I do take a deep breath and think even deeper thoughts. I promise it doesn't happen very often.

The incident that triggered this unusual meditative state for me took place about six in the morning, as I was on my way to Starbucks. Only kidding, on my way to Dunkin' Donuts. (When I get a Starbucks gift card, I give it away to a friend named Melissa.) No offense to Seattle Coffee, but I grew up on Dunkin', and I'm not sure how they legally call that other stuff coffee.

As I approached the restaurant, I noticed that there was a car trying to make a difficult move across two lanes of traffic into the Dunkin' parking lot from a side street. Without thinking, I flicked my lights twice to signal to the other car she was good to go, and she did, right into the drive-through lane ahead of me.

I did what everyone does in the drive-through lane while waiting: act bored, change the radio station, and check email. When I finally arrived at the window after placing my order, I reached for payment, but the cashier told me, "The woman ahead of you took care of it." *Bang*—6:02 in the morning, in Rutland, Massachusetts, and someone I can never thank "took care of it."

I started thinking about the dominos in this sequence of events.

First domino: A minor act of courtesy, pretty much without thinking. When it happened, I probably felt kind of good, like my courtesy merit badge was getting closer.

Second domino: A complete stranger said thank you in a very cool way to someone she will never see again. Cool.

Third domino: I was pleased at both the 100 percent discount and the thought. (Remember, it's the thought that counts. But I did get free coffee.)

Fourth domino: She must have felt good the rest of the day because of *her* actions. She knows she is a class act. I bet she had a great day.

Fifth domino: I felt good the rest of the day, too, because my act of courtesy was appreciated (and secretly I knew I could turn the experience into part of this book).

Sixth domino: I couldn't wait for my next time through the drive-through. I just had to pay for the car behind me and feel great, and I do it regularly just for the heck of it.

Eighth domino: After reading this, you might try it too.

The simple flick of headlights to let someone in became contagious. Better world, one coffee at a time.

While I won't claim let someone in while you are driving, and you'll get a free coffee, I can recommend that if you let someone in while you are driving, the world will be a better place, and you might get a free coffee.

And if the next time you are in the drive-through, it feels good paying for the car behind you, you can help make free coffee a better kind of contagious.

A Car Crashed and My Number Was Called

On a clear sunny day, I was tooling along US 3, a six-lane highway a couple of miles south of Manchester, New Hampshire, traveling about 64.5 miles per hour, if you know what I mean, when about one hundred yards in front of me, a car violently swerved to the right, then crossed  three lanes of traffic to the left and crashed into the cement retaining wall between the north and south highways. The car hit sideways, spinning at or above the speed limit, smashing against the concrete barrier, and leaving a debris field of glass and plastic all over the highway.

Just like in the movies, to my eyes, it all appeared to be happening in slow motion. Big adrenaline surge, know what I mean? There was one car between mine and the accident scene, and it slowed down in front of me in the middle lane. I came close to a stop in their trunk and checked my mirror, concerned about getting hit from behind but was able to safely swing around the mess and then realized I had to do something. My number was called. Me.

There was a car crash with potential serious implications for any passengers, and I realized that it was my job to help the passenger(s) first; there was no one else who could get there as fast as me. My number was called. I had no idea what I could be getting into, but I knew whoever was in that car was someone's brother or sister or mom or dad or son or daughter or husband or wife, and I was going to make sure I did whatever I would do if it was my brother or sister or mom or son or wife. Me.

I quickly pulled over into the high-speed breakdown lane, put on my flashers, and sprinted back to the smoking car, not knowing what I was going to find. Even now, years later, when I think about it, the same feeling of dread and shock and vulnerability settles over me. I was very, very scared and unsure about what I would do or needed to do or would be called to do. All I knew was that my number was called, and it was time to act, not freeze.

Adrenaline was surging through my system, if you can imagine, as I looked through the shattered driver's-side window. I saw a shaken-up but conscious woman, in her late twenties or early thirties, covered with white powder from the airbag as the interior filled up with contrasting black smoke. A lot of black smoke.

I didn't really understand why cars caught on fire in situations like this, but I realized that this car could ignite or blow up any second. I watch the news. As I tried to pull the door open to help the woman behind the wheel, it wouldn't budge. It had been jammed shut by the crushed front end.

Oh sh-t. It was just me; there were no other resources in that moment. The other car had a couple of people older and more infirm than me, and they were watching me, along with all the passing cars on both sides of the road. Not exactly the kind of audience that anyone wants to perform for.

And while I have pressure in my job and in my life—we all do—that pressure was nothing compared to the pressure I felt being in that situation: less than thirty seconds after I witnessed the crash, with the possibility that the car could blow up and take me with it or kill the woman trapped inside. Yeah, I was very, very scared.

I spread my legs and got a good two-handed grip on the door handle and yanked with close to everything I had. Nothing. It didn't budge. That was another oh sh-t. I tried again. Nothing. Another time. Nothing.

On the fourth try, thank goodness, the door popped open with one of those metal squeaks, or rather groans. I pushed it all the way open, the door loudly screeching the whole way as metal scraped against metal.

As I helped the shocked driver to safety, far enough away from the car to be safe in the event that it burst into flames, I said, "Thank goodness for airbags."

And she looked at me through dazed eyes and said, "Thank God my kids weren't in the car." Someone's mother.

Trucks and cars were whizzing by on the opposite side of the highway just feet from where we stood. On our side of the highway, cars were inching by, and I could hear the *crunch, crunch, crunch,* as they drove over bits of plastic and glass from the destroyed vehicle. By this time, the couple in the other car had called 911 and told us that help was on the way.

The driver seemed to be okay, but there is no book or podcast that tells you what to do when you have just rescued someone, but I grabbed a couple of bottles of water from my car. I was thinking that if I had just had a near-death experience, which I might have had, I would be thirsty. Plus, I wanted to do everything I could to help because I will tell you, I felt bad for her. I thought about cracking the cap on the water bottle for her but decided if she could do it herself, it would be an indication to me that she *was* okay.

I stood there with her for a while, resting against the Jersey barrier as she called someone who mattered to her. Not sure I remember the small talk between us because there was a lot of other stimulation. After just a couple of minutes, I realized there was nothing else I could do, because, thankfully, I didn't think she needed anything else except a new car.

The couple who stopped with me were standing on her other side, and I felt they could serve as witnesses, if needed, when the police arrived; they had the same view I had. So I walked slowly back to my car, sat behind the wheel for a few moments, catching my breath, and quietly and carefully drove off.

You just never know when something will happen. I wish it hadn't happened. I wish I hadn't been there. And I wish that I could stop thinking about it, especially when I am on Route 3 in New Hampshire. But it did. I was. And I can't.

What I can do, however, is make doubly sure that I pay close attention when I'm driving and encourage you to do the same because anything can happen out there.

I realized after that day that I need to be ready. Again. When my number is called. We all do.

CHAPTER 3: GROWING UP

The Paperboy Saga

Okay, it might not really be a saga, but it sure sounded good as the title of this story, don't you agree? It is about my experience as a paperboy and how I learned about accountability and excuses in a land long ago and far away.

Paper Route

For those younger than fifty, before the Internet and social media, before cable television and email, *everyone* got their news in something called a newspaper.

You may have even seen photos of something called the front page of a newspaper. Boston had seven daily papers. Five in the morning and two in the afternoon. Local towns also had daily papers. That's a lot of crossword puzzles.

You had to be responsible to have a paper route, as well as have an interest in generating extra spending money, and when a paper route came open because, for example, a thirteen-year-old was retiring from the business, there was a flurry of applicants for the news distributor to interview. I got the job for one of those routes. At ten years old.

The process I followed was I hopped on my bike after school, rode the two miles to the news distributor, picked up a bale of newspapers, cut the string, folded the papers, stuffed them in the basket on the front of my bike, and started the trip to delivering forty newspapers in a couple of hours.

Revenue Model

In those days, you got a quarter per customer per week from the distributor, in exchange for delivering the paper for six days. The

Sunday paper was only a morning edition, so no delivery from the afternoon team was required.

You didn't mind the sixth day, which was Saturday, because you rang the doorbell, and utilizing skills you had acquired trick-or-treating on Halloween, when it opened you announced "Collecting" in a firm voice. They gave you a buck for the subscription for the week, and if you were good that week, they might give you a dime tip, with big spenders laying a quarter on you. Some people didn't tip at all.

With forty papers to deliver, you could make $10 from the news distributor and $5–$6 from tips. Let me tell you, a ten-year-old with $15 a week was in the upper-income bracket of most my age in my town.

But this is where the accountability part of the story comes in.

First day on the job: The outgoing paperboy took me around and showed me which houses got the *Boston Evening Traveler*, the *Boston Evening Globe*, the *Quincy Patriot Ledger*, and the *Christian Science Monitor*. It was like a matrix, although I didn't know it at the time. If Excel had been invented, it would have been a lot easier. Papers on one axis, streets on another. The entire route was probably two miles and twenty streets, with one to three subscribers per street. Because it was an afternoon paper, we finished the transition day just before dusk.

Second day on the job: I didn't have the efficiency of the outgoing boy, and it took me longer. It got dark. I couldn't recognize the houses or the numbers as easily as he could. I remember trying to read details in the little book the outgoing paperboy gave me while sitting on my bike under a streetlight. I got home late. I wasn't 100 percent sure that I had delivered all the right papers to all the right houses, but I knew I was close.

Third day on the job: This was the day I learned that close wasn't good enough. Several people flagged me down and wondered where their paper was the day before, why they got the wrong paper, or why they got a free paper. This was going to be harder than I thought.

Fourth day on the job: I did it right by day 4 and breathed a sigh of relief, until my Dad got home. He indicated to me that I needed to mimeograph (copy) a half sheet of paper with my name and address, phone number, and note on it and give it to each customer when I collected for the first time on Saturday. The note said, "I am your new paperboy, and I am responsible for delivering your paper every day. I promise that it will be dry and on time. If you have any problems, call me, and I will fix them."

Lifetime lesson: And that's the day I understood what being accountable was all about, because once I handed customers that paper, believe me, I felt accountable in a whole new way. I owned it; I was accountable. The money was a great benefit to the job for a ten-year-old, but the lesson learned from my dad lasted a lot longer than the money. It has lasted a lifetime. I learned about accountability, but I also learned about excuses, because that piece of paper I handed to each customer took them away.

Excuses: What sets people over the edge more than anything else is excuses. No one likes them, no one wants them, and everyone claims they don't use them—they use "explanations." In the real world, if you have to explain what didn't happen that was supposed to happen, you can call it an explanation, but everyone else is calling it an excuse behind your back.

Sometimes it is easier than other times, but owning it and owning up to it eventually feels better and makes you a better person, leader, and employee. I owned up to it with the paper route at ten years old, and although I've slipped up plenty in my life, and still do along the way, but I always eventually remember, or I am reminded that excuses *are* for beginners and losers.

Next time you are in a discussion, and you hear yourself saying, "I meant…" or any of the derivatives, stop and think about it: Are you judging yourself on your intentions? Are you making excuses? Are you a beginner or a loser? If you are not either, don't make excuses and own it, whatever "it" might be.

When the Crying Stops

There was a movie I never saw but has been quoted over and over that "there is no crying in baseball." I broke that rule when I was thirteen years old, and it had an impact on my life.

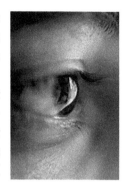

When I started seventh grade at East Junior High in Braintree, Massachusetts, I was absolutely certain that I wanted to be a catcher for the Boston Red Sox. The fact that I lacked size and talent in no way affected my ambition, so I tried out for the baseball team.

It was big jump moving from playing in Little League in the sixth grade, with bases that are sixty feet apart, to the "major league" bases that are ninety feet apart starting in junior high.

So if you are a catcher, the throw to second base to catch someone trying to steal is exponentially greater because of this change. I'm sure there is a hypotenuse or something in there somewhere to figure the difference. I chose the simpler exponentially to explain the change in distance.

The tryouts that April were the first time I had attempted to play on the big field for real. The fact that I couldn't reach second base without bouncing the ball at least once because my arm was so weak in no way affected my ambition.

After the weeklong tryouts, a list of those students who made the team was posted on the bulletin board outside the locker room, just like in a movie or two we've all seen. Try as I might, I couldn't find my name on that list, and trust me, I read it several times.

I did what any crushed thirteen-year-old boy would do: I walked home and cried the whole way. In between the tears, I rationalized that the Major Leagues often sent young players down to the minors for more experience or seasoning, and I figured that's what was happening to me.

Before I arrived home, I had already resolved to try out again the following year. That long walk with tears in my eyes was the day before April vacation, and I was jealous that all the guys got to practice the following week and not have to go to school. It must have been cool.

Wouldn't you know that the very first-period class the day after vacation for me was art. My teacher for that class was Mr. Colley, and of course, he was the junior varsity baseball coach, and yep, he was the one who cut me from the team.

It could have been an uncomfortable class. To this day, I'm not sure why I acted like I did, but as I walked into the class, I smiled (in those days, it was real boyish charm) and said, "Good morning, Mr. Colley, how is the team shaping up?"

I could tell he was taken aback for a second (writers love the expression "taken aback," by the way), and it was probably not the reaction he expected from a rejected thirteen-year-old. He said something innocuous like, "Pretty good," but when the bell rang, he asked me to stop at his desk on the way out.

He told me that one of the catchers was unable to continue with the team and would I consider taking his place? I quickly accepted, fighting back a different kind of tears.

I was so happy to be on that JV team, that I personally carried the bats to every practice that year (to a field about three-quarters of a mile away, through the woods and down the railroad tracks, the same route I had cried along earlier that spring).

My shoes were always shined, and my uniform with EAST on the front was always perfect. I was the typical runt: first one to practice, last one to leave. You know the story by heart because I didn't invent it.

That season, I played two-thirds of an inning (that's two outs). In left field. I did not bat a single time in a game, not once. But that season changed my outlook on disappointment.

I learned that when you are disappointed, there is a right way to behave. I learned that feeling sorry for yourself doesn't have as many benefits as *not* feeling sorry for yourself.

I went on to become a pretty good player. The next year, I was the last one cut from the varsity and became a captain for the first time for the JV team I barely made the year before.

My final year in junior high, as a ninth grader, I made the varsity and played with and against several kids who made it to the Major Leagues. Oh, and I still couldn't reach second base with much authority when trying to catch someone stealing the base, so I played first base and outfield using borrowed gloves, because my only glove was a catcher's mitt.

When I was no longer able to play baseball because an illness in high school caused me to miss a season, I handled that disappointment the same way: I turned to ice hockey full-time. The fact that I lacked talent and size in no way affected my ambition, and I played against about a dozen guys who went on to play in the National Hockey League, including two boys who went on to become head coach of the Boston Bruins (Robbie Ftorek and Mike Milbury).

When I flunked the eye test during the UMass Athletic Department physical, any hopes I had of playing hockey at the college level disappeared, and I handled that disappointment the same way: I focused on soccer and eventually was the cocaptain of a soccer team that was nationally ranked.

Some of the life lessons I've learned, I learned through sports, and some of the most important of those, I taught myself.

I attribute much of the success I enjoyed in sports and in my business career to my attitude and to Mr. Colley. Looking back, he probably didn't have a catcher who couldn't continue, but he was so impressed with my reaction to disappointment that he added me to the team. At least that is what I've always believed.

I wonder how many Mr. Colleys are out there? People who help us along the way because of our attitude, maybe even lying to us to do so. I may have even been a Mr. Colley a time or two myself, giving someone who cared enough a chance.

Disappointment can be a knockout blow, or it can be a catapult to success. That's really up to you, and it depends sometimes on what you do when the crying stops

Put Your Name on It

When I was fifteen years old, I saved $200 from working at the neighborhood variety store when the minimum wage was—are you ready—$1 an hour. Not a typo.

I took that hefty sum and sent it away so that I could attend the Doug Mohns' All-Star Hockey School, which took place every summer in a local rink. Doug played for the Boston Bruins and was a real star.

I knew that most campers were older kids, including many college guys, but I fancied myself as a pretty good skater, even if I was small and even if I was one of the youngest and even if I was one of the few kids on the ice wearing eyeglasses.

Anyway, when the big day arrived, I loaded up my gear, hopped in the car, and one of my parents drove me to the rink, and I was on my way to one of my first and most expensive self-improvement adventures.

I began the first of five nightly sessions at the school by getting knocked flat on my ass during the first hour of the session by someone older, larger, and probably not wearing glasses. In those days, there were no concussions, just tough/stupid kids and uninformed adults. After that hit, everyone took it a little easier on me, probably not wanting to hurt little ole me.

As the week went on, I got to play a little bit more every night, and I got a little more confidence. The last night was the night they divided us into two teams and put us in All-Star Hockey School game jerseys. For some reason, a local television station showed up to film a segment.

I remember feeling excited to go with the feeling that I had wasted my $200 and feeling like I really hadn't gotten a lot out of the experience.

As I laced up my skates before that final scrimmage, I remember thinking that since I had nothing to lose, I was just going to go out and wing it, have fun.

That night, I was skating like the wind (really, the wind!). I was all over the ice with long flowing strides, blowing past skaters bigger and stronger than me. Time after time, I skated around the net with the puck and started up ice. No one could catch me, so no one could hit me.

At the end of the game, on camera, I was presented with a trophy as the Most Improved Skater in front of my proud family. When I recently pulled the trophy out of a box, it reminded me of a couple of things.

At the time, I thought I couldn't skate any better when I got the trophy than when I started at the hockey school, but I was later proven wrong. One of other the lessons I learned was that sometimes you get rewarded when people underestimate you if you don't underestimate you.

Another lesson I learned was that the impression people have of you can be based on one incident or one event or one experience. That's a good reason to *not* have a bad day and to do your best every day.

The third lesson I learned was that I learned more than I thought I did. The year before the Doug Mohn's All Star Hockey School, I was a skater on the junior varsity team at Braintree High School, who never got into a game in a program where varsity had a record of 0–18. That is zero wins and eighteen losses, a perfect season. Think about that: zero wins, and I didn't get into a single game.

I guess I really was the worst player on the worst team in the league. Two years after the camp, however, the varsity team where I was a regular had a better record than 0–18. I think we were 8–10. I was also selected to be on the Bay State League All-Star team.

I was still one of the smallest guys on the ice, and I still wore glasses, but I guess I had some evidence that I was the most improved skater: I had a two-year-old trophy, a couple of newspaper clippings, and a partial athletic hockey scholarship offer to prove it. (Okay, it was a Division III college, and I didn't accept it, but it still counts.)

So as you look back on the learning experiences and judge whether it was worth it or not, remember that sometimes you just don't know yet.

- Sometimes you are learning things, and you don't know what you've learned.
- Sometimes you are getting better and don't realize it.
- Sometimes you are developing skills that don't seem better to you and won't until you are tested and come through with flying colors.

So lace up your skates and fly like the wind because there are challenges out there bigger and stronger than you. I suggest that you set a goal that at this time next year, there's a Most Improved Something trophy waiting for you to put *your* name on it.

More Valuable Than a Trophy

For nearly three decades, every Saturday afternoon, a show opened with the line, "Spanning the globe to bring you the constant variety of sports...the thrill of victory...and the agony of defeat...the human drama of athletic competition... This is ABC's *Wide World of Sports!*"

Sports teach lessons, in addition to the thrill of victory and the agony of defeat.

They do so for both the participants and the spectators; both are more intense for those in the action than the ones on the sideline.

Sometimes, the lessons learned take a while to absorb or process. Sometimes they arrive quickly, and sometimes they don't. This is a story about the agony of defeat that helped me gain perspective that carried over to my post-high school mindset.

The sporting experience that started my understanding took place as a high school athlete. As a senior, our soccer team had a stellar 14–2 record and only allowed two goals all season: two 1–0 losses to Needham High School. Otherwise we might have been undefeated. There was little consolation that Needham was the eventual state champion that year. It still hurt to lose those games by such a razor-thin margin. Agony of defeat is never fun.

Although we might have had the second best team in the state, and second best by only a small margin, we still were not the state champs. That experience, when I was younger, helped change my thinking, even though it seems so long ago

My thinking changed because after that season, I realized that not only wasn't I going to win every time but that I would probably come very close to winning but still fall short more than once. I started thinking that it would serve me well if I developed a perspective to call on when adverse outcomes resulted.

This is not negative thinking, as the optimists out there might claim; quite the contrary. It is a perspective that says you should try to make the most out of adversity by learning something or benefiting somehow or having the adversity make a positive difference in future outcomes.

Although they say adversity builds character, I say I have enough character, and I don't need any more adversity.

In spite of that attitude, some benefits adversity delivers, if handled with the proper perspective, are:

- Adversity creates toughness; not sure there is a better way to get mentally tough.
- Adversity develops persistence, you know, "if at first you don't succeed…"
- Adversity fosters new solutions. Without adversity, there is no penicillin.
- Adversity creates bonds among members of a group. Common shared experiences, whether positive or negative, are lasting types of glue.
- Adversity increases empathy for others. (Don't you feel bad for the players on a losing team?)

Have you ever thought that the most impressive people you know, the ones that are most admired, are those that have faced adversity and not let it stop them? In fact, probably all of the impressive people you have met in your life have overcome significant adversity in their past, even if you are unaware of what that adversity was.

How do I know this? I know this because everyone impressive you have ever met owes part of that impressiveness to their ability to overcome adversity.

The reason that I can be so sure of that is the knowledge that the alternative to overcoming adversity is to give up, and that wouldn't impress you, would it?

In fact, giving up doesn't impress anyone. The reason I can be so sure that most of the impressive people you have met in your life overcame adversity is that the times when you have impressed yourself the most were times *you* overcame adversity.

Let's face it, without adversity in our lives, we would lose one of the most important (if unpopular) measuring sticks we have. Taking pride in bouncing back is always sweeter.

If we can't take pride in bouncing back, then a huge source of our self-worth would be denied to us.

But I do feel better about myself today because I was recently reminded of the toughness, persistence, solutions, bonds, and empathy that adversity has helped mold into my character, and I hope that this paragraph has reminded you of the toughness, persistence, solutions, bonds, and empathy that adversity has helped mold into your character, because those attributes are the reasons *you* are impressive to people you meet.

So would I trade a state championship in soccer all those years ago in exchange for the lesson or perspective I took from that season? First choice, I'd like both, but if I have to choose, developing a perspective on handling adversity has been more valuable than a trophy.

Dividends from a Cheerleader Crush

Remember when you were in high school, and you wondered if you would ever use Algebra 2 as an adult? It might have been a different course (or two), but the linkage between what we were taught and what we use is not always clear. It was Paul Simon who started the song

"Kodachrome" with the line, "When I look back on all the crap I learned in high school, it's a wonder I can think at all."

I had some great teachers and went to a great school, but the class taught by Mrs. McNulty (of course I remember) had nothing to do with readin', writin', or 'rithmatic. What I learned in her class, for admittedly the wrong reasons, turned out to have had a huge impact on my life and, in fact, is still benefiting me today.

When I was a seventeen-year-old senior, a crush I had on a cheerleader turned out very well for me. Although I didn't know it at the time, my effort to impress a girl would still be paying dividends decades later.

Spur of the Moment Decision

During the second half of my senior year, I had already accumulated enough "required" credits so that I didn't have to take any specific course to graduate, enabling me to take classes of interest.

That crush I had was on a girl named Barbie, who was in several of my classes and who may have given me the time of day once or twice. Anyway, I was walking down the corridor the first day of classes and fell in beside her, and we chatted.

She turned right into a room, and I followed. She sat in the second row, and I sat right behind her and looked around. It was the typewriter room. Hmm. Typing?

At that time, boys did not take typing. When she asked me if I was really in the class, I answered in the affirmative (I signed up later). As more students filed in—it was probably a fifty-typewriter setup—I was hoping another guy would show, but to no avail. Gulp. Forty-nine women and me. Some good and bad to that equation, I guess. But all I knew was that I was going to sit behind Barbie for the semester and probably learn to type.

Typing in the Past

When this story took place, in addition to typing primarily limited to females, it was also:

1. Done on a mechanical machine. You pushed a key with a letter on it. A lever pushed that key against an ink-soaked ribbon and left a mark on the paper you had just rolled in. Don't get me started on how errors were corrected.
2. To learn how to type by touch, in classrooms each typewriter had something that could fold over the keys so you couldn't look at them. You had to type without looking at the keys! How primitive!
3. You typed the same phrase over and over and over for measured tests. "A quick brown fox jumps when vexed by lazy ducks" includes all twenty-six letters of the alphabet, of course.
4. Electric typewriters were still a few years away, and when they were introduced, the IBM Selectric, they were very expensive. The reason I mention this is that the noise in the room with fifty typewriters clacking away (I believe that *clacking* is a technical term) could get loud.

Beaten by a Girl

So when you have a crush on someone, what do you try to do? Impress them, right? And if you are in a typing class with someone you have a crush on, what do you try to do? Impress them by outtyping them, or at least keeping up.

Barbie got up to ten words per minute early in the semester without any errors. I got to ten words per minute without errors myself and was pretty proud of it.

- She got to twenty words per minute. I matched her.
- She got to forty words per minute, and I made it there as well.
- She got to sixty, as I proudly did. She has to be impressed at this point, right?
- She got to seventy words per minute, and unbelievably, I made it there as well.

Note: in typing tests, a "word" is considered five characters or spaces. If I didn't impress her, I certainly impressed me. In case you were wondering, seventy words per minute is 350 characters per minute or close to six keystrokes per second (otherwise known as flying). Barbie left me behind at eighty words per minute. The best I could do was seventy-five. My kind of failure. (For the record, we went out once on a date but never saw each other after graduation until our thirtieth high school reunion.)

Some of the Dividends

I mentioned that the competition and the crush on Barbie paid huge dividends. Here's a few:

Dividend 1: I entered college as one of the few men who could type. When I joined the fraternity, I became the house typist for almost everyone's papers and reports. Eventually I started charging for my services.

- If I simply typed the crappy, illegible report you gave me, it was one rate.
- If I corrected your grammar and spelling, it was double the going rate.

- If I stretched your paper to meet the minimum requirement (i.e., a three-page report, and you only gave me one page), it was triple base price.
- If I did original research and wrote a paper that you passed in, you paid me four times the basic rate. Oh yes. I also had my own schoolwork that involved typing, and it came in handy for that as well.

Dividend 2: I maybe wanted to be a sportswriter when I graduated from college. I loved sports, and I could write, and when you put them together = sportswriter. Shortly after arriving on campus my freshman year, I went to the office of the *Daily Collegian* at UMass and inquired about opportunities.

Since I was on the freshman soccer team, they asked me if I'd like to be beat reporter for the UMass varsity team, and I accepted. For four years during the soccer season, my byline was on the back page of the tabloid-style student paper (third largest paper in Massachusetts at the time) with a circulation of more than thirty thousand.

With two games a week, I did two "game tomorrow" stories and two "game today" stories and two "results" stories, sometimes combining them. In any case, I typed stories that appeared four or five days a week for September, October, and November each year.

Probably more than two hundred stories in my college writing career. With so much press attention, the attendance for soccer games moved from the dozens to the hundreds, sometimes into the thousands. At one point, one of the coaches said that if I could play soccer as well as I could write, I could be a star. I was not, but that typing skill sure helped me as a sportswriter.

Dividend 3: It seems everyone can type these days, and computers make it pretty easy to correct typos. In my early business career, I was able to type my thoughts on paper, and it was a big help to my career. So that crush on Barbie is still paying dividends since I'm typing this using the skills I developed trying to impress that cheerleader so many years ago.

Thirtieth Reunion Confession

At the thirtieth high school reunion, Barbie was there, still looking good, and we chatted for a while, and I told her this story. You know what she said? "You should have asked me out again."

I don't think I would be a writer if I couldn't type, so you are reading this because I can still fly like the wind on a keyboard. I get to look at the screen instead of not seeing the keys as I work, and while I may not owe it all to Barbie, that crush certainly paid more dividends than any I've had, except for the crush I've had on my wife for fifty years.

CHAPTER 4: SCHOOL DAYS

Who Moved My Cheese and Crayons?

From UberFacts: The average child wears down 720 crayons by their tenth birthday.

For those of you with small children, or expecting to have small children, you might consider heading to a discount store and buying all 720 right now.

Grandparents and future grandparents, want to be even more of a hero than you are already? Buy crayons. Can you believe each kid uses that many crayons?

I used to spend a lot of time with crayons when I was younger and when I was a new parent. I learned I was color-blind in kindergarten, when I struggled with the blue and purple crayons. In fact, my son, Joe, is my official color validator for all clothing and has been since he could talk. I won't go shopping without him.

For no apparent reason, one day I started wondering about why there may not be a single Crayola in our house. Crayons are still easy to buy; I think they are inexpensive, and there are lots of books you can get to color, as well as walls to color. Why don't I use crayons anymore? As a four-year-old, I couldn't live without them. Why don't *you* use crayons anymore? (If you do, I'll keep your secret.)

Let me count the reasons for abandoning such colorful items.

First: Crayons have a very limited use. Crayons are not good tools for the type of communication or artistic efforts we engage in as we grow. They are not very precise, they leave a residue, and they require a lot of paper for a small message. They are not renewable. Can you imagine how large your briefcase or backpack or handbag would need to be to hold all the crayons you'd need to get through the day?

Second: Crayons are very slow. Most parents might sometimes wish they were even slower so that pages would take more time to color. When we were younger, we weren't in as much of a hurry because we didn't have a next place to go or a next thing to do. I know I didn't have a wristwatch when I was four. Maybe five, but definitely not four.

Most of our day was decided for us, so we went along for the ride. Can you imagine how long it would take to write *War and Peace* in crayons? (Note: I have never read *War and Peace*, but I know it is a long book. Anyone who has read it is welcome to correct me.)

Third: Crayons are very inefficient. Crayons have a doomed storage system. With the first stroke, capacity drops. While a crayon may start out fully wrapped at a robust three inches, it is misleading.

You cannot use all three inches of a crayon. You have to stop with a minimum of about a half an inch remaining, and using it at that length takes work and super small hands, and that is only if you are desperate.

Most crayons are tossed away with an inch or so left. Have you ever thought about all the one-inch crayons that are perfectly usable but thrown away because they can't be gripped? Not to mention the peeling-the-crayon hassle as it wears down. Once that peeling started, and I couldn't read the color, I was in real trouble.

Fourth: Crayons are very fragile. If the crayon breaks because of pressure, you are left with two pieces to work it out or to throw out, and your loss is more significant than at first glance. Now you have two 1.5-inch crayons that you are going to pitch after using about one-half inch of wax. What a waste.

A classic book *Who Moved My Cheese?* by Spencer Johnson is an allegory about changes in our world and clinging on to the past when they change.

To a four-year-old girl or boy, *Who Took My Crayons?* is a better allegory and similar because both questions are backward-facing instead of forward-looking.

If you told a four-year-old they couldn't use crayons anymore, they might think it was the end of the world and throw a tantrum or two. Is that what you're going to do when everything isn't the same in your world moving forward? If so, let me know *your* tantrum techniques, and I'll write about them.

The truth is we don't use crayons anymore because they have limited use, are slow, inefficient, and fragile. Just as we have outgrown crayons, we all will be leaving some other things behind in the next few years. We have outgrown some things, and some things have outgrown us.

Change isn't always good, but without change, nothing grows. Not organizations, not people, not toddlers. Little did you know that life after crayons had pencils, pens, markers, typewriters (for me), keyboards, tablets, and hand-held devices. Imagine what you would have missed if you were still insisting on using crayons?

The more important question, in my mind, is not what was moved or taken, but rather what are you going to do about it? You have the rest of your life to figure out who moved your cheese and crayons part, but time is passing you by if you spend it on those questions right now.

Recent changes in our world require everyone to repurpose skills, time, and effort. You've done it before. Your thumbs were critical at one time for holding crayons, and you have successfully repurposed them to text on a smartphone.

So as you go through the next year, as even more changes to your routine and lifestyle are made by you, for you, and to you, as your cheese is moved and your crayons taken away, my suggestion is that you make your own choice: keyboard or crayon, stay the same or grow.

And remember that as a four-year-old, you were probably very successful at dealing with a new, crayonless normal, and you turned out okay.

Failure Depends

Many years ago, I read a study detailing the differences between those who overcome obstacles or failures, and those who do not. It was an attitudinal survey that studied what happened when people failed: how they failed, what their reaction was to failure, and how they behaved after they failed.

I'm sure the nitty-gritty data was boring, and this is not intended to be scientific review of the paper. I don't remember the source of the study or all the details, but I do remember that two simple conclusions were startling to me at the time.

Conclusion 1: Achievers don't dwell on their failures. They acknowledge they didn't hit the target, consider or determine reasons, realize that things could have been better, promise themselves to avoid the failure again, through better planning or adapting, and move on. Persistence.

Conclusion 2: Others ran their failures through their minds over and over. They dwelled on them and, in many cases, beat themselves up for a prolonged period. They made their failures worse instead of pushing forward.

The first key time as an adult where I think I came through with persistence and determination and demonstrated conclusion 1 was when I was a student at the University of Massachusetts in Amherst. I had joined Phi Sigma Kappa fraternity and developed a vision to become an officer. I'm sure I was inspired by the leaders of the chapter, because through my early fraternity experience, I had already learned some valuable lessons about getting along with others, working as a team in areas that weren't sports, and about myself.

I wasn't sure but suspected that I had some leadership potential, although I had no idea how much I had or if it would ever be activated. I know that sounds strange to have a college-age kid with self-doubt, but it used to happen.

So I did what every self-doubting kid would do: I ran for chapter president and received a single vote (out of fifty-five, and it was my vote). One vote—my own. Humbling. Did not help my self-esteem. So much for leadership. I remember wishing I had done better but moved on quickly after the election. I did win a subsequent position as the new member trainer, so I was still in the mix for something more.

I ran for president a second time (persistence or stupidity?) and received several more votes, but the election was a landslide for my opponent (still a good friend who is still in my circle of friends). I remember thinking that I might never be an officer, I would have to just be a gentleman, and I concentrated on other things until the next election and kept my goal on life support but secretly. Not dwelling on it but recognizing the reality that I hadn't done enough for the fraternity to warrant success at the ballot box for my aspirations.

The third time I ran for the highest office in the fraternity was different, and it was after everyone realized that the fraternity was at high risk for folding because we had a group of seniors graduating, another group that had discovered marijuana and wasn't interested in brotherhood anymore, and a third group that got tired of being around the group that discovered dope. It looked like we would not have enough brothers to fill the house the next fall.

We knew we needed to add a minimum of fifteen new members to fill the house (to pay the rent), so we mobilized. Every night after dinner, for a several weeks, I led a group of brothers fanning out on campus to different dorms to talk to freshmen and sophomores about joining the fraternity. This was something that wasn't typically done then, and I'm not sure it is done now.

Yes, we had people give us some static, some were rude, some kicked us out, and some jerks were interested for the wrong reasons. Not sure you are aware, but some fraternities on some campuses did not, and do not, have the best reputation.

Over the course of the recruitment period, our determination paid off, and more than twenty new men pledged Phi Sig, were initiated as brothers at the end of the semester, and the house was filled (and saved) for the next year. Our persistence and determination paid off with some great future leaders who turned out to be some of my best friends.

At the end of the semester, with elections for the fall coming up, of course I ran again. I was (finally) elected president (with all the votes but one, and it was my vote). It turned out to be one of the most beneficial learning experiences of my life, leading a group to accomplish objectives with some validation that I had the leadership gene. That's when I personally learned that nothing in the world can take the place of persistence.

To this day, when I fail—and I fail regularly just like you—whether it is something big like missing out on a major opportunity or something small like forgetting to complete some paperwork, I sometimes think back to the time I got one vote in that first election. I didn't let it ruin my perspective. Learning from that failure and taking action instead of wallowing helped me accomplish my objective.

Remember, Thomas Edison failed hundreds of times before he patented the light bulb. Not everyone hits a home run on the first pitch.

News flash: you are going to fail at something this year. Bank on it. It isn't the failing that will sink you; it is what you do after you fail. Failure happens; the impact of failure depends on how you react to it.

The Way We've Always Done It

The way we've always done it is usu-ally a pretty good way. However, the enemy of great is good. Things cannot reach great if we are working and settling for good.

This is the story of my fraternity's intramural football team leadership who embraced the we've-always-done-it-this-way mantra. It is also a story that supports one of my favorite sayings: "it is a big advantage in business and life to be underestimated." Nothing else gives you quite the same edge.

Before the story starts, a well-known secret among the soc-cer-playing community is that most soccer players are jealous, at least in the United States, of football players and especially football placekickers. In addition to football players being more popular with girls in high school, they also play in front of larger crowds on Friday night or Saturday, while for soccer, the big games are on Tuesday, at 3:00 p.m., while the buses are filling up. Hardly seems fair.

The only football I played growing up was the pickup variety behind the elementary school. And yes, we played both touch foot-ball and tackle football without any protective equipment. We were kids, and in those days, kids lived a mostly unprotected life.

At the University of Massachusetts in Amherst, intramural foot-ball was a big deal. There were six lit fifty-yard fields, more than two hundred teams, and hundreds of spectators. And yes, an occasional Friday night with lights. My fraternity team had a history of mixed results: sometimes good, sometimes bad. If I was available when there was a game, I would be there rooting the guys on.

During my first four years at UMass, because I played on the varsity soccer team, I was ineligible for intramurals in the fall (well, I might have been eligible, but the soccer coach would have kicked me off the team if I was caught playing).

However, during my second senior year (that's another story for another time), I was eligible and wanted to play; well, actually I just wanted to kick off.

Soccer players everywhere fool around with kicking an American football for fun, and I had kicked field goals by myself for years and had actually visited UMass Alumni Stadium on more than one occasion when it was empty and tried kicking on the real field just to fantasize what it would be like.

A fraternity brother named Louie had kicking duties for the team for several years, but in my youthful arrogance, I assumed that the coach-brother-captain of the fraternity's team would rather have a world-class (in my own mind) kicker, rather than an untrained leg. I was wrong.

At the first game, I went to the team captain and said, "Can I kick off to start the game?" I was told no because Louie always kicked off.

Louie was a big burly guy from Worcester. So I stood on the sideline and watched as Louie pounded the ball about forty yards downfield. Not very impressive, but we'd always done it this way, so who was I to judge?

The game continued until it was fourth down for our team, and we were still about fifteen yards away from the goal line.

But sensing an opportunity where none may have existed in the-way-we've-always-done-it world, like a little puppy, I ran back to the team captain and said, "Can I try a field goal?" He laughed at me because it was so far, but a couple of guys urged him to let me try. I'm not sure if they had confidence in me or were looking for a good laugh; I suspect the latter.

The attempt would be a thirty-five-yard field goal (fifteen yards plus a ten-yard end zone, plus ten yards behind the line of scrimmage to spot the ball). Most teams didn't kick field goals because, surprise, they didn't have good kickers. Going for it on fourth down was the rule rather than the exception. Plus, since Louie had already demonstrated that he could only kick it about forty yards with a rip-roaring running start, this was not exactly field goal territory for our fraternity team.

A short time later, we were leading 3–0, and I had kicked my first ever field goal: a neat thirty-five-yarder. To say I was ecstatic would be an understatement. I was already dating the girl of my dreams and future wife, so I knew the attracting-girls part of my new football persona wouldn't be activated, but it was still a big ego trip.

Naturally, I went back to the team captain, thinking that I had just proved myself, and said, "Can I kick off now?" I was told no because Louie always kicked off. A few minutes later, we had the ball again but had little success and were faced with another fourth down at midfield, the twenty-five-yard line.

Like a little puppy, I went up to the team captain and said, "Can I try a field goal?" He laughed again because it was so far, but after what had already happened, he shrugged his shoulders and told me to go ahead and try. A short time later, we were leading 6–0, and I had kicked my second ever field goal: a neat forty-five-yarder. To say I was borderline obnoxious would be an understatement. To say I was a little surprised would also be true. I knew I was good, but this good? You're kidding me.

Confidently, I went to the team captain, thinking that I had really, really proved myself and said "Can I kick off now?" I was told no because Louie always kicked off.

A few minutes later, we were faced with another fourth down, but we were now at our own fifteen-yard line. Staying in puppy mode but with a little bit of swagger to me, I sauntered over to the team captain and said, "Can I try a field goal?" It was hard to tell me not to try, in view of what had just happened.

It was a big risk. If I missed, the other team would have the ball on our own fifteen-yard line and was almost sure to score. If I had bet on the outcome of that kick, I might have made a fortune. As I lined up, everything stopped; even kids on the adjacent fields paused as the word spread that an idiot from Phi Sig was going to try a fifty-five-yard field goal. People were confused because the team closest to the end zone was on defense, and the team with the ball had their kicker lined up in their own end zone.

You can guess what happened next.

I took four or five steps, and I slammed that sucker fifty-five yards right through the middle of the goalposts at the other end of the field for a 9–0 lead. If anyone applauded, I didn't hear it. I was an official football star (in my own mind) after all those years.

Just as I headed toward the bench, Louie ran out to me with the kicking tee and asked me if I wanted to kick off. I said, "Thanks,

Louie." And my first kickoff almost went through the uprights sixty yards away, and we stopped doing things the way we had always done them, and no one was underestimating me anymore.

There may be something in your job that you are doing the way you've always done that may be good but may also be getting in the way of great.

There are three questions you can ask yourself if the way you are doing things is the greatest way to do them.

Why are you doing it? Because I've always done it that way, or because she wants it done that way, or because the specs say to do it that way, or it has always worked in the past that way, or I invented the way, and I'm not about to change it, or there is no other way, or that's what the book says, or I don't know another way might all be good answers, but none of them are currently guaranteed to produce desired outcomes.

How long have you been doing it? Because it's tried and true, or it's a tradition, or it is locked into the system? Where's the pay phone, the eight-track cassette, the big bulky TV with all those tubes, the VW bus, the letter sweater, the poodle skirt? All great ideas that we don't use anymore because there was a better way.

How long will you be doing it? Forever? Or for a week? Or for a year? Or until you turn forty, fifty, sixty, seventy, or eighty? When something works, we never think it won't work, but, except for Wiffle Ball, everything has a shelf life. Think about it: would you rather be the last person doing something while the rest of the world moves forward?

"We've always done it this way" through history, would have prevented the computer, the cell phone, the SUV, the Internet, and Snickers bars. What are you doing to prevent greatness from happening in your area?

Charmin—Of Course

It took me twenty-five years to graduate from the University of Massachusetts. You can look it up. I entered in the fall of 1969, and my diploma is dated 1994. The math is easy to calculate, and the story is easy to tell.

In my consumer behavior class during my final semester, the graduate assistant teaching the class gave me an 'Incomplete', for reasons still unknown. No problem, you say, just handle it.

In those days, and maybe still today, you went through a graduation ceremony; your diploma was mailed to you afterward once all the grades were in.

- As luck would have it, the aforementioned teacher disappeared and could not be found (pre-Internet, remember?).
- As better luck would have it, I already had a job by the time I was notified that I wouldn't be getting that piece of paper.
- As even better luck would have it, I was newly married, had other priorities, and a different piece of paper.

So I did what anyone would do if their teacher disappeared, and then moved away, and they got married: not a damn thing. I didn't do anything. I just let it ride.

It nagged at me a little bit, for sure. I have always been a finisher, and this was a (secret) black mark on my life. I had attended college for five years, was in debt (I paid $49.86 per month for seven years), and had no degree to prove it.

Just so you don't think less of me, I never lied about it. My resume always stated, "Attended University of Massachusetts 1969–1974." Was it my problem if hiring managers jumped to conclusions? Quite frankly, it was the knowledge gained, the experience of college, living in a fraternity, and playing on the soccer team that facilitated my career, not a piece of paper.

After a few years of marriage, we moved to California, even further from Amherst and even further from resolving. I moved up the ladder without the piece of paper. Then we moved to Memphis, still working up the ladder without the piece of paper.

Sometime in the winter of 1994, the nagging thought in the back of my brain got to me, and I decided to look into what it would take to get the piece of paper that wasn't hanging on my wall. I made some calls.

First, I checked with the University of Memphis and learned that they had a summer course in consumer behavior for three credit hours. I needed four but felt I could work something out. Then I called the Marketing Department at UMass. I'll never forget what the person on the phone said, "Mr. Doherty, we didn't have computerized records when you were here, so we'll have to look in the basement for your file. Can you call back in a couple of weeks?" No problem.

At this point I wasn't sure if any, or all, of my previous college work would count or if it had expired. In the hope that things would go my way, I registered for the 7:00 a.m. summer session class in Memphis and dutifully called back the Marketing Department in two weeks.

I'll never forget what the same person I had spoken to the first time on the phone said, "Mr. Doherty, were you in Phi Sigma Kappa fraternity?" Shocked, I meekly answered in the affirmative. She said, "The dean would like to speak with you."

Totally freaked out and not sure what was happening or why, anticipating bad news, like I had to do all four years over again, the dean got on the phone and said, "Ed, this is Eric. You're going to do the work."

As you can imagine, I was confused for a minute, and then it dawned on me. The voice was familiar. Then I realized that Eric, the dean, was a fraternity brother and past president of Phi Sigma Kappa back in the day. He grilled me on why it took me so long and why now. He then repeated the message that I had to do the work. His message was, "We'll work with you to get your degree, but we're not just giving it to you. You have to do the work and attend the classes and get a passing grade." Deal, Eric. It's a deal.

So a few weeks later, I started the class, and of course, I was the oldest student in the room. I was approved for the three credits and an independent study credit in marketing. I was pursuing something called a degree in absentia.

There was one incident in the class that is hard to forget. It has to do with Charmin Ultra Soft and me. The teacher was talking about the difference between commodity items and differentiated items and said that toilet paper was a commodity. I raised my hand to disagree. The twenty-somethings in the class knew they were in for a treat, and they got it. I debated with the professor for a few minutes that I'm very sure everyone enjoyed.

The next day, I got to the classroom early so I could arrange to have, waiting on the teacher's desk, a roll of Charmin Ultra Soft, not an apple. No message, no comment.

Of course, when the rest of the class filed in, there were giggles galore (what a cute phrase that is: giggles galore). The teacher looked at the toilet paper, looked at me, and didn't say a word. The following day, at the start of the class, she said something like, "Toilet paper is not a commodity product. Thank you, Mr. Doherty."

The rest of the story: One day, years later, after we'd moved back to Massachusetts, I decided to stop in the new wing of the business school to see how it came out. As I was wandering around the lobby, this guy was walking down the stairs and said, "Can I help you?"

I said "No, I helped to pay for this with a donation, so I wanted to see what it looked like."

He said to me, "Me too."

I turned and saw his face and simply said to him, "Hi, Eric."

It was the marketing dean and fraternity brother I had met forty years before and who, fifteen years before, had supervised my degree in absentia. We went next door and had a coffee and covered the decades since we'd both lived in the house. As we were leaving, the last words I said to him were, "Eric, I want you to know that I really did do the work."

He said, "Of course."

CHAPTER 5: THE WORLD OF MCWORK

Like a Pencil Snapped in Half

This story starts out in Brattleboro, Vermont, about five or six weeks after my wife and I were married. I was a manager trainee for McDonald's, and I was part of the team scheduled to work sixteen hours a day opening a new store.

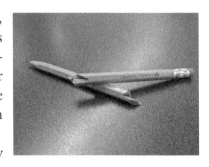

My wife and mother-in-law drove me up from Massachusetts and came to pick me up when my week was over. What happened on the way home changed the next seven years, but no one knew it at the time.

After graduation, I moved into the apartment in Leominster that my bride and I would occupy after our wedding that summer. It only had a beanbag chair, which I slept on, and a refrigerator and a little black-and-white TV. My wife was working at the Foster Grant sunglass factory and would pick me up in the morning, I'd drop her at work, and then we'd hang out. I had a job when I graduated but promptly quit when I moved away from Amherst.

One day, after dropping her off and running some errands, I went into the McDonald's restaurant across the street from where she worked to grab some fries. Sitting there, with no job and no money and an impending wedding, I went to the counter and asked for an application, figuring I could make a little money and stay busy.

They were skeptical but hired me, and I soon impressed them with my grillwork (I had worked fast food in high school). One day the area supervisor, Peter, stopped in and asked to speak with me. He offered me a management trainee position, and after some thought, I accepted it. I thought the wedding announcement in the newspaper would read better if I was a manager trainee rather than unemployed. So after our wedding, I started as a salaried manager at McDonald's with no real plan other than to keep looking for a real job.

After a few weeks, I was offered the chance to go to Brattleboro to open the store, and it sounded interesting.

When my wife and mother-in-law picked me up, I was pretty tired, so my wife drove our little green Toyota Corolla the two hours back from Vermont and dropped her mother off. Then I took the wheel for the eight-or-so miles to our apartment. Our apartment now had a bed, a couch, a beanbag chair, a little black-and-white TV, and a refrigerator.

About one hundred yards from the driveway to the apartment complex, a fourteen-year-old kid in a stolen car crashed into the back of our little Toyota and spun the car around at least 360 degrees and shot it into a Sunoco station. It rested about a yard from a gas pump. My wife had been sleeping when we were hit and woke up groggy. My arm had been on the stick shift, and when we were hit, my arm snapped back and actually broke the seat in half, pushing the top half of the seat toward the rear, with the headrest parallel to the floor. The investigation showed that the broken seat stopped the trunk from crushing us.

My wife asked me if I was okay, and as a recent college athlete familiar with bumps and bruises, I mentioned that my arm was broken. Just like that. I just knew. Somehow we both climbed out of the windows because the side doors were crushed shut, and I sat on the ground leaning against a gas pump until the ambulance came to take me away.

Just like in the movies, the EMTs cut my jacket and shirt off me and stabilized my arm. When they wheeled me in through the emergency room, I remember looking at the ceiling passing by as I grimaced in pain on the stretcher. I always wondered what that view was like.

A couple of things happened really quick in this postmidnight emergency room. First, the attending physician held up a pencil, and with his two hands, he snapped it into two pieces and said, "This is what happened to your arm." Ouch!

My wife came in shortly after that and said she talked to Peter, the area supervisor, and he said the company would take care of my salary for as long as it took for me to recover.

I thought I was hallucinating. I had only worked for the company for a couple of weeks. Even though I knew that it would be months before I could return to work, and they were going to take care of everything? Wow. I don't know if Peter came to the hospital or spoke to my wife on the phone; painkillers, when you snap your arm in half, will do that to you.

The next day, we ordered a recliner because the doctor said the only way to heal the break was to keep the separated bones vertical so they would grow together. That meant that these newlyweds would have unusual sleeping arrangements.

My bride would use the bed; I would use the new recliner and sleep sitting up. For three months. I recovered from the close call by January, but it took me seven years to recover from the loyalty that Peter had shown me and my wife at a most critical time in our journey together.

Now don't get me wrong. I didn't stay in a job I hated for seven years to pay them back. I was pretty good at the restaurant management thing.

But the top two reasons I stayed were, first, I was learning so much about business, marketing, human resources, finance and accounting, leadership, pressure, team building, construction, even television commercials (another story for a later day).

I loved being a leader and developing people, and the franchise company that I worked for was a great place to do that. I was also doing some training and on the new franchisee tour list, meaning that when someone was granted a franchise after putting down their quarter of a million bucks to get started, they were sent to spend a week with Ed to see how a "real" store was managed.

The second reason I stayed was because when my back was up against the wall, or up against a gas pump and my arm had snapped like a broken pencil, someone saw the potential in me and had my back. So I wasn't really paying them back for the salary; I was paying them back for seeing my potential, an even more valuable gift.

Hamburger University: Learning to Learn

The first store I managed was store 343 in the chain of more than 38,698 today. When I started, McDonald's road signs read "13 Billion Served," and when I left, they read "49 Billion Served." Today, they just say "Billions and Billions" because changing the sign took too much time too often, but last I checked, it was over 300 billion served.

Not sure if "served" refers to customers or burgers.

I opened a couple of stores in Boston, one in Downtown Crossing, which at the time was only the seventh urban location in the world. I opened another across the street from Fenway Park.

During that time, I learned a lot about leadership, training, finance, marketing, and equipment. I learned how to learn one Sunday night in a part of a motel that was under construction, and it helped the trajectory of my career.

I have an unusual advanced degree. It is in hamburgerology from Hamburger University, class 213, in 1976.

Even though I did decently in high school and did well at the University of Massachusetts in Amherst, looking back, I realize that I learned how to learn at Hamburger U, and the experience helped me for the rest of my career.

I know, I know. I don't act like I have an advanced degree, but I will tell you that the two weeks I spent in the Chicago area that January were a little bit harder than any two weeks I spent at the University of Massachusetts.

So yes, Hamburger U is a real school but doesn't have a football team or a basketball team.

It is a private corporate learning center. Or today, I should stay "centers" because now there are locations all over the world since McDonald's are all over the world. At the time I attended, there was only one with a couple of classrooms, tucked into a space between a motel that served as a dorm and a very, very busy McDonald's.

The school was founded in 1961, in the basement of that McDonald's in Elk Grove Village, Illinois, by Fred Turner, the first grill man for McDonald's and, later, their CEO for twenty years. Over the past fifty-five years, more than 275,000 people have attended Hamburger University at campuses in Illinois, Tokyo, London, Sydney, Munich, São Paulo, Shanghai, and Moscow.

Believe it or not, students at the American campus can earn up to twenty-three credits toward an associate or bachelor's degree at 1,600 US colleges and universities, the American Council on Education reports.

Here's the story of my hamburgerology degree.

I took a part-time job at the local McDonald's while waiting for our wedding date. The area supervisor talked about me becoming a manager trainee. It wasn't on my radar, but as we sat there, I thought that the upcoming wedding announcement in the paper would read better if it said, "The groom is in the management training program for McDonald's" instead of "The groom slings burgers," or "The groom lies around all day watching game shows and soap operas."

I said yes to the salary offer of $135 per week for a sixty-hour week. Still not as much as my wife made, but it was more than watching game shows and soap operas paid and way more interesting for me than selling life insurance.

After our honeymoon on the cape, I started the job and got to wear a shirt and tie instead of a smock. My hat color changed from blue to orange, and I was off to the races. My schedule was simple: Sunday through Thursday, 3:30 p.m. to close (midnight or 1:00 a.m.), and Saturday 11:00 a.m.–7:00 p.m. I know you are jealous.

My wife's schedule? Monday through Saturday, 7:30 a.m.–3:30 p.m. If you are a clock expert, you might think that we didn't have the same day off, and we almost never saw each other. You'd be partially correct. I drove her to work each day; a coworker gave her a ride home.

We both maintain that *not* seeing each other too much in those early days may be the reason we are still together.

Before you could be *the* store manager of a unit for the franchisee I worked for, you had to attend/graduate from Hamburger University, so when I was told I was heading to Chicago, I was thrilled. If/when I was promoted, I would get a big raise and work mostly days and get to see my bride more often.

There were about one hundred people in the class, and I remember that I graduated in the top ten.

The curriculum surprised me. First of all, while there were some management concepts covered, it was mostly an equipment-maintenance course. We studied grills, fryers, refrigeration, heating, ventilation, and air-conditioning, point-of-sale machines, multiplex postmix beverage machines, and more.

We actually had electives in ice machines, grills, and point-of-sale systems based on the brands in our home location. That's right, you either attended a Frymaster or Henny Penny deep fryer course.

McDonald's took equipment maintenance so seriously that after graduation and during my career there, I actually installed several fryers and grills. No big deal.

The company even required managers to tell the service repair person when you called what the issue you were calling about was. You didn't say the ice machine isn't working; you said that the sight glass is cloudy.

There are two things I remember most about the Hamburger University experience, since I was not, and I am still not, a technically savvy kind of guy.

First, speaking of ice machines. The machine at my new store was going to be a Manitowoc, but I had no experience with that brand. I was a Kold-Draft guy. So I was instantly lost when the ice machine elective class started.

And in case you don't know, ice is made by running water over a cold surface, and the shape of the cubes is related to the type of cold plate, and each brand of ice machine uses a different method; that's why the cubes are shaped differently. Some aren't even cubes.

To this day, when I see ice in my glass at a restaurant, I mentally log the type of ice machine they use. I know, silly.

One Sunday night during my two-week stay in Elk Grove, before my Manitowoc final exam, I had a thought that maybe if I could find a similar ice machine and watch it work, I might do better on the test.

There was a new wing of the motel that wasn't opened yet, and sure enough, there was a Manitowoc ice machine at the end of the unfinished hall. A small machine, but it made ice the same way. I opened it up and watched it make ice for a while. Then I shut it off and took it apart and put it back together. It was the night I learned how to learn. I set a goal, devised a plan, watched, listened, and then had hands-on experience.

I aced the exam the next morning.

The second thing I remember was the final exam on equipment. It was two parts.

Part 1, they put a detail of a piece of equipment on the big screen.

For example, they would show a close up of a pressure valve or a pilot light. We'd have to identify the part, identify the equipment it was from, and describe what the part did or what it was used for and how to maintain it. Brutal.

Nothing compared to part 2, which was a sound test.

They played the sound of a piece of equipment over the speaker system. You would then have to identify the piece of equipment that the sound came from and the part of the equipment that was making the sound.

You then had to write down if it was a good sound; i.e., the equipment was in working order or not or a bad sound. If it wasn't in working order, you had to describe what the problem was and how to fix it.

Students knew in advance the nature of the test, so we studied a little differently. Details were important. Asking questions was important. Verifying understanding was important. If you didn't do all three, the final exam was an excruciating experience.

Fortunately for me, I had already started to learn how to learn, and I aced that test. Even today, when I am in a restaurant, and I hear a sound coming from the back, a strange thought will sneak into my head, and I'll say something to myself like, *That's the carbonator pump safety valve opening and air releasing from under the drip tray*, or something similar.

Don't worry, I don't tell the manager. If I am in a McDonald's, s/he already knows.

An All-Nighter with Larry Bird

In the fall of 1979, my wife and I attended the very first regular season game that Larry Bird played for the Boston Celtics. When he was announced that night, a creative fan released a dove that flew around the old Boston Garden. Little did I know that less than six months later, I'd be with Larry Bird at a restaurant all night.

Some aspect of that evening impacted me so many years ago, although I'm not sure exactly what it was. I will tell you that Larry is as authentic in person as he appears on TV, and he doesn't go around thinking he is better than everyone else. He can also really eat.

I guess the thing that I thought about him then, and think about him now, is that he was and is a hard worker, and one of the reasons I say that is that the night we were up all night together must have tested him.

Most people old enough are familiar with the Larry Bird and Michael Jordan commercials for McDonald's in the '80s and '90s. These were commercials where one or the other called the trick shot they would make.

In these famous TV spots, each all-star legend would shoot a basketball and bounce it off a building or a bridge, hit a sign, have it bounce twice and maybe hit a light pole, and then *swish* through a basketball net. It started on a court, then they moved to the stands and bounced it off the scoreboard, and it kept getting trickier. Basketball players recognize this activity as the game of horse. After calling and making the shot, they'd then challenge the other to match it. Eventually, they started on the top of a skyscraper, and the shots always ended with a *swish*.

Few people know where the inception of the showdown-style spots began, but it was in Boston, during Larry Bird's very first TV commercial, because I was there. Not only that, my sister and my wife were in the commercial as two of the extras.

Larry's first commercial took place in April of his rookie year in a McDonald's near Fenway Park that is now the site of a twelve-story multiuse building.

It started one day, in the winter of 1979, when the operations director for the franchisee I was with, Peter, came to the store and indicated that the advertising agency was going to use the store to film a commercial with Larry Bird, about to wrap up his first year with the Celtics, and already quite a celebrity in Boston.

Because it would be his first TV spot, everything had to be perfect. He was going to film the spot for a brand-new product: a McChicken Sandwich. Up to that time, believe it or not, McDonald's had spent twenty-five years testing fried chicken, and it just didn't catch on. The introduction of the McChicken was hoped to be the breakthrough product for the five thousand stores in the system, to be tested in the New England market.

Because I supervised the restaurant, my job was to find the extras, make sure the restaurant was clean, direct all nonunion staff as needed, and then, believe it or not, make sure that the HVAC and exhaust system was shut down for each filming sequence to avoid background sound. I guess I was an assistant producer, but no one called me that. Usually they just said, "Hey, Ed."

Part of the assignment was easy: the full- and part-time managers of the store, including several college students, plus a sister and a wife, would be the extras in the commercial. Nepotism? No, practical. My sister worked there, and we needed a crew person in uniform, and my wife was so beautiful, why wouldn't I start her on the way to Hollywood?

The filming took place in that brand-new McDonald's, close enough to Fenway Park that when they played the national anthem at the park, you could hear it in the dining room.

So there I was for the first commercial and the first bank-it-off-the   moment in McDonald's/Larry Bird history. It took place about 3:30 a.m., but I'm getting ahead of myself.

The restaurant closed at 4:00 p.m. for the shoot and quickly filled up with the real nepotism crowd: friends of his agent, all kinds of marketing, and McDonald's brass. In the 160-seat restaurant, there were probably more than one hundred hangers-on in the building. Lots of suits.

A Winnebago pulled up about 4:30 p.m., and that's where Larry Bird would be hanging out between the takes.

Once all the lighting was set, the sound was checked, and twelve freshly prepared new, never-before-seen McChicken Sandwiches were ready, we shut down the HVAC fans and began shooting. Except every time Larry Bird squeezed a sandwich to take a bite, the chicken slipped out due to the special sauce and lettuce on the caramelized bun.

For the rest of the night, we made a version of the McChicken Sandwich without sauce to prevent this squeeze out, which looked bad on film. The sandwiches didn't taste as good but looked better to the camera, and the breaded chicken patty stayed between the bun halves.

Lights, camera, action! "Larry Bird, what are you doing here?" Stop. Let's do that again. "Larry Bird, what are you doing here?"

Cut. Let's try that one more time. Before we were done—over a period of six or seven hours—Larry had bites of dozens and dozens of McChicken Sandwiches. The damn actor hired for the part just couldn't get it right. He was standing on a milk crate leaning over a half-wall, staring at Larry Bird. Everyone but Larry appeared frustrated, but he stayed cool.

On each break, Larry would head to the trailer. And each time the filming started again, as it got later and later, the crowd of onlookers would get smaller and smaller. By the time we had our union-prescribed lunch break at 11:30 p.m., all of the big shots had gone home, and it was just Larry, the crew, and the extras (including a six-year-old boy who was sleeping in a booth and who, by law, should not have been in the building at that hour on a video shoot.)

Naturally on the break, we served—what else—McChicken Sandwiches to the crew and extras, and guess who took one? Yep, Larry Bird. I was impressed, not only with the size of his digestive system but by the fact that he was putting his mouth where his money was.

The other thing that impressed me about Larry Bird? Once the crowd of spectators left, he stopped using his trailer and just hung out with us in the restaurant dining room, shooting the breeze. That's right, I sat next to Larry Bird and talked basketball at one o'clock in the morning.

Once the incompetent actor who took way too many takes to get "Larry Bird, what are you doing here" was done with that single line to everyone's satisfaction, the fun started. The rest of the filming consisted of Larry crumpling up the bag his sandwich came in, shooting it at the menu board, having it bounce off, hitting the top of the register where my sister Susan looked surprised, and then landing in the hands of the six-year-old boy, who promptly slam-dunked it into a trash receptacle.

That segment didn't take too many tries, maybe only a half-dozen. When the director yelled "That's a wrap" (yes, they really did say that), everyone was free to leave.

That was right around 4:00 a.m., and we all were tired and worn out, except the six-year-old kid who slept in a booth most of the night.

The thing I always remember about that night was the fact that Larry Bird ate a McChicken Sandwich on the break. After taking bites of dozens of them, made incorrectly for the camera and many of them cold, he dug into a perfectly made hot, fresh one and finished it, sitting around a large table in the lobby with a bunch of McDonald's employees, shooting the breeze. For some reason, that had a big impact on me.

He was taking the money to endorse a product, and he apparently actually liked the product. In some ways my all-nighter with Larry Bird mirrored his eventual hall of fame career; he led by example, was authentic, and did his best. What a great formula for the hall of fame and everyday leadership.

Excuses Are for Beginners and Losers

We are all fascinated by excuses. Whether they are from government leaders, corporate executives, Hollywood celebrities, or teams eliminated from the playoffs, we frequently talk about excuses.

We actually do more than that. We judge the excuses and drop them into two categories: valid explanations or flimsy attempts to pass the blame. We all do it, but have you ever wondered why we do it and how we categorize them? Or more importantly, how others see our excuses?

I was told that excuses were for beginners and losers by a college student, who may have never realized how and what he taught his supervisor many years ago, in a long-gone restaurant visible from Fenway Park.

I've never forgotten the lesson, although I've fallen short of its ideals many times. My memories, the thoughts, and lessons I learned follow. You might need a mirror to finish the story.

One day, when I was managing that restaurant years ago, a part-time shift manager-college student reinforced a lesson I originally learned as a paperboy. His name is Carlton Knox.

It was a payday, and when he received his check, it was wrong. It was short by a couple of hours, and that meant it was short a lot of money for a college kid. He confronted me about it. I apologized for the error, gave him an explanation, and maybe indicated that I must have had a problem reading his time card and told him I'd add the hours and the money to his next check. I turned to walk away. As I did, he stared at me and said, "Excuses are for beginners and losers. Which one are you?"

I was taken aback! (Another phrase I've always wanted to use in a sentence.) I mumbled something else, not sure what, and apologized again. I might even have pulled the amount out of my pocket and offered it to him, I don't remember, but he stomped off, not ready to join my fan club at all.

I thought about his comment long and hard. I was certainly not a beginner, so apparently I was a loser, at least based on the evidence? From his perception, he didn't care which I was because I had impacted his wallet.

Looking back, it changed my approach. Evidence of that is I'm repeating the quote decades later, I remember his name, and I've shared this story with teams throughout that time. All of us know that sticks and stones may break our bones, but words can have a bigger impact.

Think about a teacher, mentor, supervisor, or partner who said to you, "That's an excuse." How did that make you feel? See, calling each other out for excuses is one of the ultimate judgments people pass on each other, and it doesn't feel very good.

Excuses are for beginners and losers, Carlton told me, and we generally don't want to be considered in either category, ever. So how do we avoid excuses? Well, the first step is probably understanding the difference between an excuse and an explanation.

It turns out that, just like beauty, the difference is in the eye of the beholder. An excuse and an explanation can be the same thing with the same words, just viewed from different perspectives. In fact, the definition of *excuse* at Dictionary.com includes the word *explanation*: "Excuse: an explanation offered as a reason; a plea offered in extenuation of a fault or for release from an obligation, promise, etc."

Most of us live in a double-standard world when it comes to excuses, and that could be because of human nature.

We all tend to judge ourselves based on our intentions and to judge others based on their actions.

Some familiar examples?

- Get stopped by an officer of the law for going just a little too fast? We give an explanation that she hears as an excuse.
- Forget to bring milk home? We give an explanation that he hears as an excuse.

- Late for a meeting? We give an explanation that the others hear as an excuse.
- Miss a deadline? We give an explanation, but no one is happy with our story.

It's almost like every time we are sharing why something didn't happen as anticipated, that it comes with a checkbox where the listener can check one.

___Excuse   ___Explanation

Interestingly enough, whether a reason is viewed as an excuse or an explanation by someone else comes down to their value judgment of the quality and scope of the excuse. Think about these explanations/excuses for the same level of tardiness:

- Ten minutes late for a meeting because you helped deliver a baby in the parking lot? Explanation accepted; you're a hero. Especially if you are not a physician.
- Late ten minutes because the line at Starbucks was slow? Borderline acceptance by a few but not accepted at all by Dunkin' Donuts fans. It was your own fault.
- Late ten minutes because you stopped for a Three Musketeers bar? No one thinks that is justified. A KitKat bar maybe, but not a Three Musketeers bar.

When we hear it, we judge it.

And we all regularly use phrases like these to mitigate our excuse/explanation: 'I tried to, I meant to, I planned to, I intended to, I was going to.'

These are go-to words when we are probably judging ourselves by our intentions. But by doing so, we are likely making and accepting excuses from ourselves. The reason? These are all behavior-excusing phrases and the kinds of phrases used by—you guessed it—beginners and losers.

When we don't make excuses, we get more things done more often and are a little better at judging ourselves in a manner similar to how others judge us—by actions. Excuses can pop into our heads just before failure or the realization that we are not going to hit the goal we wanted or expected.

Our typical first reaction sometimes is, it couldn't be me. Our last reaction is to hold up a mirror. Maybe holding up the mirror first could save everyone a lot of time? Hard to do sometimes.

Here's an example to illustrate the difference between intentions and actions.

Let's say that you had a friend with a serious cut that you had bandaged to stop the bleeding but needed to get him or her to a hospital or urgent-care facility right away, but when you arrived, it was closed. What would you do?

There are only two choices: go home or find another facility. And if you kept going and that next facility was closed, what would you do?

There are only two choices: go home or find another facility. Some people would keep going until they found a facility open; others would say, I tried, I wanted to, I intended to, I meant to. Sorry, pal. All these are words that excuse the behavior of not delivering the goal of better treatment. Why they were all closed is another matter.

But what if you are a beginner? It is best to let those that will be judging you know. You don't have to shout it or wear a sigh, but maybe both can work depending on the situation. When I ran a restaurant company, I had all first-week servers wear a button that said, "I'M TRAINING AND I'M TRYING," and it was incredible how the customers were more empathetic to them. If they had worn a button that said, "I'M THE BEST SERVER IN AMERICA," I don't think the empathy would be as high for an error.

Of course, I never posted a sign that said, "THE KITCHEN HELP IS TRAINING AND TRYING. GOOD LUCK WITH YOUR FOOD." That would have been overkill. You probably can't say I'm training and I'm trying in your role, because it is not true.

So if we are not beginners and not losers, what are we? A producer.

We produce results. In fact, we were hired or promoted or assigned or were born into a role where we are expected to get results. If we don't, we might want to consider the fact that we might be exhibiting beginner behavior or loser behavior because both categories don't know how to get it done.

If we have a reputation or image as a producer or someone who delivers, when we give an explanation for the occasional nondelivered item, we are more likely to be judged as providing an explanation rather than making an excuse. If we don't have that credibility because of past performance or newness, then Carlton is right.

Moral of the story: Don't expect everyone else to be as easy on you as you are.

The next time you give an explanation/excuse, think about the fact that excuses are for beginners and losers and judge yourself based on your actions, not intentions, and you will do better.

CHAPTER 6: CALIFORNIA DREAMIN'

It's All Your Fault

We called her Nana.

Five siblings shared the role of making sure that our ninety-plus-year-old mom had a daily visit from one of us. When it was my day or days, I'd stop by and do a couple of simple things on a list she sometimes made for me.

Occasionally, I did the dishes, organized the refrigerator, and took out the trash. I was in the restaurant business for several decades, so not only are old habits hard to break, I happen to be very good at most of my old habits. Two of my sisters performed much more important and frequent functions.

As part of my visits, I provided a detailed update on, well, what I was up to: where I'd been, how I'd been, and with whom I'd been. (Does anyone know if it is *who* or *whom*? I think it's whom, so I'm going with it.)

One week after a particularly robust report to her on my volunteer service to organizations old and new, some medical experiences, a live music event or three, a run or two, and a little bit of travel, she looked me right in the eye and said, "You lead a very, very interesting life. And it's your own fault." It gave me pause. My mother was a profound philosopher.

I realized I do lead an interesting life, now that you mention it. Driving back from my mom's apartment, I thought about the fact that I've always led an interesting life. I mean always.

I've had years where I went to more than 120 live music shows, and others where I went to seventy Major League Baseball games, and years where I traveled on private jets (the reason I don't like riding on roller coasters).

I've run half-marathons, a whole marathon, been in dozens and dozens of football, basketball, and hockey stadiums. I've met governors, ambassadors, and senators, not to mention country stars

Shania Twain, Kenny Chesney, and Keith Urban and rock legend Peter Frampton. I even shared a pizza with a guy named Wayne Huizenga, the owner of the Miami Dolphins, and went drinking with a guy named Al Copeland, the founder of Popeye's Chicken, in San Francisco.

And of course, being married to the girl of my dreams, currently my proofreader, for more than many years has been very interesting as well.

So I've led an interesting life. Buy why? Accidental or planned? I started thinking about whose job it is to make our lives interesting. Who did we assign that responsibility to? When did we assign it? The reality is my mom was right: if your life is interesting, or if it is not, it is your own fault. No one cares about your life being interesting as much as you do. No one has more at stake than you do.

If you look at the work side of things, the question could be posed: Whose job is it to make your job interesting? If you totally rely on your company or supervisor to make your job interesting, you probably have a boring job.

When you think of the most interesting parts of your job or your personal life, my guess is that you had something to do with it by customizing the role or creating that twist or that enhancement to something basic you really find interesting.

It's not too late to make your life interesting. Here's a simple example of a time where interesting life was the goal.

I worked in California with a guy from New Hampshire, Bill Garrett, and we would commiserate that we were too far from Fenway or the Garden or Foxboro to attend games, and we missed the experience. In those days, for example, there was one year the Celtics won the world championship, and the games were not even on TV in Los Angeles. Not. On. TV. It was hard to get a Boston sports fix out there.

One night, while sipping cheap chardonnay on Stearns Wharf in Santa Barbara harbor (the best place in the world to drink and a very interesting place on its own), we came up with the idea to make our lives as New England sports fans more interesting.

Within two years, we had seen the Patriots play in Anaheim and Seattle. We saw the Red Sox play in San Diego, Anaheim, Oakland, and Seattle, plus the Celtics and Bruins play in Los Angeles. I can assure you, our lives were more interesting as a result. We timed our travel and work schedule to be in those cities when one of our favorite teams was playing. It actually wasn't that hard.

I use this example to illustrate the fact that many people don't lead interesting lives because they give away the capacity to do so. Living an interesting life isn't their goal. Many people settle for boring.

Why wasn't last week an interesting week for you? Who did you assign the task of making your week interesting? What do you think could make your life interesting this week if your goal was to make your life interesting? (While keeping it legally, socially acceptable.)

As you go through the week, ask yourself questions about interesting. For example, are you watching TV because you're bored? Or are you bored because you are watching TV? The world doesn't owe you interesting; you owe you interesting. Whether you have an interesting life or not, it's clearly your own fault. It's your own fault.

Feedback Is a Gift

We are all good at some-
thing. Some are good at multiple
things. The single fastest way to
get better is to get feedback, but
few are good at providing it, and
fewer still are good at receiving it.

Every year during the performance review season, I tried to
encourage people to receive feedback that would help them.

Some accepted feedback and improved. Others were the "smartest person in the room" and rejected it. In my mind, an absolutely
terrible career and financial decision.

This story is about a time I received some very blunt feedback
and how it changed the course of my business career, for the better.

Every time I see the Texaco sign, I think of this story.

Earlier in my career, I had a job as the regional operations director for a national restaurant chain, and my territory consisted of
Central and Southern California.

Altogether I had fifty-six restaurants within my area of responsibility, millions of dollars in revenue, and thousands of employees,
and I can tell stories for days about the two years I spent in this
market.

I was a couple of months into the job, and it was time for the
regional vice president to tour stores with me. Touring stores is the
technical term for visiting a lot of stores in one day, meeting the managers and staff, doing a quick inspection, maybe having a cup of coffee, or discussing a marketing promotion or policy and moving on.

We left our Santa Barbara office about 7:00 a.m. and drove
one hundred miles to Los Angeles and visited ten to twelve locations
before calling it a day. Because I did this type of thing regularly, there
was a Texaco station in Camarillo, on the Ventura Freeway, about
halfway back, where I always stopped and filled up my tank at night
on the way home, so I was ready for travel the next day (in this job,

I drove more than fifty thousand miles a year, so full-tank planning was important).

I had my Texaco credit card in the car visor, I had a receipt envelope between the seats, I knew the station and the pump to pull into, and I really had the simple process down pat.

As we pulled out of the station to head back to the regional office, the RVP said to me something like this, "After spending the day with you and visiting your stores, I have identified what you do best." I was pretty excited to have this senior person share his thoughts with me until he said, "Getting gas." In response to my quizzical look, he said, "Ed, you really know how to get gas, but unless you do a better job at a lot of other things, you aren't going to make it."

Getting gas. High praise in the LA world, but not exactly the type of feedback I was looking for.

Over the next six months, in part because I was so receptive to his feedback, our weekly one-on-one sessions turned into private training classes rather than pounding sessions.

He would share a concept or critique my work, and I would try the method or revise my methods and report back. Gradually, my numbers and other factors improved, and on subsequent store tours, the cleanliness, organization, and management team knowledge and professionalism improved as well.

I became better at more than getting gas, although it remained a strong suit. In fact, I became better at a lot of other things, and about a year later, when that VP was promoted to manage the Northwest US and needed a right-hand person to manage the San Francisco region for him in his new role, guess who was selected? The guy who, at one time, could only list getting gas in the excellence column.

The lessons he taught me kept getting applied in my new role as director of operations in Northern California, and my skills developed and expanded, and eventually when he moved into the corporate office, guess who became the new regional vice president for San Francisco and Seattle? Me and my Texaco card.

There is no guarantee you will be promoted if you accept feedback. There is also not a guarantee that you will be happier or feel better about your personal life if you get feedback. But there is a guarantee that you will not progress and develop at the same rate if you create a feedback-free bubble around yourself.

In my career, I have observed that the most frequent waste of talent happens when someone doesn't accept feedback. We've all heard of the glass ceiling. Some people carry around their own glass because they reject feedback that doesn't agree with their self-perception. Almost everyone reading this knows someone like that. If it's you, I recommend a different approach.

My business career is not the result of being told that getting gas was what I did best. What changed the trajectory was someone taking the time to give feedback to someone who wanted it. In this example, if I had rejected the feedback, I might be in a very different place. Who knows?

For the feedback loop to work, it requires us to:

Perform: Demonstrated performance or activity with someone paying attention. That means either someone who has to pay attention or someone who cares.

If you don't have someone paying attention, find someone who cares. And if you don't have someone who cares, find someone who is paying attention. Your attitude about accepting feedback has a huge impact on this.

Permit: The person or persons paying attention need(s) to be authorized or have permission from *you* to give feedback.

Feedback may be hard to receive, but in my experience, it is even harder to give. Rarely have I provided feedback without permission to do so. It just doesn't work well. The best way for you to grant permission? Ask for feedback. That not only grants permission but demonstrates your attitude about accepting feedback and has a huge impact on this.

Process: The feedback needs to be accepted, understood, and processed. Listening and hearing needs to take place so that the feedback is understood. Whoever gives you feedback knows that you get it by the light bulb over your head when it clicks on. Your attitude about accepting feedback has a huge impact on this.

Plan: The feedback needs to be incorporated into future planned behavior. Talk is cheap. The way you prove you have processed feedback is by your future actions. Your attitude about accepting feedback has a huge impact on this.

Progress: Follow-up feedback on progress or performance also needs to take place. The person who is paying attention or the person who cares (in a perfect world, the same person) needs to circle back and verify or validate the change. Your attitude about accepting feedback has a huge impact on this.

If you had any doubts before, you should feel pretty comfortable that your attitude about accepting feedback has a huge impact on your future. Who do you know who could tell you that the best thing you do is get gas?

Don't Try This at Home

We all develop our own leadership style if we are tasked with
leading others. Even if we don't
have direct reports, we might have
peers or friends to influence, and
we develop a style, if not a reputation, that clings to us.

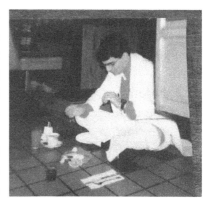

There is a style that you don't
need to take a college course to
understand, and you don't even
need to read a book.

I have always found that leading by example, or at least trying
hard to lead by example, is at the core of most good leadership styles.
It has been my personal model, and I try very hard, every day, to lead
by example.

The opposite of lead by example is hypocrisy, and that is a turn-
off for almost everyone, and the quickest way to lose a team, lose
respect, and lose the label leader.

There is also an expression, "It's hard to get in trouble with your
mouth shut." This is a story of a time where opening my mouth,
implementing a cliché, and leading by example worked well in an
effort to inspire others to raise standards and excel. It involves a waffle, a tuxedo, and a marching band.

After a fairly successful stint in the Los Angeles-Santa Barbara-
Orange County area, I was promoted during a reorganization to
lead a group of sixty-eight locations representing almost $50 million
in revenue from an office in San Francisco that covered Northern
California and part of Nevada. The territory included Sacramento,
Lake Tahoe, and Reno, and yes, lucky me, the Napa Valley wine
country.

A well-known secret of multiunit supervisors everywhere
in every occupation: the first task in a new assignment is to clean
things up. That might mean the finances, the inventory, the human
resources, the landscaping, or the management team. It might also

mean the sanitation, and in my case, for this new region, it meant all of the above.

Early on, things were so bad that I wasn't sure if I had been promoted or punished with the new role. There weren't many locations in my new territory where I'd let my wife or mother use the restroom—always my standard for a clean restaurant. Insider tip: if the restrooms are clean, the kitchen is clean too. Take my word for it.

The only good part of the job was a cool office on the twenty-fourth floor in downtown San Francisco.

Some of you may know that California has a different kind of health code. Violations are considered, or were considered then, criminal acts. That's right. In addition to closing the restaurant for serious violations, those responsible can be put in jail. Back in LA, during my first month on the job, I actually appeared in court on behalf of a location I hadn't visited yet, with a judge who threatened to put me in jail unless I cleaned it up. (For the curious, I was successful and didn't serve time.)

Anyway, my point is that the health departments in that state don't mess around, and before I tackled the finances, the inventory, the human resources, the landscaping, or the management team, I had to get things cleaned up.

My plan was simple: Visit each restaurant regularly. Make suggestions on improvement. Recognize progress and results.

Regular visits: I decided that I would announce my visits rather than surreptitiously sneak in, although trust me, I did do that a time or two. I was more concerned about what the store teams knew than what they used. Until I knew what their actual level of knowledge might be, I would be unable to understand how to solve any issue. My logic was simple: If something was wrong on an announced visit, they either didn't know it was wrong, or they didn't know how to fix it, and teaching was the solution. The gap between what they knew and what they used I referred to as the hypocrisy gap.

Suggestions: I rated each restaurant on each visit either green for good, yellow for getting there, or red for this place really sucks. On every visit, I did something to advance the cause of cleanliness. It might have been done with words of praise to maintain the standard, or it might have been done through more direct words (remember, feedback is the breakfast of champions). I will confess that in many of the stores, I showed the manager how to clean a toilet, and in other stores, I was on my hands and knees scrubbing floors and baseboards, while still in others, I cleaned built-up grease in the grill or fryer hood area. I spent a lot on dry-cleaning my suits in those days.

Recognize effort and progress: We are always judged on two things at once, regardless of our job or our occupation:

- At the start of our assignment or project or job, we are judged on our effort and our progress.
- Once we've been in place for a while, and we know better, we are judged on our progress and our results.
- Ultimately, we are judged on our results and our results.

And that's how I judged the restaurants. I expanded the inspection program after a few months and announced that any restaurant that earned a green rating for the quarter would earn a plaque for excellence that I would present on my next visit. I published and shared the results in a weekly newsletter to all the stores.

I didn't realize how neglected the market really had been until my first tour presenting the plaques. I was surprised initially that there were families showing up for the presentations, including kids skipping school. In some of the smaller towns, the newspaper showed up, along with elected officials and local celebrities.

Something that I was simply doing to clean things up turned out to activate pride and provide recognition that had been sorely missed.

Let me mention here that I wasn't visiting the stores once in a while; I was in the field four days a week, sometimes five. I averaged more than one thousand store visits a year when I was based in San Francisco. Divide that by sixty-eight stores. On a typical tour, I would hop in the passenger seat with the first regional manager, drive around to all his or her stores, strategize on the highway between stops, and at the last store, the next RM would meet us, and I would continue on the journey.

What was happening before my eyes was simple: the region was getting better, and here's an example of how the standard was raised:

- Let's say on a Monday, a particular store is not very clean.
- On Tuesday, they find out I'm coming with their regional manager.
- By Thursday, they have raised the cleanliness level three notches.
- On Friday, I show up, it looks pretty good and then leave.
- On Saturday, the cleanliness level drops two notches, but it is still better than it was the week before; it moved up a notch.

This is the three-steps-forward-two-steps-back approach. Although it worked, it didn't work as fast as I had hoped, or I was impatient. It didn't matter; I needed something more, and I found it.

After a tour of some stores in the Napa Valley, I came up with an idea. At the next weekly meeting with the regional managers, I uttered the immortal words that helped turned the tide.

I simply said, "My definition of a clean restaurant is one where I can eat off the floor. The first restaurant that meets that standard, that's what I'll do."

The team buzzed. And the questions started: Off the floor? With or without a plate? When? I announced that on the next tour of sixty-eight, whichever restaurant was the cleanest would earn the reward of having me come in and eat off the floor during regular business hours.

The chase was on. The number of green stores doubled; the number of red stores almost dropped to zero. The winning restaurant was located in San Jose on McKee Road. Bonnie was the manager's name, and Bob was the regional manager.

I showed up on the big day wearing a white tuxedo. Not to be outdone, the regional manager had hired the local high school marching band, and they were playing in the parking lot when I arrived.

A reporter and photographer for the San Jose *Mercury News* were on the scene for the future front-page story.

I walked in, sat down next to the counter, and smiled for the cameraman, who was on a ladder above the designated spot. There was a place setting ready: knife, fork, spoon, napkin, and menu. The server came over, took my order for a waffle special, with scrambled eggs with bacon, coffee, and grapefruit juice, and I tried not to pass out from the adrenaline pumping through my veins.

The order came on a plate, and the server pushed it off onto the tile floor. Now what? I picked up a piece of bacon. Okay, it had started. I had ordered a waffle, figuring it would sit nicely on the floor and not be too messy, but I forgot about waffle syrup. With all eyes on me and spectators jostling for a better view, I lifted the small glass carafe of maple syrup (with a flourish?) and drizzled it on the waffle and watched as the syrup ran through the grout between the tiles. Oh my. Don't try this at home.

After that breakfast, I spent more time cleaning up the other things—the finances, the inventory, the human resources, the landscaping, and the management team—because understanding the cleanliness standards was no longer a regional issue.

My standards were clear, I meant business, and I had led by example.

National recognition for the region and for me wasn't too far behind. When the chairman of the board asked me what my secret was to turning around the region, I told him I had four secrets: When I started the transformation, I recognized effort and progress. Then I transitioned to recognizing progress and results. We were now in a space where results and results were the things I recognized.

He said, But that's only three."

And I said, "And I try very hard, every day, to lead by example."

CHAPTER 7: WALKIN' IN MEMPHIS

Shockingly Hypnotic

Shortly before finishing my freshman year at UMass, I got the great news that one of my new fraternity brothers had helped me score that summer job at the General Dynamics Shipyard in Quincy, walking distance from my home. The position would be as a union pipefitter (third-class unskilled), making the incredible sum of $2.89 per hour when the minimum wage was $1.60. (Of course, gas was 36¢, and the average apartment rented for $108 per month.)

If I wasn't going to be rich working that summer, I was going to be damn close, I thought. The good news continued. I had been working in high school as a grill man at a fast-food burger place and would also be working there for the summer as a shift manager during evenings. Two jobs, about seventy-five hours per week. Sweet.

Since I came from a large family, when I went away to school that prior fall, my bedroom space was reallocated to a younger brother, but we had a great couch that was to become my sleeping space. Since I ended up working Monday through Saturday at the shipyard, from 6:30 a.m. to 2:30 p.m. (yes to union overtime!), and Thursday through Sunday nights at the restaurant (3:30 p.m.–1:30 a.m.), I slept very little anyway.

Being new to union work, I learned firsthand of the tension between management and labor almost immediately. I was part of a gang of pipefitters, about a dozen, who were working on a US Navy ship that, as soon as it was finished, was designated to head to Vietnam since that war was in full force.

The gang would gather at 6:30 a.m. in a designated spot below deck and await instruction from a white hat before heading off to specific jobsites or projects. All managers wore white hard hats, maybe a throwback to cowboy days? Us pipefitters had baby-blue hard hats.

Each of the other trades had their own color hard hat. There were chasers (red), carpenters (green I think), and so forth.

The second day on the job, all twelve of us were standing around waiting to start work, and a white hat made a beeline for me and demanded to know why I was standing around doing nothing. I don't remember what I stammered, but I remember he told me not to do it again, or he'd write me up. Hmm.

My mentor that summer, an Irishman named Ray, told me when we got to the jobsite that the white hat targeted me because I wasn't holding a cigarette: the union contract allowed smoking, but if I was standing around doing nothing, the contract didn't protect me. Interesting.

The next day, when we were standing around waiting to start, I bummed a cigarette from Ray to hold, and the white hat backed off.

The third day, when he realized I was just holding an unlit cigarette, he came at me and said, "Light it."

By the second week, other members of the gang were tired of me bumming cigarettes and told me to buy my own, which I did. Can you guess what happened next? Yep, I became a smoker. Courtesy of a union contract, an intractable white hat, and the United States government.

In those days, everyone smoked.

- I can remember the fog when my parents had people over for cards or a dinner party. Most homes had ashtrays everywhere, and they were a great gift idea at Christmas.
- Up until the '90', airplanes had smoking sections in the back, and as soon as that seat belt sign was off, twenty-four or thirty-six or forty-eight people lit up. Hard to believe if you weren't there.
- Training classes and meetings had a smoking side and a nonsmoking side. Of course, restaurants had smoking and nonsmoking sections. You get the picture. Everyone smoked. Everywhere. All the time. Inside too. Can you imagine?

My pipefitter job started me on two decades as a puffer. Of course, I tried to quit intermittently. My problem? I really liked to smoke. Blasphemous, I know. But I did, and my efforts to stop were stopped by the fact that deep down inside, I wasn't committed.

Serious attempt 1, Los Angeles, California: Many years later, I have a newborn baby, and I have an additional reason to quit, but I know I need help. These were the days before nicotine patches and gum and other quit-smoking aids.

I had heard about Schick shock aversion therapy from a newspaper account or a friend (remember, no Internet either). So I investigated the concept. Here's the definition:

> Aversion therapy is a treatment method in which a person is conditioned to dislike a certain stimulus due to its repeated pairing with an unpleasant stimulus. For example, a person trying to quit smoking might pinch his or her skin every time he or she craves a cigarette.

Two to three times per week, I would go to an office in downtown LA with two packs of cigarettes, each with twenty smokes, for the session.

I'd sign in and then move into what was basically a 3×4 closet with a desk.

The desk was covered with thousands of cigarette butts in overflowing ashtrays and a set of electrical contacts that I would rest my wrist on. (Tongue twister? Rest my wrists.)

The technician would fit a string around my smoking hand ring finger. We were ready to start.

In case you were wondering, the closet/room stunk to high heaven.

Definitely wanted to hold my nose. It was that way by design. They rarely cleaned it, hoping to maximize every client's distaste for the smell of cigarettes.

For the next hour, I would smoke all or part of twenty to thirty cigarettes. Yes, you read that right.

Every time my right hand lifted up a cigarette to my mouth, my left wrist experienced a mild shock, like snapping a rubber band against the arm. The room had no ventilation, did I mention that? It got smokier and smokier and stinkier and stinkier.

There were various exercises, for example:

Speed smoke: I would have sixty seconds to puff a complete cigarette down to the filter. Suck, suck, suck as fast as I could, no break, no pause, until it was gone. That probably took about 25 percent of the smokes.

Smoke gets in your eyes: Then of course, there was an exercise where I smoked a cigarette with my face parallel to the ground so that the smoke went directly into my eyes. Another 25 percent of the butts were burned that way.

To be honest, I don't remember the other exercises too well; the passage of time and our natural erasures of bad memories may be factors.

Did I quit? If I answer sort of, those current and former smokers will understand. I stopped smoking compared to the two-pack-a-day habit I formerly had but became expert at sneaking cigarettes and quite proficient at bumming them. The practice maybe moved me to half-a-pack a day but didn't really do its job.

Remember, I loved to smoke, but deep down inside, since I wasn't fully committed, even the birth of a new baby couldn't help me, and the aversion therapy that made me avoid smoking in closets only partially worked.

Serious attempt 2, Memphis, Tennessee: Fast-forward just a couple of years. We've relocated to Memphis for work, and my wife leaves a newspaper ad for a hypnotherapy session to be held at a hotel ballroom in a couple of weeks, where the charlatan has the capacity to hypnotize up to three hundred people at once to quit smoking.

I signed up, not because I had stopped enjoying a smoke in key places of my day, but smoking was becoming a hassle. A real hassle. No longer were there ashtrays in every room and office.

- Not only that, but now people had the audacity to ask you to smoke outside! A real pain.

- Not only that, but you were also being viewed as a lesser human being for smoking.
- Not only that, what was originally 45¢ for a pack of cigarettes was now more than a buck, and that translated to hundreds of dollars per year. Yikes.

So I signed up to be hypnotized in a ballroom with three hundred people. But something was different.

Don't get me wrong, I was skeptical. Very skeptical. I was also absolutely certain that I was not hypnotizable. Even then, my mental discipline was famous, and I knew no guy on a stage in a ballroom in Memphis, Tennessee, could possibly have the power to hypnotize *me*. No way. But I really wanted to quit and didn't care if it was a quick fix. I wanted to check all the boxes until I quit, and if hypnosis was one of them, so be it.

The instructions said to bring your cigarettes to the event. The ballroom was packed. There was one of those aluminum ashtrays on every seat. The deal was the program would be in two parts. Part 1: you could smoke, and the hypnotist would explain some things about the process, habits, and more.

At half-time, he instructed us to take our smokes, have one last cigarette on the break, and to throw all the tobacco away before coming in for part 2. The hotel provided large barrels for everyone to toss their butts.

So behind the Hyatt Hotel, with the noise from the traffic on I-240 in the background, I threw away my last Marlboro and came into the ballroom, hopeful but still skeptical in spite of what he had told us before the break—that the key was to become a nonsmoker rather than to quit smoking. The concept was to replace the negative of quitting with the positive of becoming.

The lights were dimmed. Soft voice. He stated the start time of the exercise, then started a large timer on the stage and spun it around so we couldn't see the elapsed time.

Everyone relaxed, appendage by appendage.

Then he said something like, "You won't want a cigarette with coffee," and I was thinking, *Damned if I don't*. And he said, "You won't want a cigarette first thing in the morning." And he kept going, listing just about every situation he could think of where I could possibly want a cigarette.

About halfway through the litany, I started hoping really hard that I was hypnotized and that I wouldn't want a cigarette with a beer or any of the other situations. But I wasn't sure that this was going to work.

The lights were turned up, and we all returned to full consciousness. He asked a single question that changed my life. He asked for a show of hands for those who believed that we were hypnotized for less than a minute.

A smattering of hands. Then he asked the same question for various intervals, and I raised my hand that I believed we had been in the exercise for about four minutes.

He then told us to look at the timer he spun around and our watches, and I freaked out. It was—*gulp*—almost twenty minutes. Are you kidding me? Me of the powerful mind? Me of the mental discipline? Me who could not possibly be hypnotized just went through an experience I thought lasted four minutes and was actually twenty?

Maybe it worked. I drove home without cigarettes and arrived about 8:30 p.m. I told my wife I was going directly to bed, since to the best of my recollection, I had never smoked while sleeping. I wanted to get eight or so hours under my belt as a nonsmoker before being tempted. When I woke up a nonsmoker, I had an urge to grab a cigarette, but it strangely passed in a few seconds. Then I had a cup of coffee. Small urge. Same pass. Then I drove to work. Same urge. Same pass.

That first day, I had the urge every ten minutes, but they all passed. The second day, the same urge, but it was every thirty minutes. The third day, every couple of hours. By the end of the week, the urges were sporadic, a couple a day, and passed. By the second week, the urges were gone, and I happily agreed that I had been hypnotized to become a nonsmoker.

I'll never know if I was able to be hypnotized because I was committed to being a nonsmoker or if I was committed to being a nonsmoker because I was hypnotized.

But it helped me in a very specific way that might not be apparent. It changed the way I thought about the way I thought. I realized two things from that rainy night in Memphis.

First, most of us are not as smart as we think we are, and it is important to seek out people that are smarter or who have expertise greater than our own. Whether that is financial, nutritional, conditioning, or other types of advice. Since that night, I have been zealous in connecting with those smarter than me, whether they be employees or functional experts.

Second, I realized how many times we fool ourselves into failure because we "think" we are committed. You have to know you are committed; you have to be all in.

Successful people form the habit of doing the things that failures don't like to do, and one of those things that failures don't like to do is to be all in.

When I look back at those things that I succeeded at, and those that I didn't, I could make a case that the main difference was my commitment level.

I'll never know if I was able to be hypnotized because I was committed to being a nonsmoker or if I was committed to being a nonsmoker because I was hypnotized. To be completely honest, I don't even know if I *was* hypnotized. It doesn't matter today, but I do know that I was committed to being a nonsmoker, and it is more than three decades later.

(Hypnosis is not a panacea for smoking addiction and doesn't work for everyone. This story should not be considered an endorsement of hypnosis; it is only a story about what worked for me. What worked for me was a commitment at a level higher than I had experienced before. If you are a smoker, best of luck in shaking it. See below for another reason.)

The commitment to be a nonsmoker has saved me a lot of money, according to an article in the *Worcester Daily Voice*.

A pack-per-day Massachusetts smoker will spend $3.17 million over a lifetime on cigarettes, lost income, health care, and other financial losses due to tobacco addiction, according to WalletHub's

"The Real Cost of Smoking by State." Massachusetts is the most expensive state in the nation in which to be a smoker.

The study considers several categories, including out-of-pocket costs for buying cigarettes; financial opportunity costs, which include how much a person would have earned by investing the money in the stock market instead of smokes; health-care costs; income loss due to absenteeism, workplace bias, or lower productivity due to smoking-related health issues; and other costs such as higher homeowners' insurance premiums and the price of secondhand smoke to others.

Annually, tobacco use costs a Massachusetts smoker more than $66,000 per year, the study said.

Keeping Score—The Right Way

When my son was almost two years old, our family moved to Memphis, Tennessee, from the Los Angeles area, and we lived there for a little over ten years, so we had the full Memphis experience.

We all (as opposed to y'all) went to Elvis Presley's Graceland about a dozen times and wrote our names on the brick wall outside the mansion, with thousands of others, more than once.

We've had barbecue at the Rendezvous Restaurant. It is literally in a dark alley, underground, behind a dumpster, where the average waiter has more than twenty years of service and is as likely to tell you what you should order as take your order.

More than once, my wife and I had the chance to catch the blues at Lou's, an authentic southern blues club overlooking the Mississippi River, just off of Beale Street.

In a city without snowplows, except at the airport, I once paid an entrepreneurial truck driver $20 to push me up a modest incline on my desperate way to the airport during the one unforgettable snowstorm. Imagine six inches of snow that is packed down by the cars, never plowed, and treated by sprinkling ashes on the road after it snows.

We ate catfish regularly, including, of course, an Easter dinner at a friend's house our first year in town.

For the most part, we loved living there. It was slow-paced, inexpensive, easy to get around. Our town house on a small lake was the perfect place for our son to grow up within walking distance of the elementary school.

Oh yeah, and my son and I won a Father's Day father-son golf tournament on a course on the campus of the old Holiday Inn University in Olive Branch, Mississippi, in a most unusual manner for a most unusual reason.

Growing up: When Joe was three years old, as part of a plan to help him reach his potential, I took up golf so I would be able to play with him when he was older. As a youngster, he was able to walk in a limited manner. Not for long distances and not exactly gracefully, but he could still walk. He didn't use a walker in grade school and didn't use a wheelchair until junior high, as a result of major spine surgery.

So we were excited when a new golf driving range opened up just across the state line in Mississippi, about ten minutes away. We'd head down there and take turns whacking away at a basket of balls for an hour or so, and then head to the clubhouse for a root beer and some video games or Skee-Ball. We were probably one of the best customers, and of course, everyone knew our names.

Clare, the sister of the owner, worked there most nights, and the place was open year-round. There were times Joe and I were the only customers, and we'd hang out after using the driving range and play pinball or other games. I think we had a frequent bucket card or something. We eventually got to know the owner's whole family, and in fact, Joe had one of his birthday parties there; a good time for all the kids and parents, especially the dads, if you know what I mean.

Holiday Inn was founded in Memphis, and their university, where hotel managers were trained, was located about fifteen minutes away in Mississippi and had a great (I mean easy) golf course, in addition to a hotel and conference center. When I played golf for real, which wasn't very often, it was most likely at this course (renamed Whispering Woods and now closed).

One year I saw a poster touting a Father's Day Golf Tournament, a father-and-son event, where team members would alternate shots for eighteen holes. Perfect for my son and me. A great time to be with the guys and be together. To make things even and more interesting, a double-blind bogey handicapping system would be used.

Non-Golfers: Attention

Please ask a golfer you know for a better explanation than what follows. It is hard to explain if you don't golf.

Definition Section

Golf handicap: Wikipedia says, "A golf handicap is a numerical measure of a golfer's potential that is used to enable players of varying abilities to compete against one another. Better players are those with the lowest handicaps."

In handicap stroke play competitions, a golfer's playing handicap is subtracted from the total number of strokes taken to produce a net score, which is then used to determine the final results.

Blind Bogey Handicap Net Score:

I had never heard of this type of system, and here is an explanation from the Internet:

The blind bogey holes are checked, and strokes over par on those holes are totaled. That total is then doubled. That is the golfer's blind bogey handicap allowance. That allowance is then subtracted from the golfer's gross score, the result of which is his blind bogey handicap net score.

In other words, in a tournament using this system, holes are chosen at random, and scores on those holes are subtracted from the total so that golfers of unequal skill can compete. The worse the golfer, the higher the blind bogey golf handicap and the lower the net score.

So for this event, the final scores would be whatever was shot minus this blind bogey golf handicap to level the playing field or level the greens, whichever you prefer.

When we showed up for the event, we were excited to learn the owner of the driving range and his son, about eighteen years old, would be in our foursome, and we set off.

Their cart kept score, and after each hole, we'd announce what we shot, and so would they. After only a few holes, my son became suspicious about how they were counting, and so I started paying closer attention.

Sure enough, they must have flunked math when they were in school, because the sevens and eights and nines were becoming fives and sixes and sevens regularly. My son asked if we could keep score the way the other golf cart was keeping score, and I told him that we'd play it straight and track our actual performance.

We might be bad, but we would be accurate. It wasn't worth it to fudge the numbers. (Quick note: I am the nerd who gives back change when the cashier has given me too much.)

I know there are readers out there who use the scorekeeping method members of our foursome used. My understanding is that it is pretty popular method, even used by a former president, to tally scores. I don't golf anymore, so I wouldn't know.

To be honest with you, I felt bad when we put down a couple of twelves and at least one fourteen, because it was mildly embarrassing. But we weren't there to impress; we were there to share Father's Day on a beautiful course together.

We finished the eighteen holes, shook hands all around, and went to enjoy the postround barbecue behind the clubhouse. Barbecue in the south is like lobster in Maine, crabs in Maryland, blackened red snapper in Louisiana, tacos in California, or pizza in New York—they do it right.

It took quite a while for the tournament managers to calculate the scores of the one hundred-plus golfers, since they had to select the holes for calculating the handicaps, then apply them to the scores and tally it up.

We were minding our own business when fourth, third, and second place teams were announced. And then they announced the winners of the entire event as Joe and Ed Doherty from Memphis.

We looked at each other in surprise, got up from the picnic table, and proudly received the biggest freakin' trophy I had ever seen.

The trophy was awarded to us because in the double-blind bogey system, we didn't cheat, and that actually helped us. Our bad holes that were accurately recorded ended up being subtracted from our overall score as our golf handicap and gave us the lowest net score.

Moral of the story: When we got back to our house and took a photo with the trophy, we both knew that without the double-blind bogey golf handicap system, someone else would have won the trophy. But the purpose of the system was to create an equitable playing field so everyone had a chance to win. It worked. We did.

We also knew that playing the game honestly contributed to us earning the trophy. We will never know if we were the only golfers that day recording every stroke, but what we have always known is that by recording every stroke and playing the game right, we won. It worked. We were not just walkin' in Memphis but walkin' tall in Memphis.

It's Always Today, Isn't It?

We are all persistent. We all pound our way through obstacles and problems. Some of us brag about how resilient we are or how tough we can be when faced with problems or how we've responded under intense pressure. All of what we say and believe is true.

We can think of dozens of times we didn't give up, didn't back down, or didn't buckle under extreme situations. As proud as we are of the things that we were able to overcome, sometimes or many times in our life, we have been faced or will be faced with a mountain we are not strong enough to climb or a river that is too deep for us to cross or a wave that is too big for us to withstand.

It happens.

You can be the toughest person on the deck (or the meanest SOB in the valley, as some say), but when the biggest wave hits, your resolve will not keep you dry.

Many times in our lives, the size of the wave we are facing is simply too big for us to withstand. It could be the birth of a premature baby. It could be a serious personal crisis. It could be an inherited disease. It could be an addiction. It could be a financial crisis. It could be rejection by a loved one. It could be the loss of a job. It could be the death of someone close. It could be any of a thousand major waves that sweep us away.

There are times in our lives when we will face a wave bigger than we have faced before, and it will knock us over. There is no shame in being overwhelmed by a big wave. Houses, beaches, and roads have all been destroyed by big waves. Cities have been devastated by waves bigger than expected.

What separates the mediocre from the good and the great from the near-great is what happens *after* the wave hits. How quickly and solidly the road, or country, is rebuilt, how soon the life is put back together, or how effectively the beach is restored.

The list of big waves thrown at us is almost endless:

- The entrepreneur who loses it all and then rises again.
- The addict who kicks the habit and stays clean.
- The town that was hit by a tornado and comes back bigger and better than ever.
- The pitcher who has arm surgery and makes it back to the big leagues.
- The person who is fired and then comes back to lead the company.
- The child who has leukemia and beats it.

Those are also examples of the people and things in our society that we really admire. Everyone gets knocked down and will continue to be knocked down. We admire most those who overcome adversity to succeed.

I admit that when you are lying flat on your back after taking one of life's devastating blows, it can be hard at that moment to realize it was the size of the wave and not you. But the length of time between being knocked down and getting back up obviously determines how quickly you will return to where you belong.

So the next time you are faced with a mountain too high or a river too deep or a wave too big for you to handle, remember that what you need to do is focus not on what you just didn't do, or couldn't do, but what you need to do next.

Many years ago, my four-year-old son got it right. I was sitting on a lawn chair in the front, and he was riding his tricycle around, and he rolled up to me and said, "It's always today, isn't it, Dad?"

Yes, Joey, it is always today.

- Yesterday is gone, and what you did or didn't do then is not nearly as important as what you do today or tomorrow.
- What happened yesterday determines your history.
- What happens today determines your future, and you determine what happens today.

- You determine what happens today, and it is always today.

If a four-year-old could recognize that, it should be easy for us. May all your waves be small and your resolve be strong today.

CHAPTER 8: ROCKIN' AND ROLLIN'

Paddle Equity

When my son, Joe, was in high school, we got a ping-pong table, like lots of families do, and put it in the basement. Since he was new to the game he spent plenty of time getting frustrated when he couldn't make a shot or return a volley.

Most of his frustration was the result of being in a wheelchair and having a different view of the table with no chance to deliver a wicked overhead smash in my face. To people using a wheelchair, the table is at chest level or neck level. Imagine eating pasta from a table at that height? Stick a napkin on your shirt.

Speaking of height, my standing height and superior mobility was tough to beat, so my son's goal in the basement when he first started playing was simply to learn how to play well enough to make our games competitive. He gradually progressed in skill and confidence over time, but I remained the most skilled volley person in the family and could win most of the time if I put my game face on.

I've never been one to throw a game or let the other guy win, although I might occasionally let up a little bit with a family member, except when it comes to Scrabble. I play that game to win, no matter whose feelings are hurt. One day, as we entered our private basement ping-pong stadium, I glanced over at an old rolling desk chair in the corner, and a light bulb went off in my head. I grabbed the chair and moved it to my end of the table and sat down.

Joe's eyes opened wide when he realized what was happening. In an instant, his perspective on ping-pong morphed from an activity with his dad to something different, because now the game was more equitable.

My height privilege was, well, gone. More than that, Joe actually had more experience and skill than me at this closer-to-the-ground version of ping-pong. We played that day, and every day thereafter, with me sitting in a chair.

Playing ping-pong with a person in a wheelchair when you are sitting down levels the playing field pretty fast. All of a sudden, the games were more competitive and more interesting for both of us. My son developed more confidence, and his focus turned to winning, like it is now when he crushes me in Words with Friends. We probably played twice as often because it was just more fun.

Well, that, plus I'm the type of guy who wants a rematch when I lose, and the apple doesn't fall far from the tree.

Sometime later in that school year, my son's gym class was forced inside on a rainy day, and the ping-pong tables were put out in the gym. The instructor was quite surprised when my son was the first one to grab a paddle and rolled over to one of the tables.

He held his own with the standing unnamed opponent, in spite of the kid's height privilege. But Joe was so confident in his ability (did I mention the apple doesn't fall far from the tree?) that he challenged his next opponent to play him sitting in a chair.

The instructor was all over that and rushed to put a chair across from my son, instantly realizing there was some type of life lesson awaiting the whole class.

Awkwardly the students must have instantly understood how their inherent height privilege was going to be taken away and how that leveled the playing field. So I imagine another kid with courage or someone who also saw the lesson about to unfold or some other cool kid took the challenge. The whole gym must have stopped as the match started.

Of course, Joe smoked that kid and all comers that day in this new equitable ping-pong contest because he was very good at this particular version of this particular game. Each kid he played probably loved playing that way, something new and innovative, and they all had an experiential lesson in height privilege.

Eventually word of all this made its way around the school, and Kings High School had another cool kid, this one in a wheelchair. The gym teacher liked what he saw so much that most rainy days, he pulled out the ping-pong tables in Joe's class. In fact, I think I remember my son beating the teacher a time or two that year.

Each person having the same paddle = equality. Playing ping-pong in a chair = equity.

We see both equity and equality in our daily lives in ways we take for granted or overlook. Take shoes for an example. Shoes are sold on an equity basis; it would be tough if everyone had to wear the same size shoes, wouldn't it? Not to mention dresses or hats or shorts. Clothing, to sell, has to be equitable; it has to be what is needed. In fact, would there even be malls if clothing wasn't sold on an equity basis?

Sandwiches, on the other hand, are sold on an equality basis: your size, age, height, and whether you are in a wheelchair or not have nothing to do with what you get. Can you imagine buying a Big Mac and getting ten all-beef patties, special sauce, lettuce, cheese, pickles on a sesame seed bun because you are seven feet tall? Not a good use of three thousand calories anyway.

Coffee uses both equality and equity to sell: Your coffee sizes were predetermined to be small, medium, large, extralarge, ginormous, and a boxful (or if you speak Seattle, they are tall, grande, venti), but you can equitize your cup with cream or sugar or sweetener or even low-fat something to make it taste terrible if you'd like.

Even though I was Joe's dad, I had no idea what he was really facing when we started playing ping-pong, and neither did any of his classmates that rainy day.

There is an old expression my father used a lot about problem-solving that says, "If you can't raise the drawbridge, lower the river." Sometimes I think when we are faced with an obstacle, and we can't raise the drawbridge, we stop at that instead of looking for ways to lower the river or play from a chair. Equity is something that benefits everyone and, like this story, in many cases doesn't cost anyone anything. Equity is not a zero-sum game; there can be more than one winner, just like ping-pong when you bring your own paddle and chair.

The Horizontal Ellipse

For everyone feeling sorry for themselves today, this is the story of a sixteen-year-old kid who was knocked on his back, literally and figuratively, and got off the mat through hard work and, of course, persistence. It is the story about how Algebra 2 almost knocked him out and how he fought back to win and learned a valuable lesson about persistence.

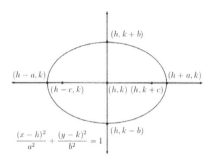

If you remember, Algebra 2 is the subject that was invented by someone who hated high school students, to confuse them and complicate their lives. If you are a parent, you get to go through it again when your child goes through high school.

There are so many formulas. They run together, and when you think you have the right answer, you don't, and when you get the right answer, you are not sure how you got it. (Kind of a metaphor for life, but that is a theme for another day.)

At the start of my son's junior year in high school, he unavoidably missed the first six weeks of class because he had major surgery on his spine. Sure they sent homework to the house, but that can be hard to do after major surgery.

When Joe finally started school, with a lot of time and hard work, it was fairly easy to pick up and catch up with social studies, science, English, and other subjects.

Algebra 2 was another story entirely. You just can't miss the first six weeks of Algebra 2 and survive, but we had to figure out a way. We didn't figure much out in the first quarter, and he received an *F*, but it might as well have been an *H* for *hopeless*.

I was the incompetent homework helper, and we were so lost, so far behind, so confused by Algebra 2 that we were this close to giving up. We eventually decided to start an intensive search for a tutor. We advertised, we asked for referrals, we tried everything, but no one showed up to rescue us. Eventually, we did find a tutor—me.

Not anyone's first choice, believe me. I was not really qualified for the job. Not an ideal solution. But we were accountable, and we really had no choice. So we put together a plan to outwork Algebra 2 by doing hours of homework *per night*.

We figured, when totally lost and when in doubt, try hard work.

He did all the assigned homework and every problem he could find in the earlier chapters. He went online and took practice tests at some website. He emailed another website with our questions and struggles. He did this every night during the second marking period, including Saturday and Sunday; although occasionally he took a night off, sort of, to go to a basketball game.

Even that occasional night off was a little different. At the time, we had front-row season tickets for a Minor League Cincinnati basketball team, and believe it or not, he brought the Algebra 2 book to games. During warm-ups, or if play was boring or during time-outs, sitting in our floor seats, he worked on Algebra 2.

The ushers used to look at us like we were crazy. Who brings textbooks to basketball games?

After a few weeks, we both developed a rhythm and started to grasp *some* of the concepts. I would stop at a FedEx office location on the way to work, copy the *next* chapter, and review it during lunch. I might also do some of the problems so that when I got home at night, I could help with the homework.

For the second marking period, Joe earned a *C*, and let me tell you, I was impressed. It was a big accomplishment.

Unfortunately, the year continued, the material got tougher, and neither of us had ever been accused of being a math genius, so the hours every night continued. Joe actually tracked the hours he worked on a master document (of course it was an Excel spreadsheet), so we knew he was averaging between two and three hours per night in the dining room doing the work.

In fact, to make it easier, we converted our dining room to an Algebra room and even put up a whiteboard to make it easier to work through problems together.

My son's study hall teacher, Ms. Woods, was so inspired by the effort and progress Joe was making, she did something absolutely remarkable: she gave up her free period in the morning and attended an Algebra 2 class *every day* with my son's teacher so that she would be able to assist my son when he came in for study hall at the end of the day!

She gave up her single free period to help one student! For the third quarter, he earned a *B*, and you wouldn't believe how very proud and happy we were with that, including Ms. Woods.

Going into the fourth quarter, we really knew how to attack Algebra 2, even though Algebra 2 still knew how to attack us. Although the material didn't get any easier, the teacher was inspired by his progress and effort, his study hall teacher was highly motivated by his progress and effort, and he was becoming the talk of the Math Department.

The story of the kid who missed the first six weeks of class and grabbed a *B* was clearly teacher's lounge material. None of that enabled him to reduce the amount of time he spent on the material, because as you know, horizontal ellipses wait for no man!

But there *is* a lot to be said for the cumulative effect of effort, because when the stuff got really hard, Joe had the habits, had invested the time, had the support system and the motivation to handle it well.

He handled it so well, unbelievable as it still seems to us; his persistence enabled him to earn an *A* in Algebra 2 for the final quarter. An honest-to-goodness, no-favors-extended *A*—one of only two in his class. The climb from *H* to *A* literally inspired everyone who witnessed it, including his parents.

His teacher wrote a note saying it was the most remarkable experience she had ever had in fifteen years as a math teacher. She had never seen anything close to my son's performance and climb from hopelessly behind to superior results. Even now, when I think about it, I burst with pride at what he did. Pure hard work, really hard work was important.

An inspired volunteer in the form of his study hall teacher, studying during halftime, and a whiteboard in the dining room were also keys to his success. But the most important component?

Persistence. He just never gave up, took a day off, made excuses, justified a break or any of those other things that we do when we are too lazy or not motivated to go the extra mile.

Joe was a persistence machine that wasn't going to be stopped. We didn't know when he got that first-quarter F that he would earn a fourth-quarter A, but we did know that whatever the grade was going to be, it would be a grade that reflected he'd done his best. He walked away with the hardest earned A in quite possibly the history of Algebra 2, but there was another reward for the persistence.

Prior to that year and Algebra 2, my son hadn't expressed much interest in going to college; although he had decent grades and was in the college prep track, but not that inclined. As a result of what he learned about persistence, hard work, study habits, and applying himself in Algebra 2, by the time he graduated from high school, he did so with the state of Ohio giving him a scholarship to the Raymond Walters Campus of the University of Cincinnati. He went from hopelessly behind to college graduate because of his persistence.

So even if you are hopelessly behind, as you read this today, and feeling a little bit sorry for yourself, realize that what you are doing is *not* Algebra 2; you are likely well trained to do your job, there are no mysterious formulas to memorize, that you have a solid support system in place, and you are not sixteen years old with a first-quarter F to deal with.

Considering those facts, if applicable, it is probably time to stop feeling sorry for yourself, even though you can justify it, and get on with solving those problems you face.

If you want to get an A when it really counts, if you want to inspire others to help you, you need to get moving. Nothing in the world can take the place of persistence. Talent will not; nothing is more common than unsuccessful men with talent. Genius will not; unrewarded genius is almost a proverb. Education will not; the world is full of educated derelicts. Persistence and determination alone are omnipotent. The slogan Press On has solved and always will solve the problems of the human race (and Algebra 2 problems as well).

So press on, and in case you forgot, the formula for a horizontal ellipse is still $(x-h)2/a2 + (y-k)2/b2 = 1$.

We Sang to Shania Twain

For several years, I ran a restaurant company in Cincinnati, Ohio, with twenty locations franchised from Perkins Restaurant and Bakery. They required a percentage of revenue to go to media advertising, mostly television. In the local market, we devoted a smaller portion to radio promotion. In addition to paid advertising, our company supported local charities, mostly with donated food to nonprofits requesting auction items or other support.

Since the Perkins concept was originally founded in Cincinnati, we were well known in the community. During the years I lived in the market, we made a donation here, a donation there, and so forth. We had also done some promotions where our local restaurants were drop-off points for things collected for the community.

Sometime during the height of her popularity, the promotions director of Y96, the young country radio station in the market and a station owned by the group that we were advertising with, approached me about using the restaurants as collection points for the canned food drive that country music star Shania Twain did in advance of each of her concerts that summer.

Shania's nonprofit, Shania Kids Can, was dedicated to helping disadvantaged kids and, in those days, collected canned goods as well as donations. The radio station approached me because the original drive was not going as well as they had hoped. They reached out to see if our restaurant group could help. After discussing it with the team, we agreed, and the eighteen locations in the market turned into drop-off points, and we worked to fill a Shania Twain-painted tractor trailer with food over a three-week period.

Promotional announcements and radio spots urged the local community to visit the restaurants and bring a can of food. The restaurants gave a generous discount to those who did. It was kind of

a perfect advertiser-station partnership. As part of the "shrewd" nego-
tiations on my part, the plan was that I would present one of those
big checks to Shania Twain before her show in Cincinnati. Original,
I know. The fact that my son, Joe, was a huge Shania Twain fan and
could accompany me to the check presentation was a bonus, not to
mention the thrill of a lifetime for him (and me?).

The night of the show at the Riverbend outdoor amphitheater in Cincinnati, we were there early and were waiting when Patty
Marshall, the promotions director, gave us the bad news: Shania had
been filming late in New York City the night before and was waffling
on whether or not she would be available prior to the show for the
check presentation.

Crushing news to my fourteen-year-old son, who saw his thrill
of a lifetime dissolve. After a slight pause, Patty said to me, "Here's
what we'll do if she cancels. Joe is going to meet Shania regardless,
even if I have to hop on stage during the show and have you pass him
up to me."

In that one moment, in that one sentence, in that one thought,
the word *loyalty* was redefined for me. Patty was going to take care
of us, she was going to deliver, and she would not be stopped. I
had stepped up when she needed me, and she was going to step up
when we needed her. Loyalty defined. However, about thirty minutes
before showtime, Patty waved us backstage; the check presentation
was on. Joe and my wife and I were ushered into a cramped space,
sweat dripping off everyone. We were in the room with the megastar
Shania Twain and a few radio station personnel. My son's smile may
not have been equaled before or since. Plus, before the check presentation, we had another assignment: to sing happy birthday to Shania
Twain. That's right, it was her birthday.

As a result of this experience, I can say we sang to Shania Twain
at the Riverbend amphitheater in Cincinnati for the rest of my life,
like I just did. The fact that I was not on stage with her is irrelevant
to the boast. The fact that she smiled and engaged with my son made
my day, my week, my month, my year. It was the thrill of a lifetime.

We presented the check, took the photo, chatted for a bit, and
left the backstage area and enjoyed one heck of a concert. We col-

lected a few thousand bucks and ten thousand pounds of food—five tons. Not a bad rescue.

I remember three things from that night: singing happy birthday to Shania, the look on my son's face when he met her, and Patty Marshall's loyalty. Some things are just cool.

Welcome to the Jungle

Advocacy means different things to different people, and equity and equality are in the news a great deal. Advocating for fairness, at least to me, supersedes all other kinds of advocacy; it is a crusade.

This story is about a time my son and I advocated for change, for a fair outcome, and left behind a benefit that hundreds, or maybe even thousands, of people in the past several decades have enjoyed. It is also a story of mismanagement, but that is less important than the more obvious lessons.

That's the thing about change; once it's changed, it's changed. As you will see, we started out simply wanting to go to a football game in a new stadium. We weren't being treated fairly, so we did something about it with a lot of help from others who used their resources and commitment to fairness to make a difference.

Welcome to the Jungle: In the summer of 2000, the Cincinnati Bengals were about to open a brand-new stadium, a gift from the taxpayers of Hamilton County in Ohio, as an incentive to stay in Cincinnati. Threatening to leave town was a pretty popular business model for NFL teams in the 1990s.

As local residents, we followed the ballot measure, the funding, the construction, and eagerly awaited the first exhibition game so we could see inside the multimillion-dollar edifice. (Apologies, but I've always wanted to use the word *edifice* in a sentence, and now I can cross it off my bucket list.)

Because my son uses a wheelchair to get around, we have been in the habit of prescouting everywhere we go for the first time: restaurants, venues, and stadiums. We look first for parking and then for overall accessibility. Imagine our surprise when we learned that there was no handicapped parking for this brand-new stadium! See, you are surprised, too, and you probably have half the knowledge of the Americans with Disabilities Act that we possess.

(The Americans with Disabilities Act [ADA] and Section 504 of the Rehabilitation Act of 1973 prohibit discrimination on the basis of disability in admission or access to, or in the administration of, programs, services, and activities for the public.)

The situation was that the stadium was built on public land and managed by the Bengals. The parking lots around the stadium were also on county land but managed separately. Following me so far? The county (or the Bengals, I'm not sure which) sold season parking passes with their season tickets. If, for example, there were one hundred spaces in a lot, they sold one hundred season parking passes without regard to handicapped parking. That's right, the correct number of handicapped spaces were painted on the asphalt but not available to handicapped fans and used by fans without placards or license plates. One hundred spaces equals one hundred season parking passes without regard to disability status.

The team's theme was "Welcome to the Jungle," but it appeared that those with disabilities were "Unwelcome in the Jungle."

Having lots of experience at being underestimated, I went right to work.

- I called the Bengals to describe the issue. They said they couldn't help me because the county controlled the parking. We could park in a downtown garage instead, I was told.
- I called the county Commissioner's Office. They couldn't help me; the parking passes had all been sold. I could park in a downtown garage instead, they told me.
- I called the attorney general for the state of Ohio. His office couldn't help me; in his mind, it wasn't an ADA issue (they were incorrect).
- I called the National Football League Offices in New York City. They couldn't help me; they said it was a local matter and referred me to the Bengals.
- I called the Department of Justice in Washington, DC, multiple offices. They couldn't help me either, but I don't remember why; it might have been because no discrimi-

nation had taken place yet. I thought if I called them back after a few games, I might be able to make a case.

- I called many people back, hoping to get a different voice and a different answer, all to no avail.
- I called—you get the picture. Anyone and everyone I could think of. The more I called and was *not* helped, the more determined I became. Okay, the angrier I became as well.

I kept a meticulous log of the two dozen people I spoke to: date, time, and response. The local ABC television station really appreciated my recordkeeping when I provided my log to them, but I'm getting ahead of myself.

I called the Bengals one more time, because a friend had a contact there, and if you can't come in through the front door, a side door is good before you knock the doors down.

I happened to be donating blood when the Bengals called me back. In the spirit of compromise, I suggested to this executive that if there were no more spaces, that perhaps a remote lot or a downtown garage with a shuttle to the stadium would work well, just like the University of Cincinnati used for their events to accommodate handicapped parkers.

When he told me that they wouldn't do that because we'd blame them if we missed the kickoff, little did he know the fuse he ignited or that the blood tech had to grab my arm to keep the needle in.

I told him he didn't have a chance. When he asked what I meant, I simply said, "To you, it's only a job, but to us, it's our life. You'll give up. We won't." I was fighting mad.

Remember, news of the stadium opening was *the* big news in Cincinnati, and everyone talked about it all the time: at lunch, at social events, on sports talk radio—it was everywhere. I personally had three rather innocent conversations that turned out to have a big impact.

First, I was talking to the general manager of a local radio station. He knew my son used a wheelchair, and when I told him what I had been up to, he volunteered to have the station rent a parking lot and provide a shuttle to the games as a public service. Of course, I agreed, and of course, I went on the radio and talked about the issue and thanked them for their generosity. Warm 98. Dan Swenson. A great guy who created the first domino.

Second, I was having lunch with one of my company's vendors who happened to be a heavy advertiser on the market's premier sports talk radio station, including the afternoon drive-time program, hosted by Andy Furman. The vendor told me to reach out to Andy (currently heard nationally on Fox Sports Radio) and arrange a time to come on his show and tell the story. JTM Food Group. Tony Maas. A great guy who set up the next domino.

Third, the president and general manager of the ABC station, Channel 9, was on a nonprofit board with me, and in casual conversation, I mentioned the situation, and he thought it would be a good topic for his investigative group, the I-Team, to take on as a project. When I told him about my documentation, that sealed the deal. WCPO. The late Bill Fee. A very big domino was set up.

Here's how the dominos were knocked down.

The parking lot that the radio station donated went into effect for the second game. It was used and reported on. People seemed happy with the solution, and I think the Hamilton County commissioners and the Bengals may have crossed this issue off their list of problems as solved. Not so fast.

Next, I was booked on that drive-time sports talk radio show on WLW to call in for a ten-minute segment. I had the private number that guests use to call in; it was very cool.

Much to my surprise, the host started taking calls, and before I knew it, my ten-minute segment turned into a ninety-minute talk-fest with callers ranging from wounded veterans to senior citizens to other disabled families checking in and, of course, supporting the cause. You could feel the momentum building. Lots of people who knew me heard me and reached out. Shortly after that, Channel 9 did an introductory piece to their investigative series. It outlined the issue, the problem, and some of my efforts.

Eight Days in October

1. *Sunday:* That next Sunday, it was game day. I met a videographer at the television station, he hopped in the passenger seat of my van, and during the game, when the lots were packed, I talked my way into every single parking lot around the stadium, and he captured on video either empty handicapped spaces that could have been used or, even better/worse (take your pick), video clips of cars in handicapped spaces that didn't have a placard or a plate authorizing the use of such a space.

2. *Monday:* When that story ran on Monday night, during the six and eleven newscasts, the fan started spinning—if you know what I mean—and I knew it was just a matter of time.

3. *Tuesday:* On Tuesday, a Cincinnati newspaper called me and wanted us to come to the stadium for an interview and photo for a story to run later that week.

4. *Wednesday:* Wednesday, a high county official called me after the whirlwind of publicity. It continued to be a hot topic on sports talk radio every day, and the TV station was promoting the I-Team investigation around the clock. I remember our conversation like it was yesterday because I was a little over the line on the belligerence scale. Remember, it was our life and just his job.
    Important official: We are trying to work with you, but all the publicity is causing a problem.
    Me, just a dad: Problem? You'll soon be spelling problem—C-N-N.
    Important official: C-N-N?
    Me, just a dad: Yes, if this isn't resolved, I will arrange for hundreds of wheelchairs to ring the stadium at the next

home game. That will be on CNN, and then you will really have a problem.

I don't really know why I said that or where it came from. What I knew was that it was time to fix the problem.

5. *Thursday:* The next day, I got a call from the same official, who wanted to share with me that the suite holder lot on Second Street at Pete Rose Way, the one closest to the stadium, would be converted to a handicapped parking lot before the next game. With one hundred spaces. It was the next-to-the-last domino. (*Penultimate?* Is that the right word?)

6. *Friday:* The newspaper story ran on Friday, and instead of more advocacy, it was more of a victory or celebration article.

7. *Saturday:* I had a lot of email appreciation, and of course, the topic was still buzzing on sports talk radio.

8. *Sunday:* On game day, we loaded up our van and brought friends and family to tailgate in the new lot. Dan Swenson from Warm 98 stopped by, and I think Bill Fee from Channel 9 visited as well. The TV station may even have done a recap of the story. While tailgating, I called the pre-game show, hosted by Andy Furman, thanked him live on the air, and shared the good news. He said they should name the lot the Ed Doherty Memorial Lot. I told him I was still alive but thanked him again for his help. WLW. Andy Furman, advocate for fairness.

9. *Today:* To this day, that lot remains in use for those in wheelchairs, disabled men, women, and children and those who just can't walk that far, and the phrase "Welcome to the Jungle" continues to apply to all fans.

CHAPTER 9: FLYOVER COUNTRY

Nobody's Perfect, That I Know Of

Most of the vehicles I've driven have had a sunroof. I'm not extrovert enough to drive a convertible, and a sunroofed vehicle has all the benefits of a rag top with the utility of a glass roof in bad weather and winter.

I pulled into my driveway after a long early spring day. I had driven home with the sunroof wide open. Temperatures were probably in the high fifties or low sixties.

I'm sure I had dinner a little later and might have even sat out in the yard for a while with a nice glass of cheap chardonnay or watched the Red Sox game on TV.

I remember it was a clear and remarkably beautiful evening, filling me with all the promise of a great spring and summer on the way.

I think I went to bed about 11:00 p.m. and slept soundly until the thunder woke me up about 4:00 a.m. When I rolled over, barely conscious, I could hear the rain pounding—I mean pounding—on the roof. The roof? When I shot up, half-awake, it occurred to me that I wasn't sure whether or not I had closed the roof of the car after dinner.

Half-awake or half-asleep, depending on where you fall on the glass half-full spectrum, I bombed downstairs clad in gym shorts and a T-shirt, running out the front door in the driving rain in forty-degree weather, car keys in hand.

The shock of the cold driveway on my bare feet helped me concentrate—try it sometime. I reached for the top of the car, hoping to touch glass. Now fairly wet and at least three-quarters awake, and may I add, remarkably refreshed by the driving rain, I realized that no, I did not close the sunroof and that water had been filling up the passenger space of the vehicle for about twenty minutes.

I did what you do at 4:00 a.m. in the driving rain in your driveway, with the sunroof of your car wide open and not quite fully awake: I jumped in to turn the key and close the roof. I still remember the shock as my gym shorts and T-shirt hit the forty-degree puddle of water on the seat.

Now fully awake, I closed the roof, got out of the car, and stood in the driving rain in my driveway, in the dark, with very, very wet shorts and T-shirt, and laughed.

The moral of the story? Several.

- No one is perfect—not you, not me.
- Sometimes we get distracted on a beautiful day.
- Everyone forgets something important now and then.
- We all get shocked sometimes when we sit down, and conditions have changed.
- We all wake up at a different rate, with different stimulants, although I don't recommend driving rain; coffee is better.
- We all need to laugh at ourselves now and then, and of course, if you have a sunroof, close it at night.

Shut Up and Color

Have you ever been in a social setting and heard a phrase over your shoulder that made you stop talking and try to listen in on the conversation behind you?

I was at a neighborhood social gathering when, from somewhere behind me, I heard the phrase, "Shut up and color," and it grabbed my attention.

I couldn't imagine what the subject could be, so I tilted my head and listened in to what was going on next to me. Two of my neighbors were talking about one of their mutual friends, an elementary school teacher in a nearby town. One shared that this teacher, when she was too busy to prepare a lesson plan for the following day, used to say, "Well, I guess my lesson plan tomorrow is going to be to tell the kids to 'shut up and color.'"

My first thought was to wonder how many of *my* days in school were shut-up-and-color days for my teachers?

I recalled a lazy third-grade teacher who used to have us copy the problems on both sides of the math paper. That must have been a shut-up-and-color technique.

I also remembered having a few teachers when I was older who let us work on our homework during class. Was that the high school version of shut-up-and-color? Come to think of it, isn't every study hall a shut-up-and-color period endorsed by the principal?

As I walked home that night, I remember thinking that shut up and color was really not a good attitude for a teacher to have about being a teacher and disrespectful toward students.

Now I know a lot of great teachers and don't mean to imply that they all use this technique. I also understand that teachers can't always be 100 percent honest (particularly during parent-teacher conferences). But what makes the shut-up-and-color mindset difficult for me is that it combines two negative traits: a lack of preparation, combined with the assumption that the kids could be or would be fooled.

And the more I thought about it, the more I recognized that even as adults, we're told to shut up and color more than we think by the ill-prepared people we encounter. Anyone who is supposed to deliver a service or provide support and doesn't plan ahead and ends up wasting our time might as well be handing us a crayon.

Can you imagine asking the receptionist in a doctor's office, after waiting forty-five minutes past your appointment time, when you'll be called and having her say, "Shut up and color?" Oh, that *hasn't* happened to you? Sure it did; she just used different words.

Can you imagine pulling up to the drive-through, and nothing comes through the speaker, and you say, "H-e-l-l-o-o?"

Then from the speaker box, the reply is the terse, "Hold on, I'll be right with you," which, translated, means of course, "shut up and color."

How about waiting for a hair appointment? Aren't those year-old magazines the equivalent of coloring books? We're so well trained when we see a magazine in a waiting room we know we should shut up and color.

Even that popcorn they give you at some restaurants gives you the same message. In fact, I've been to several restaurants where they actually let you color on the paper tablecloth. Hmm. Brazen!

If your favorite sports team hasn't won a championship in a long time (I forget *that* feeling, being in Boston), at the end of the season when they say, "Wait until next year," they are sort of saying shut up and keep coloring.

Most of us couldn't or shouldn't add a shut-up-and-color safety net to our own personal planning no matter how much we see it in daily life.

That's partly because we probably deal with a more sophisticated audience, whether at home or at work, than the teacher who coined the phrase in this example.

But the best reason to avoid the use of shut up and color is that it usually reduces your credibility in some way. Can't *you* tell when someone is telling you to shut up and color? It's an attitude that is pretty easy to see through.

Effectiveness, whether planning for fifty or for one, starts with great preparation, and while it might include great crayons and a killer coloring book, it also includes a healthy dose of respect for the audience.

You can fool some of the people all of the time and all of the people some of the time, but you can't fool all of the people all of the time; there just aren't enough crayons around to do that.

Inspiration from a Trash Can

Consider taking some of your inspiration from a trash can at your local gas station, convenience store, drugstore or fast-food restaurant.

Why is it there?

It may seem like an easy question for you, but what would happen if there weren't any trash barrels at fast-food restaurants or post offices or Walmart?

No trash cans at the highway rest stop filled with paper cups from a hundred miles away. No trash cans at McDonald's filled with Dunkin' Donuts trash. None in front of the Shell station filled with plastic bags from a supermarket. What would you do, what would we all do, if there were no trash cans at these places?

First of all, you might not even notice, and you would just empty the trash from your car in a trash can at home, right? Would you throw it on the floor of the post office or between the gas pumps or on the front lawn of a school? Unlikely. Today.

Yet many years ago, before littering wasn't cool, that is exactly what some people did. I know it must sound as strange as describing a pay phone to a teenager, but people actually threw stuff out of their car. In an immensely innovative moment, businesses came up with the brilliant idea of placing trash cans at the sites of the crimes, and it worked.

Brilliant! Brilliant? Think about it: there are actually businesses—millions of them—who will gladly accept your trash when you visit because:

Are they afraid you will litter? Not really.

Are they interested in the intrinsic value of trash? Not likely.

They do it because they have always done it—it solved a problem years ago; it is built into the system ("Hey, where's the trash can. We can't open yet."), and they still do it because they've always done it. What do you or your business do every day because you've always done it?

My personal fascination with trash cans is decades old, and I was fortunate to have the ability and authority to validate the assumptions above in the real world.

True story: I removed all the outside trash cans from the twenty-two restaurant locations of the company I was managing. Just took them all away from the front doors and parking lots and threw them in the dumpsters.

The local employees were afraid of what would happen because all of the newly departed cans were filled every day, requiring time to empty them, new bags to insert, and dumpster space.

Within the first week of this radical new plan, do you know what happened?

Not a thing.

Within the first month? Not a thing.

Within the first year? Again, not a thing.

Decades later, there are still no trash cans outside most of those restaurants. (I'm sure someone not quite as "trash woke" as me replaced some of them.)

No one complained, no one noticed, and no trash was strewn about the front entry of the stores. Nothing happened because all the people with trash in their cars threw it away somewhere else. Well, actually the company saved about five thousand cubic yards of trash-removal costs for dumpsters we didn't need picked up as often and tens of thousands of dollars in labor cost for the cans we didn't empty.

What is your trash can? Do you have one?

What are you doing this week because you did it last week? What can you eliminate, and no one will notice? Want more time to work on the important things?

Start with not doing the things that no one cares about. Eliminate the trash cans in your world that solve problems that don't need to be solved. No one will notice if you stop doing those things.

Throw the trash can away; it won't be classified as littering.

Oh Well. Now They Know

One day, shortly after moving to Tennessee, a coworker was raving in the break room about his church and his pastor, and he invited me to a men's club meeting at the church. I didn't really know anyone in town; I didn't really know what a church men's club was either, but it seemed like a good thing to do.

When I walked into the meeting room at the Church of the Resurrection, there was a group of guys already there, and the pastor, Monsignor Peter Buchignani, was hanging out with them, and everyone was laughing and joking around.

It was obvious he was a great down-to-earth guy. The evidence for that thought was that he was drinking a beer and smoking a cigarette when I walked in, and my first reaction was, *This is my kind of church*, especially since I was a beer drinker and a smoker at the time.

Maybe not the perfect reason to join a church, but the end result sometimes is what counts, and that visit led to another, and in short order, I knew I was official when I received a stack of dated donation envelopes for the basket passed during mass.

As newcomers in a strange town, in what, to us, was a strange part of the country, the sense of welcoming and sense of belonging offered by the church was just what we needed.

But along the way, I became frustrated at a couple of small things that actually impacted my life and, potentially, the lives of dozens of others. No, it wasn't as serious as the church scandals that would eventually come to light. It was simpler: poor planning.

We enrolled our son in the preschool part of the religious education program. Those kids met during the 9:00 a.m. mass. As parents with young children know, the formula is: *drop off before the service + pick up after the service = peaceful, fidget-free service.*

However, there are basically two things that can go wrong with this universal formula, and we encountered both of them almost immediately.

Frustration point 1: We'd stand in a line outside the classroom after mass with twenty other sets of parents, and the class would run long. What sense did this make? It wasn't a surprise that mass was going to take fifty minutes. How could you not be ready?

Frustration point 2: The running long issue was supplemented by another kind of frustration—it seemed like every other week, we were taking some kind of preschool artwork home that wasn't dry yet, so we had to carry it horizontally to the car and carefully place on the rear-window ledge (when cars had rear-window ledges) for the ride home. Open a window by mistake, and you had blue and yellow paint on the seats as the artwork blew off. Did the lesson plan actually state, "Wait until just before pickup to use paint?"

Those who know me well can guess what I did next: I volunteered to teach that preschool class the following year, along with my wife, so that at least one class would end on time and have dry artwork for the ride home. My style was to do something about it rather than simply complain.

On the first day of our first class, when the new "teachers" presented during the meet-the-parents session, we told everyone to come to our room first if you have multiple kids in different grades, because we will always be ready, and we do all of our artwork at the start of the class, not the end. Some readers may find it hard to visualize me in a class of preschool kids, and looking back, I find it hard to visualize me in that space as well. I think my wife did most of the work.

Over the course of our one year in preschool, we became pretty popular with parents. Let me rephrase: we were rock stars. Finishing on time with dry finger paintings? Who wouldn't love us? Even if we did have funny Boston accents.

The director of religious education, who was desperate for a third-grade CCD (Confraternity of Christian Doctrine) teacher, also noticed us, so we signed up for that class the following year. One year of preschool is probably enough for most preschoolers, and it was definitely enough for us.

Little did I know at the time, but for seventeen years, I'd be a third-grade CCD teacher. For nine years, every Wednesday, I'd head to that same church in Memphis and have a group of twenty to twenty-five third graders spellbound.

Right after we relocated to Cincinnati to the Church of the Good Shepherd, they put out an appeal for a third-grade teacher, and I answered that call and held class for another eight years. I was pretty familiar with the subject matter and curriculum. But I also had some secret methods that made being a teacher a little easier.

Secret 1, only one rule: I had only one rule, and I stated it at the start of every year and every class, and when the inevitable rambunctiousness started up (try spelling that word without spell-check), I would ask for silence and then ask the kids to state what that one rule was. My rule? I am the only comedian. I could be funny, at least to an eight-year-old, and I didn't want anyone to be funnier or funner than me.

Secret 2, pencils: My biggest secret weapon was pencils. Every third grader needs pencils, and I had a system where a kid who gave the right answer would get a colorful pencil, or sometimes I'd state, "If everyone is quiet for the next minute, everyone will get a pencil." It worked great. I'd use them as bribes—I mean rewards during the class. I even had pencil exchange nights where, for example, if you didn't want the My Little Pony pencil you got last week, you could exchange it for a baseball pencil. The kids were also allowed to negotiate with each other during these pencil exchanges.

Secret 3, parents: The rule in both parishes was that a parent of each child needed to sign up to help for one class and be a coteacher with me. The parents would get to see what we were doing and get into the curriculum a little bit. My methods were not a secret.

Secret 4, coaching, sort of: What I knew, as a parent, was that when the kids were picked up and placed in the back seat of the car, Mom or Dad would ask, "What did you learn today?" Of course, the usual answer was, "Nothing." I set about to change that. During the last five minutes of the class, we'd rehearse the answer to that question, sometimes with a rap (yes, that kind of rap), sometimes with a memorized sentence. We'd usually do this sitting on the floor with a clapping tempo to the words.

I turned out to be a very popular teacher. The parents liked my humor when they were in the classroom. They liked my planning when the kids were lined up and ready to go at the end of the class. And they liked the fact that the kids actually said they learned something.

I liked teaching the class because after the first year, I didn't have to do a lesson plan. I simply used the one from the prior year, so my investment was only the drive to the church, the class, and the drive home.

But what I liked most of all was the number of bad days I had at work that dissolved the minute I saw the enthusiastic third graders.

Teaching that class and going from high pressure, demanding, problem-filled days and settling into a job where I was volunteering and doing good in the world really helped in a lot of ways.

Disappointment during the day was offset by the vibe of doing good and making a difference. Balance. Perspective. Peace. Lots of benefits to me and a real-life example of the more you put into it, the more you get out of it.

I have always been busy (and hopefully productive), and I wouldn't have volunteered for seventeen years if I wasn't getting something out of it. I think the experience helped me understand myself, my faith, and my priorities. Although you may think of me as grown-up, I like to think I am still growing, and the time as a CCD teacher was a big part of that growth.

As our relocation to Massachusetts was upon us, I started what I knew would be my last class at the Good Shepherd with mixed emotions. Over the years, more than five hundred kids had heard enthusiastic classes on my favorite commandment (Honor thy Father and thy Mother; they take care of you now, and you will take care of them later), but I knew my teaching career was over.

At the very end of the very last class, as we were all sitting on the floor practicing what to say when we got in the car, and to kill some time, I asked if there were any questions.

A little girl in the back raised her hand and asked in a soft voice, "Mr. Ed, what's a comedian?" All those years, all those kids, all those pencils, and I never defined that word for the third graders. Oh well, they know now.

CHAPTER 10: HARD TO HIDE
A GOOD ANYTHING

It's on Sale for $11.95

I pulled into an inspection station in Ohio and was told the car I was driving flunked the emissions test. Apparently, there is a test performed on the gas cap; you know, that thing you unscrew behind the little door prior to pumping gas? Who knew?

I was told that I needed to replace my gas cap. Having never actually bought a one before, I asked the attendant where I could get one. He indicated there was an auto parts store only four miles away.

I drove there with assurance that if I returned quickly with my shiny new gas cap, I could be reinspected and be certified to drive in Ohio without doing significant damage to the environment. I pulled into the unnamed auto parts store and asked for a gas cap for the exact make and model car I was driving.

The grease-under-the-fingernails kind of clerk opened a giant book, twice the size of the Yellow Pages (remember those?) and looked and studied and peered. He may have asked me a few questions. I could feel my anxiety rising, as I thought to myself, *I'm not looking for a fuel injector for a 1968 Dodge Dart or a part for a SpaceX rocket. What's going on here?*

After several minutes of awkward silence, he simply said, "No."

To which I (most likely sarcastically?) responded, "No what?"

He said, "No, we don't have that gas cap. We don't stock many gas caps."

Relying heavily on my superior interviewing skills, I managed to pry from him that there was a competitor about two miles farther away on the same route.

What was supposed to be a quick trip to get a sticker for the car just became more complicated and was turning into not a great way to spend an afternoon; I'm sure you know the feeling. So when I pulled into the competitor, an AutoZone store, I was starting to believe a gas cap might be a rare spare part, and I was wishing they would hurry up and invent Amazon so I could find one on my front porch.

I was also a little bit discouraged. Since I was still highly motivated to cross this inspection thing off my to-do list that day, I went into the store and asked the well-groomed clerk in the red sweater for a gas cap for the Sebring convertible (told you it was a while ago) that was at fault.

While smiling and without losing eye contact with me, he quickly reached under the counter and pulled a box out and said, "Here you go. It's on sale for $11.95." I was a little bit taken aback after my previous attempt. (Only writers use the phrase "taken aback," and we love it when we can do so.)

Being the curious sort, I asked him how he did that and wondered if he knew I was coming. All he said to me was, "There's an emission inspection station about six miles from here, and we always have people come in looking for gas caps all the time, so we keep them right here under the counter." I thanked him, he thanked me and even helped me install the gas cap (you have to connect that little plastic cord that prevents you from losing it).

A few minutes and six miles later, I left the emissions station with my inspection sticker and the air in Ohio a little safer to breathe, but I also headed home with a great lesson about customer service, anticipation, planning ahead, and the importance of quality team members.

Service: We are all serving someone in our roles. It could be customers, it could be volunteers, it could be each other, it could be someone from another company or another office, or it could be a family member or members. It's all called a form of customer service.

The old cliché if you are not serving the customer, you are serving someone who is serving the customer is universally true for most roles. Everyone can tell the difference between the two approaches to customers in this particular story.

Good customer service is hard to hide, easily spotted, and shared with others (and I've shared this story for many years), and I'm sure you have your own story that you repeat at the drop of a hat.

Anticipation: We know what is coming much of the time. Yet people buy shovels after the snowstorm or umbrellas after the rain. With just a little anticipation, like connecting the dots after a couple of people have asked for gas caps, we can be expecting something to happen that happens and be ready.

Planning ahead: We waste a lot of time searching for things that we once had in our hands. Some studies have shown that the average office worker spends a week a year looking for things on or in their desk (probably more now that the desk is in the bedroom or dining room). Moving those gas caps to a convenient spot right under the counter to save steps and time is good planning. Isn't planning ahead a universal way to impress yourself and others?

Quality team members: That second counter person with clean fingernails, a bright-red sweater (he probably didn't like to wear), gave a much better impression than the grease-stained industrial-style-shirted confused clerk in the first store.

One of the easiest things to recognize is a quality team member, whether it is an usher at a baseball game, a hostess in a restaurant, an Amazon delivery driver, or the clerk at an auto parts store. Quality team members make everything easier, and a poor team member makes everything more difficult: a steep hill to climb. But there was an even bigger difference between the locations, and that was management.

Management: In order to make it from the emission control station to AutoZone, potential customers *all* stopped at the other store since the clerk at the emissions control facility was sending them there.

Think about it. The first store had everything going for it: it was closer, flunkers were referred to it by the facility, it had a steady stream of drivers who were ignorant about gas cap protocol, and more. The second location, two miles farther away, was at a significant disadvantage. The difference between the two stores was made up for by a customer service focus, anticipation, planning ahead, and quality people or what some would call good management. Where do you keep *your* gas caps?

It's Hard to Hide a Good Restaurant

I would be lost without clichés. Sometimes I brag that I am a cliché machine.

IT'S HARD TO HIDE A GOOD RESTAURANT

Clichés and analogies are my friends because they enable me, and you, to get a message across by creating a common image or agreement about a subject or a topic. The last time I checked, agreement was in short supply in our country, so I am doing my part to help everyone come together by using clichés.

"It's hard to hide a good restaurant." With a few decades in the restaurant industry, this cliché was born there but has a much broader application. It is an expression I use regularly in a variety of circumstances because it sets the stage for a lot of analogies.

Note that it is also hard to hide a good car dealer, a good grocery store, a good contractor, a good coffee shop, a good shoe store, a good hairstylist, a good gym, a good nonprofit, a good golf club, a good consultant, a good fraternity or sorority, a good—well, you get the picture. If an organization does a good job, customers will find it, whether it is on main street or in the back of an industrial park

In fact, one time I walked into a packed new business, Seven Saws Brewery, in the back of an industrial park in my town. The brewery founders did an outstanding job of hiding it: no signs, a half-mile off, and not visible from main street and not really advertised or promoted.

The 250–300 customers who were there the night we found it found it too. The place had no kitchen, only a food truck outside, a beer-only liquor license, no real decor except for big windows looking at the tanks, but that wasn't enough to keep it from the public.

Two days before, we visited a brand-new restaurant which shall remain nameless for legal reasons. It was a converted Friendly's that seemed to take years to remodel. Right on Main Street, across from the US Post Office, on perhaps the most visible corner in the entire town.

145

If the brewery had a traffic count by its front door in the dozens, this place had a traffic count on Main Street in the tens of thousands. After one visit, we won't go back, and I won't share the details, but we were very disappointed in almost everything about the place.

Two new businesses, about a mile apart. One totally hidden, another with the greatest visibility and the anticipation that goes with months and months of visible construction.

It's not about the location; it's about what's inside. The point of the cliché "it is hard to hide a good restaurant" is that customers are smart about how they spend their money.

They are not always right, but they are always fair, and if you offer good products and provide good service, they'll find you, no matter how hard you make it and no matter what your business is.

On the other hand, if you don't offer both good products and good service and an appropriate atmosphere and attitude, they will only find you once, because they aren't searching for mediocre places to spend their money. They'll ignore you.

Buzz, Buzz, Ding, Ding

Being in the restaurant industry for so many years means there are things I can't unlearn. Unfortunately, or fortunately, when I go into a restaurant, I see things that others may not see and form conclusions that others may not form.

The following thoughts were inspired by an uninspiring visit to a bakery café.

I originally was going to title this "The Chicken or the Egg," but that didn't seem right. Then it was going to be called "Leadership or Talent." That seemed like a boring title, and I knew that "Buzz, Buzz, Ding, Ding" would be a title that would get it read.

See, I was right.

Leadership-Talent Matrix

What matters more, leadership or talent? Which is more important to a successful team?

What better way to organize thoughts about this than a matrix, right? Plotting leadership and talent on two axes helped me think through the answer.

Simplistically there are four basic states of this dynamic and every unit of every organization, and in fact, every team in every league falls into one of four general categories:

- Excellent leadership, excellent talent
- Excellent leadership, marginal talent
- Poor leadership, excellent talent
- Poor leadership, marginal talent

Champions and Losers

You don't need to be a genius or have a business degree to figure out that excellent leadership and great talent is the combination most likely to win a football game or market share and the best combination for a business and a professional sports team (see New England Patriots, Golden State Warriors, and New York Yankees).

It also doesn't take much to avoid betting on the poor leadership-marginal talent combination in business or with a professional sports team (see the Baltimore Orioles, New York Jets, and New Orleans Pelicans).

How Do You Know?

Where the debate takes place is when there is only one or the other, which combination is more likely to succeed? Excellent leadership with marginal talent or poor leadership and excellent talent?

The question is, what is more powerful, leadership or talent?

Since we all have experience working for bad leaders, we'd most likely say nothing can overcome poor leadership. Some of our favorite sports teams have had more than enough talent to win but not enough leadership to succeed.

Sports Validation

If we look to sports for metaphorical validation that leadership is a more significant factor contributing to success, there is plenty of evidence this concept is generally true.

A great coach can make up for the deficits of his players with a strong game plan, in game adjustments, and hundreds of minidecisions, not to mention selecting the right talent. The same applies to all types of organizations.

Regardless of how talented they might be, skillful players cannot completely compensate for a coach with a weak game plan, a lack of understanding or awareness of what is happening on the court, field, or ice, and playing the wrong players at the wrong time in the wrong positions. This also applies to all types of organizations.

More Useful Question

But a more useful question might be how you know whether a substandard operation is leadership or talent or both. Here is a description of the experience I had that prompted me to ask the question. It is a story about a poorly managed business. But before I begin, I would like to state my credentials:

- Customer: I had my first restaurant meal at the age of five or six at the now-defunct Howard Johnson's, and I have been eating out since then. I average multiple meals outside the home per week.
- Experience: For more than thirty years, I worked for national chain restaurants, ranging the gamut from fast food to pizza to quick service to full service to twenty-four-hour service, with locations from Seattle to San Diego to Florida to New Hampshire and most states in between. I spent a lot of time evaluating operational performance and visiting locations, sometimes as a big shot from the home or regional office.
- Consultant: As a consultant, I am required to look insightfully at things I observe, analyze them, and come up with recommendations for sustainment or improvement.

How to Tell It Is Poor Leadership

I have a home office, but I also have branch offices throughout the state and country in the form of a national chain of bakery cafés that offer surprisingly strong and free Internet access.

I most often frequent my branch offices in specific cities near clients or contacts, including a location that will remain nameless because it is the subject of this story, and I don't have a legal department.

For the most part, these locations have created a certain standard of expectation for me, as most chain operations do. Since I am probably a visitor two to four times per week, I have a good feel for those standards and operating systems, as well as the strength of their coffee.

I don't normally jump to conclusions on one visit unless bad management hits me over the head. Even then, not only for these branch offices but for any business, I am the type of guy who gives most a second chance.

Before you jump to the conclusion that the story that follows happened the way it did because it is hard to get employees, you should know that I discounted that theory because I observed plenty of employees on duty, very few customers, and only one order at the pickup area.

Here's my tale:

- *Too busy:* I headed to the counter, and the employee behind the counter was a little too busy with something to help me, so she called someone from the back. The first tiny alarm bell went off in my head.
- *Uh-oh!* The fetched employee took my order for a bagel and coffee, and I gave him my phone number. He told me the price was $6.72. I told him the reason I gave him my phone number was because I was in the monthly beverage club: pay one price, and get unlimited beverages all month. He said it didn't register.
- *Request:* I said, "Please call the manager." He didn't and mumbled something. He comped the coffee another way, and I was glad because I didn't have time for a debate, but another bell went off, this one a little louder. I took the buzzer he offered, one that I understood would light up, flash, and vibrate when my order was ready, calling me to the pickup window.
- *Empty:* I went to the counter where the coffee urns, sugar, sweetener, lids, and cream were located and picked up the half-and-half pitcher; it was empty. I turned around, saw a different employee behind a different counter fiddling with something, and brought the pitcher over to her and said,

"This is empty. Can you please refill it?" She nodded. At this point, I may have lost track of the number of bells in my head going off about the operation of this place.

- *Minimum effort:* I went back to the counter and started mixing my brew while waiting for the cream.
- *Huh?* A minute or two later, she called out to me from behind the counter, "Do you still want the half-and-half?" She left the pitcher on the counter near the cashier stand, a mere ten steps away, and disappeared. I went over and picked it up. I should have brought my cup to the cashier stand, used the half-and-half, and left the pitcher there, but I was too polite and brought the full pitcher back to where it started. Besides, the bells in my head were playing Beethoven's "Fifth."
- *Buzz, buzz, ding, ding:* I walked by the pickup window on the way to my booth to put down my coffee and fire up my laptop, but I thought I saw a bagel waiting to be picked up but figured that it couldn't be mine because the buzzer they had given me hadn't buzzed, flashed, or vibrated. I peeked at the slip under the plate, and sure enough, it said "Edward." It was mine. *Ding, ding, ding, ding.*

I sat down and looked around, and there was only one other customer in the dining room. No clusters of seniors drinking coffee that are common to this chain. No moms with strollers taking a break after the school bus pickup that are common to this chain.

I wrote down some thoughts, shut down my laptop, finished my bagel, grabbed my coffee, and moved to another branch office a few miles away.

Second Chance

How can I be so sure that these small irritating broken promises to me as a consumer are evidence of poor management? I couldn't know for sure. But in predictable give-them-a-second-chance mode, I came back two weeks later.

Guess what? No half-and-half. I brought it to the counter, like the last time, but there was no one there. I just left it by the register.

Guess what? No one showed up to greet or service the four or five customers mingling in front of the counter. Because I was in a hurry, and my mind predicted that it would take a while to get half-and-half, I picked up the almond milk pitcher to give it a try instead.

Guess what? Empty. I put it on the counter next to the unclaimed empty half-and-half pitcher and went back to my table, finished my business meeting, and got ready to leave. The person who I was meeting with wanted to order a bagel to go and got up to order.

Guess what? After a while, when the buzzer didn't go off, we found it at the pickup station ready to go and getting cold.

Bad employees can produce a one-time bad experience, but bad management consistently produces bad experiences.

The next time those bells go off in your head that something isn't right with this business, trust your gut because when the bells go off in your head, you can be sure that they aren't going off in the manager's head, where they belong.

Buzz, buzz, ding, ding.

Managers Get the Employees They Deserve

At the height of the it's-hard-to-get-good-help era, I went out to breakfast at the 122 Diner in Holden, Massachusetts, about two miles from our house. Sunday morning, 9:00 a.m., packed house. Great food, great service, and plenty of employees.

Make that plenty of trained, motivated, and enthusiastic employees. As I sat there watching the eight front-of-the-house employees expertly interact with guests, deliver each other's food, pour coffee refills around the room, and grab booster seats for little ones, I was thinking to myself that the so-called employee shortage wasn't having much of an impact on this operation.

My immediate conclusion was that there must be good management or good ownership or both, because this small-town restaurant was cranking and supporting the theory it is hard to hide a good restaurant.

My thoughts shifted to why. Why did this location *not* have an employee problem? And as I looked around and saw many of the employee faces that I've seen over the years, I realized that it had enough quality staff because the good ones stayed. I also saw new faces and realized that the good employees probably referred their friends and that the restaurant had a reputation in the town for being a good place to work.

(Disclaimer: I have no interest in this business, do not know the manager or owner, and only visit one to two times per month. No one in the business knows me.)

One of the ongoing debates in all industries is the subject of why employees quit.

It amazes me that this is even a discussion, since we all know why employees quit, don't we?

Forget the human resource surveys and exit interviews; those are likely accurate but dominated by very disgruntled or kinda-sorta-unsure vanilla responses. I'd also be less than honest with you if I didn't admit there are times when I've wanted an employee to quit. Not all turnover is bad, although all turnover reflects a judgment error of some kind.

What you are about to read doesn't contradict the surveys or what you've observed with your own eyes or through your own experience, but it is maybe a little between-the-lines insight.

From my time as a people manager, with accountability for literally tens of thousands of employees over the years and with the knowledge that thousands of employees have quit the business units I've supervised, I believe there is a much simpler explanation for why people quit a job.

You might think the answer I'm going to give is money, but it's not. While money is obviously a factor in 99 percent of the decisions we make and not limited to employment decisions, I don't believe it is the primary reason people quit jobs.

It's the manager. People quit managers more than they quit companies, but in all fairness, to most employees, their manager *is* the company or at least the part of the company that impacts them the most.

My mother's Uncle Joe, a man of wisdom, used to tell me when I was a kid, "It is doubtful that an organization ever became disappointed in an employee before the employee became disappointed in the organization." Replace the word *manager* for *organization*, and you have it right. When people become disappointed in their direct supervisor, they quit or go over her/his head with other consequences.

Why are managers the reason that people quit? Well, the most obvious reason is that managing is not easy. In fact, managing is hard. Managers struggle to manage. The evidence includes the number of books on management at Amazon or Barnes and Noble. (If you go to Amazon and type *management books* into the search box, it will show more than one hundred thousand titles.)

In my years of managing and managing managers and managing the managers of managers, as well as training managers, here is my version of the three things that managers struggle with the most.

Failure to Prioritize People

Most managers, especially those promoted up through the ranks, have a high degree or expertise in a field or technical knowledge. That's what gets them promoted.

Unfortunately, once they become part of management, that technical expertise is *not* what they are judged on, not what they earn their living by, and not the expectation of employees they supervise.

No, they are judged based on their ability to give direction. Many new managers believe that supervision is in addition to their "expert" function, and it is just the opposite. Supervision is the primary, first, and top priority of a manager, and the technical part or the expert part is secondary. Many new managers fail to understand this and fail at managing. If you are a manager, your primary role is to manage others, not be the technical expert.

Lack of Style Adaptability

Most managers like a certain style of managing or use one style of managing. You hear terms like *autocratic* or *participative*, or *employee-centric* and other terms du jour for the latest fad.

The reality is all those styles work but only for employees who respond well to those styles. From my restaurant background, new servers, those who have never waited on tables, need to be *told* what to do; i.e., suggest dessert, not participate in the discussion. Veteran servers, on the other hand, can likely decide what dessert to sell and when to sell it.

To use a directing style with the veteran servers will move them to move on because of micromanaging, and to use a participative style with new servers will move them to move on because they are overwhelmed. Failure to vary the leadership style based on the skill, ability of readiness of a follower for a specific task is a blank check for turnover.

Selfishness

I have been in several situations where the management or leadership was poor, and I came to the following conclusion: it wasn't because the leaders didn't care or didn't try or were intrinsically bad.

Rather it was because they were in over their heads and/or doing something for the first time. I believe that there is no difference in impact, whether someone is in over their heads or doing something for the first time; it is not fun to be an employee in that environment. Why? Because in those situations, as an employee, you see more than the leader and constantly and consistently wonder why?

My explanation for why this is true is that when you are in over your head or doing something for the first time, you are too worried about yourself—how you are doing or how you look—to worry about your employees. Even if employees don't verbalize it, they know. They always know.

If you are a manager of people, consider the following to improve your team's results:

Make supervising people your number 1 priority.

"I am never too busy to talk with you" is a great mantra for a leader to share with her or his staff. In homage to human resources research, the number 1 factor employees use to evaluate a boss is the answer to the question, do you care about me?

Care more to reduce turnover.

Vary your approach.

Treating all the same is fine when it comes to company policy, fairness, equity, and the law. But treating all employees the same when providing directions ignores the fact that they come from different places with different experiences.

Vary your style based on who you are managing and the task they are performing. One size does not fit all in management. A new employee and a twenty-year employee do not have the same skills, abilities, and readiness for all tasks.

Take the time to assess where each employee might be in relation to the assignment you are giving. Gray hair doesn't automatically mean expert, and youth doesn't automatically mean green behind the ears. Everyone teaches us how to supervise them; we just need to pay attention.

The Situational Leadership model and Situational Leadership training is an excellent source of information and skill development in this area.

Find as many mentors as you can.

There are only two ways to move out of an in-over-your-head situation or a time where you are doing it for the first time. The first is to push through it, collect the scar tissue that comes with a rough experience, and learn from it. The second is to get a mentor.

Mentors can diminish the gap between your personal experience and the experience you need to be effective. Mentors can not only be found in other areas of the organization or outside the organization, but sometimes they can be found among the employees supervised.

Being the boss does not come with a requirement to know all the answers. Being the boss comes with the requirement to make the right decision, regardless of where the insight came from.

Word Travels Fast in a Small Town

So I don't know anything about the management or ownership of the 122 Diner, but I will tell you that in the words of Miranda Lambert, country music artist, "Everyone dies famous in a small town," and if the 122 Diner did not have good employees and good management, it would be gone, just like the restaurant it replaced.

Good and great managers minimize turnover by:

1. Caring about their employees and putting supervision first on the priority list
2. Varying their leadership style based on the employee's skill, ability, or readiness
3. Focusing on making the right decision instead of being the smartest person in the room.

My guess is that they consistently do all three of these things at the 122 Diner.

They may not have zero turnover, but they have a great team to supervise; they have the employees they deserve.

CHAPTER 11: DANCING WITH THE STARS

Part 1: Brave or Stupid?

Many years ago, an executive with a local health insurance company asked me if I would volunteer for a fundraiser for a Boston neighborhood civic association. The event was Dancing with the Stars of Boston. Much to my surprise, and the surprise of many in my business and social circle, I said yes.

During six weeks of training, I put my feelings, my experiences, and my attitudes into words, in diary fashion. Spoiler alert: I didn't win the competition.

Log Entry: April 18-INTRODUCTION

More than forty-five individuals voted in my informal poll, and the vast majority wanted the show to go on, so I guess this is going to happen on June 4.

Some of the advice I received before deciding:

- "Please don't. Love, Mom"
- "I vote yes. How bad could you be?" Paul, a friend.
- "I'll be there. Fifteen lessons, wow, sounds fun." Joanne, sister.
- "I would watch! And am sure that since you were a soccer player, you're coordinated enough to do a great job!" Sandy, a friend.
- "Funny. Quickly tell them no!" Brian, brother.
- "I couldn't do it…but all the stars say step out of your box…It's the best thing they've ever done." Susan, sister.
- "I am speechless!" Sherry, a friend.
- "Your willingness to make a fool of yourself to bring some great attention to your nonprofit is admirable." Paul, brother.

Log Entry: May 9 A NEW PAIR OF SHOES

I put two dimes in the parking meter and was thrilled that I had a spot directly in front of the store I had been trying to find in Wellesley. I think the fear hit me for the first time when I opened the door to the shop. Earlier, when I just "thought" it would happen, I was actually quite calm.

When my professional ballroom dancing instructor, Carol, asked me why I had agreed to do Dancing with the Stars, I really didn't have a good answer, because I'm not really sure why I'm doing it.

Maybe it's because I am afraid to bungee jump? Maybe I haven't read a good book lately? Could be because two of my nieces, Shannon and Ryanne, were dancers, and they would think I was cool?

- The fear didn't hit me at my first lesson when I walked into the studio and saw the mirrored walls and the parquet floor.
- It didn't hit me when I met Carol, the professional instructor who would be tasked with managing this impossible dream.
- It didn't hit me as I learned the basic steps of the foxtrot, waltz, rumba, and cha-cha (I quickly knew I was *not* a cha-cha kind of guy).
- The fear didn't even hit me when I learned how to hold my hands and how to let Carol's arm rest on mine while I touched her shoulder. Advanced stuff.
- I was actually pretty relaxed through that whole first lesson, bending my knees, putting my foot down toe first—you know, that basic stuff that we dancers do.
- I think the fear hit me for the first time when I opened the door to that little shop.

As the door closed behind me, I could see a little girl in her new pair of shoes, with taps, showing mommy how she could make noise with her feet. I could see the displays with leotards and leggings and the other stuff that dancers, young and old, need to be dancers.

I didn't see too much merchandise a guy my age could use, so I kept my glance downward. I could see a dad reaching into his wallet as his teenage daughter with braces smiled that special smile that only daughters have for their fathers, and the clerk made a joke about today not costing $200.

I thought of my brother, who must have been in shops like this, with a wallet like that, probably dozens of times with his two daughters, who had been dancers since learning to walk.

Without daughters of my own, it was a slice of life that had escaped me. Without any interest in dancing, it was a slice of life I never wondered about. Now I was faced with the cold hard reality that I was in Capezio's Dance Theater Shop with a 10 percent discount card I had snagged at Arthur Murray's Dance Studio.

It all happened so fast I could scarcely believe that I was a preferred shopper at a store that specialized in dance supplies!

That was when the fear hit me, and it hit me pretty hard.

I knew for certain, in that place and time, that I was completely out of my league, that I had no business being involved, that I was going to make a complete fool of myself, and that I really didn't want to spend a hundred bucks on "male ballroom dancing shoes."

Yep, if I was quick, I could sneak out of that place and get back to the car—too late. "Can I help you, sir?" the owner inquired while fitting an eight-year-old with some ballet shoes. *If my friends could see me now!* was all I was thinking.

So in short order, there I was, sitting on the bench next to a future ballerina, wondering if there was a market for gently used male ballroom dancing shoes. All I could think about was how I could unload the shoes I hadn't even bought yet when the event was over.

That was when the second wave of fear hit me. I trembled as I tried the shoes on, I was shaking as I paid, and in a trembling voice, I indicated I didn't need a bag; I was good to go.

As I walked past the leotards and special socks that stood between me and the door, clutching my very first pair of male ballroom dancing shoes, I told myself I had nothing to fear but fear itself. But that thought changed to the thought that I actually had a lot more to fear than fear itself.

I was sneaking into a new world, like landing on a different planet. These dance people were serious! I was a pretender, and everyone would soon see through my charade.

Could I actually be a dancer in thirty days? How long did it take us to get to the moon? I briefly contemplated faking an injury, just like you would in my situation. By the time I reached the car, I had decided that if, or since, I was going to do it, I would at least do it with enough energy to surprise. That became my goal, born out of fear: to surprise.

Surprising is a lot different from excelling; I agree, but maybe not. If I go through this and do something no one thought I could do in a way no one thought I could do it, that's sort of like excelling, isn't it? Nah, I didn't think so either.

Log Entry: May 10-DANCING EVERYWHERE

The first lesson wearing my new dancing shoes went by quickly. On the day before my second lesson, I was hoping *not* to surprise any construction workers in the vacant office space. I had been struggling a little bit with transitions from one kind of step to another, and I knew I needed to miraculously get better before my 3:15 p.m. lesson if I was going to have any hope of surviving.

Unfortunately for me, I was coming off a late night in Boston, and I had a busy day ahead of me. There might not be any time to practice, so I knew I would have to improvise. I wasn't sure if I was going to practice my steps in the basement, the men's room, the halls of the office, or the halls of Montezuma. Eventually, I came up with an idea.

So there I was at 6:15 a.m., in a vacant open office space that was under renovation in the building where I worked. There was no carpet, no walls, and no construction workers at that hour. I had the whole damn ballroom (I mean office space) to myself. Can you picture me with earphones playing "Mack the Knife" and foxtrotting around the room, holding my imaginary partner? Neither can I, but that's exactly what I was doing.

For forty-five minutes, I pounded that cement floor with my tasseled loafers until I could at least go around once without losing my steps, the beat, or my mind. It was the kind of act you might hope to see on YouTube.

On the positive side, I hadn't come close to falling on my butt! When you are grasping for straws, remaining upright counts as positive reinforcement. As always, the thought *If my friends could see me now* wasn't too far from the front of my mind. Today it was preceded by, *I hope the carpet guys don't see me now*, because I was sure at any moment that the construction crew would show up and have a good laugh at my expense. Maybe a preview of reactions to come?

Log Entry: May 23 Sixteen Seconds

So there I was, flying around the vacant office space in our building feeling pretty good by my low personal standards and feeling very much like a light-footed dancer—you know, doing the knee dips and stuff and wiggling my hips when I really got into it—when I noticed a sound. I turned around, and that was when I realized I was still alone, but my fingers were snapping to the music in my head.

Part 2: Mack the Knife Arrives

Oh my gosh! I was turning into a *GQ* kind of guy right before my eyes! Could it be that I was actually enjoying this stuff? Nah. Just a fleeting moment, and the fear returned anew. That shark in the "Mack the Knife" song may have pretty teeth, babe, and he may keep them pearly white, but
this whole process was getting out of hand, particularly later that same day when my professional dance instructor told me I did (and I'm quoting here) "an awesome job."

The Song

"Mack the Knife" or "The Ballad of Mack the Knife" (German: *"Die Moritat von Mackie Messer"*) is a song composed by Kurt Weill with lyrics by Bertolt Brecht for their 1928 music drama *The Threepenny Opera*. The song has become a popular standard recorded by many artists.

"Mack the Knife" lyrics:

> Oh, the shark, babe, has such teeth, dear
> And it shows them pearly white
> Just a jackknife has old MacHeath, babe
> And he keeps it out of sight
> You know when that shark bites with his teeth,
>   babe
> Scarlet billows start to spread
> Fancy gloves though wears old MacHeath, babe
> So, there's never, never a trace of red.

When it comes to finger snapping to "Mack the Knife," I have what it takes. Whether I can dance to the song is another matter, but I am ready *to-day* to snap my fingers for two minutes and sixteen seconds if I have to. (In response to numerous inquiries, no, I am not wearing one of those cute little vests, and I am *not* waxing my chest.)

You may be saying, "Everything seems to be coming so naturally to you, Ed," but you would be wrong. Finger snapping, I get an *A*; fedora management, I get a *C*. That's right, I start the dance with a fedora (that's a hat) in my hands, and I have to put it on my head *while I'm strutting*.

This is a basic variation of the walk-and-chew-gum-at-the-same-time theme we are all familiar with. I have to strut and twirl a fedora at the same time. You don't want to know how many times it takes to get this one right. Thursday, I will show my professional instructor that I have the steps, the finger snaps, and the timing down to move on to the next part of the choreography.

I'm pretty sure, but not certain, that when I stride triumphantly into the Arthur Murray studio in Natick for my next lesson, I *will* have memorized all sixteen seconds of the routine. That's right, to this point, all I have rehearsed and worked on is the first sixteen seconds of the routine. I am a master at the first sixteen seconds of "Mack the Knife," but how I am ever going to learn the remaining two minutes of this dance is anyone's guess.

Less than two weeks to go to learn two minutes of dance routine. Can I do it? Let's see, with two double lessons this week and two triple lessons next week, it is going to be close. But if I'm already up to twinkle steps, then the sky's the limit for me. (Yes, twinkle steps is a real term.)

I know I will be on that stage with the lights shining in my face, very much hoping not to crap my pants. I finally have the fedora flipping down, and my son observed a practice last week and indicated that I was better than he thought I would be, but this close to Father's Day, he's not likely to be slamming me.

I have put those earbuds in every day and danced by myself, mastering those sixteen seconds—in my driveway, the basement, the kitchen, the bottom floor of the parking garage at Post Office Square, and on the steps of the statehouse. I play the song "Mack the Knife" pretty much nonstop in the car, visualizing each of the steps. I know this much at this time: I might be bad, but I'm not terrible, and in fact, I may even be proudly mediocre.

My mom was a great ballroom dancer and has encouraged me. She believes I have the genes to do this. After today's lesson, I will know more about how much work I have to put in and how many of the most critically needed genes I might have. I'm thinking maybe bungee jumping would've been a better choice for whatever midlife crisis I'm living out on this one.

I am still learning. I was a little surprised today when I learned that I can't walk backward and wiggle well enough to include such a showstopping step into the routine. It has been replaced by walking backward and basically bumping butts with my partner. And while I have no formal training, and we practiced very little, apparently I am a good butt bumper naturally.

I also learned that even though the likelihood that I will drop my partner at the grand finale when she falls over my bent leg on her back is slim, she is still nervous. That's her problem. I'm nervous about the whole damn dance; she can be nervous about the last two seconds.

I also learned that I need to develop an "attitude" and ham it up. I'm just not "Mack the Knife" yet. This could be the hard part. In machinelike fashion and with hard work, I guess I always knew I could memorize the steps. If you can memorize all those formulas for algebra, you can memorize dance steps.

I guess I also always knew that I would eventually find the courage to get on the stage, because I have a lot of experience being afraid in front of a crowd, and I have always managed to face the audience. I'm just not sure I can get an attitude I don't have.

Log Entry: May 29 LIKE FATHER, LIKE SON?

At today's lesson, my wife dropped in because the curiosity factor was killing her, and she may have insightfully saved me without realizing it.

At dinner, we didn't talk about my routine much, but she said something that put a tear in my eye then and has one there now. She said when she was watching me prance around the room, it reminded her of my father; "Mack the Knife" was his kind of song and his kind of attitude—Sinatra-like.

It's been decades since anyone said I reminded them of my late dad, but I realized she was right. If I'm going to find that attitude for the song that they want me to have, I guess I can stop looking around and start looking inside. My father could have an attitude, and he could ham it up. I guess maybe I'll just bring him on stage with me and see what happens. Maybe he's been with me all along, and I just couldn't see him. It wouldn't be the first time I had help from him I didn't know I had.

Log Entry: May 30 DARING, SCARY AND NUTS

I guess this will be my last entry until the contest. The next time I write, I will have completed one of the most daunting tasks of my life. To get up on stage and do this with no dancing experience or ability is stupid, outrageous, daring, scary, and nuts!

But like the sign hanging on the wall in the men's room at the Natick Arthur Murray studios says, "Life is not measured by the breaths we take but by the moments that take our breath away."

Someone's breath is going to be taken away next Wednesday, and although it could be mine because I could forget to breathe, maybe that's enough. And while I can honestly say I have never been inspired before by any sign on any men's room wall anywhere, the next time someone asks me what my goal is for this event, I'm going to look them right in the eye, with an attitude of course, and say, "To take your breath away." Let's get this thing over with.

Part 3: The Peaceful Warrior

Log Entry-June 4: The Big Day

It is four in the morning. I'm up and ready to go. Today is the day of the big Dancing with the Stars of Boston competition, the final step of the journey. Strange things happen when you change your goals.

As long as my goal was to surprise people with my dancing performance, my attitude and effort reflected that; I tried very, very, very hard to learn and was normally diligent in my preparations. Extra work and maximum effort came easy to me.

As soon as my goal shifted to the take-your-breath-away objective, my whole world changed.

- Just like my dad, I realized I can be "Mack the Knife."
- Just like my mom, I realized I have a dancing gene or two.
- Just like my son, Joe, I realized I don't give up.

At the same time, I realized how talented my professional partner, Carol, was and how patient she had been with me and how much I depended on her. I realized that my routine was really "our" routine based on our collective abilities—not just hers and not just mine. I realized that the routine is really "cute," as the other dancers say; it is a good song with good choreography.

I recognized that as a professional, Carol has more at stake than I do, and so does the Arthur Murray Studio in Natick. I realized that it was the journey, not the event, that I have been writing about, because it is the journey that is most important and interesting.

It isn't the four weeks and twenty-three forty-five-minute lessons, sprinkled with a few high fives, but many more "breathe," and "keep your eyes up," and "put some personality into it" comments that I will miss. I realize that I will miss being with a very wise person and a special person who was able to handle this quest with me. Think about it: would you want to teach *me* to dance?

The pride on her face at my happiness when I finally hit all the steps in the final rehearsal was obvious (there may have been some relief in there too).

Recently I reread some of the quotes people sent to me when I polled the audience on whether I should volunteer for this event. The responses mostly fell into two categories: some felt it would be funny to see the finished version, but even those who didn't think it was a good idea, including several family members, never doubted whether I could do it, and I guess, deep down inside, I stopped doubting it too.

Each of the people giving a response had an opinion. My professional dance partner had no choice and no opinion in the matter. I showed up with two left feet, she started working with me, and moved me to the point where *our* goal reached "to take your breath away." I'm not sure who is more amazed that I can do this routine, Carol or me.

As I said to the entire staff at the dance studio, who turned out for my dress rehearsal, when I walked out of the studio for the last time, "The miracle has already happened. I'm a dancer."

It doesn't matter to me what happens tonight; I know we'll do a good job. We've already impressed ourselves. Thank you, Arthur Murray Natick. Thank you, Carol. Your professionalism, your welcoming, your support, your patience, your encouragement took *my* breath away.

I'm not sure who created that take your breath away quote hanging on the men's room wall that I've latched onto. What I do know is that I'm not afraid anymore. It has been a short journey and a totally unexpected one. I've come a long way from that scared little guy buying male ballroom dancing shoes with a preferred customer card in that little shop in Wellesley.

I could tell I had changed by the look in the eyes of those observers at the studio yesterday for my last visit. I could tell that by Carol's eyes when we finished rehearsals. I could tell that by the look in my eyes in the mirror this morning.

Log Entry-June 5: After the Show:

As I get ready to head to sleep after an exceptionally intense day, I know it has been quite a journey and quite a test. What I learned on the journey still benefits me, and I feel great that I passed the test.

I know that when I stepped out on the stage and started twirling that fedora, it was a moment that took more than one person's breath away. That was when the line between bravery and stupidity was crossed, and I successfully made it back. You figure out which side I started on.

A phrase I remember from my fraternity initiation ceremony was in my mind as I left the stage that night. In that ritual the leader said, "When you face up to the fears that confront you, many times they disappear." The founders of the fraternity were right on many things, including this one.

The photo of our bows after the routine captures one of the most relieved moments of my life: The dance is over. I didn't trip. I didn't split my pants. I made most of the steps. And of course, people were laughing with me, not at me.

If you are a fan of the television show, many participants say stepping out of their box was the best thing they've ever done. Maybe not the best thing for me, but right up there. I feel so good about this I may take up brain surgery next—it can't be any harder.

Or maybe I'll try out for the Boston Celtics Dance Team? Now *that*, my friends, would take someone's breath away. Ta-dah! The end.

Postscript: So I did not drop her. I didn't come close.

During the training for this event, in her wisdom, she recommended that I read a book called the *Peaceful Warrior* by Dan Millman, and in the preface, he says: "I call myself a Peaceful Warrior... because the real battles we fight are on the inside."

CHAPTER 12: NOT RUNNING ON EMPTY

Personal Best with a Twist

The Fourth of July makes most Americans think of backyards and barbecues and fireworks and beaches. It makes me think of those things, too, but I also  remember something else involving an American flag.

Do you have any idea how motivating a personal best is to a runner or any athlete? If you are a runner or a weight lifter or a field goal kicker or a swimmer or a golfer, you do.

Reaching for a personal best is so powerful that aching muscles do not hurt *that* much. It is so powerful that you cannot wait for the next time. It is so powerful that nothing can ruin your day. It is so powerful you just have to write about it, so I do.

When I was training for my first half-marathon, I achieved a personal best with an unexpected twist, and the twist turned out to be more memorable than the personal best.

My training assignment at daybreak on a Sunday morning was to run 9 miles. At the time, I had never run more than 7 miles and didn't exactly feel as fresh as a daisy after that distance. I couldn't imagine how crappy I'd feel after nine miles. But since it would be necessary to run 9 miles if I was going to run 13.1 in a half-marathon, I was ready to try.

Regardless of how many times I've done it since then, let me assure you, nine miles is a long, long way. My wife was very concerned about this feat of daring, so I promised her I would run a route on Main Street, where someone could see me or help me in the event I, ahem, struggled with the assignment.

Like many runners who follow the same course in their training runs, I had memorized every mile on Main Street for shorter distances, so I knew exactly how far I had come and how far I had to go on an out-and-back route, but the nine-mile stuff was a little new to me. Of course, being a planner, I drove the route the day before and realized that nine miles is a long, long way. On the scouting ride, I was having even more doubts about this idea, thinking about excuses or, I'm sorry, valid reasons to not try nine miles. Wouldn't six miles do? Maybe seven? Is it time to twist my ankle, mildly?

As I left my driveway very early that Sunday morning, with the thought that I wouldn't be back for almost two hours (are you kidding me, two hours?), I did what I do best: I put one foot in front of the other, and I was off, hoping this was going to just be me pounding through the miles and bringing along stubborn persistence.

I was feeling pretty good as I reached the 4.5-mile turnaround point and started back. In fact, the first 5.5 miles were uneventful. No special aches, pains, trips, or slips. Then I saw it. In front of one of the restaurants on Main Street, there was an American flag lying on the ground.

I realized it was one of the town flags that had broken free of the light pole above. I paused, unsure about what to do next. The flag itself was longer than the pole it was attached to, so I couldn't lean it against anything because the stars and stripes would still touch the ground. I didn't want to tie up the flag; it seemed so unprofessional. And there was really no place to put it or bring it at that time of the morning, almost nothing was open. So I picked it up and started running.

Can you picture it? There I was, running down Main Street, holding an American flag that is literally flowing behind me. I really didn't know what else to do. I didn't want to kill my nine-mile training run time by looking for some place to put it, so just on reflex, I grabbed it and ran and decided that I would drop it at the police station, always open, and conveniently on my route, only about three miles away.

I have anticipated your questions.

Did cars honk driving by me as the town started to wake up? Actually, dozens of them. Did I feel like a patriot? Absolutely. Did the miles fly by? Assuredly so. I really do not know if I had ever taken a step with an American flag flowing behind me in my life, but on that Sunday, I took about three thousand of them, and it felt great.

What did I think about when I was running? As the son of a veteran, I could not help but think about servicemen and women, alive and dead, including my dad, who had run to our flag, with our flag or for our flag.

I thought a lot about the symbolism of what I was doing and how people driving by must have been assuming something about this gray-haired dude running with an American flag. But what did they assume? In America today, where there are so many divisions, I sincerely hoped that everyone who saw me just smiled and felt good about being an American.

I hoped they were thinking, now there's a guy who cares. As I reached the police station, I hit the pause button on my Fitbit, ran inside, turned in the flag, explained where it fell from, and resumed my run, all in less than twenty seconds.

I missed the flag as I finished the rest of the long, long route, and I started to feel the aches and pains that naturally come the first time you run nine miles. The running was noticeably harder once I dropped off the flag. Maybe I had been running on air?

When I finally crested the last hill and hit my driveway, a mere one hour and forty-five minutes from when I started, I remember thinking I was proud of three things: I was proud to finish such a long run. I was proud to set a personal best distance mark, and of course, I was proud to be an American. I also wished I had a hot tub, but I took a nap instead.

Inside the Orange Barriers and Arena

Life would be a little boring if we achieved 100 percent of our goals, wouldn't it? Oh sure, it would be fantastic but a little boring.
What that means, I think, is that failure is important to a nonboring life? It is the doubt about success that can drive us to achieve.

I'm sure you have set a goal but realized almost immediately that you were going to fall short and fail.

When that happens, we intuitively know we have limited choices.

We can stop, quit, and live to fight another day.

Or we can pause, re-evaluate, reset the goal, and keep going.

Or we can keep going without a reset and see how far we can get or how close we can get to the goal or, inversely, learn exactly how far short we will fall.

I was faced with those three choices (again) in downtown Boston one year at the Boston Athletic Association 10k Road Race (6.2 miles for the metrically challenged).

When my day started out, I was concerned with the rising temperatures, approaching eighty degrees, and the rising humidity, approaching 80 percent. It might hit ninety degrees before the race was over. Hot-weather running is a challenge for everyone.

I had planned ahead but not well enough. I'm sure that's happened to you. I left a cooling cloth in the car. I had also packed a water bottle that I had planned to spray my face with if I got hot and left that in the car as well. My preparation did not earn an *A*.

But I had known in advance that the day was not going to be a personal best-achievement day because of the weather, and I had planned to run a slower race and stay safe. At my age, the thin line between bravery and stupidity is a dangerous line and one that I regularly flirt with. Too much heat in my body would be stupid and could impact my ability to fight another day.

So while I was waiting for the event to start, I got philosophical and asked myself the following question: Why run a race that I cannot win (and never could) and cannot set a personal best? As I walked around and stood in line for one of the 250 porta-johns, I wasn't sure what my actual goal was going to be for the day.

I remembered when I first started my running career, my goal was modest: not to finish last. Since then, I've earned a wall full of finisher medals that are reminders that I've done pretty well at times. But I still couldn't figure out why I was running.

I only had to wonder for about a mile after the event began. At that point, it was so hot that I had to stop and walk. I know when I'm hot, and I know when to stop. And when I'm very hot, I stop. Let me assure you, I was totally ashamed of myself.

I had five more miles to run, and I was already wiped out. I was not going to hit a personal best, and I was also not going to run 6.2 miles. No, instead I was going to drag my ass through the streets of Boston with prodigious levels of sweat and would be walking more miles than I was going to run.

Choices: I wasn't going to call off the event; I couldn't send six thousand people home until another cooler day. I couldn't stop, turn around, and go home and keep my reputation intact. I had to keep going, so I did, and I had to develop a goal for this disaster on the fly.

I realized that I was in downtown Boston. On a sunny June morning. With six thousand others. When I looked around, I felt a little better because there were so many people walking instead of running. (Misery loves company, no matter what you've been told.)

So I set a very unusual goal: to enjoy myself any way I could. Strange goal, I agree, but I was desperate. I realized that one of the ways we enjoy ourselves is through memories, and I drifted into the past as I passed through the present. I literally took a stroll down memory lane.

- As I walked behind Kenmore Square and the famous Citgo sign, I saw the secret parking space that I used to use for

Red Sox games, thanks to a BU professor who moved his car out of his space for me to use when I needed it.

- I also saw the spot close by where my battery died years ago, and Triple A came to help me in less than fifteen minutes. (Most AAA experiences are not good memories; this was an exception.) A couple of good memories to fuel my new goal, so I jogged a little bit. Very little. I was hot, so I walked again.

- Less than a mile later, I was in front of the Boston University's classic buildings and thought of one of its MBA graduates, my dad. I jogged one hundred yards in his memory. In a little while, I passed in front of the Paradise Rock Club, where my youngest brother, leader of the band Gang Green, used to play and where I attended a fundraiser for him after his stroke.

- At the turnaround point, I could see everyone behind me, so I knew I wouldn't finish last and jogged a little bit to make sure. We were outside Nickerson Field, and I thought of the night when I was ten years old, and I attended the very first Boston Patriots game.

- Good memories. I then remembered that I played there once on the UMass soccer team and watched one of my brothers play there for Braintree High.

- When I went by the studios of WBUR, a public radio station, I remembered when I once did an interview there for the nonprofit I managed. Boy, this stretch of Commonwealth Avenue had a wealth of memories.

- And then I thought about the time I met my version of Mr. Bojangles in the same neighborhood. An eighty-year-old guy chewing on a cigar stub who told me the story of how he and his wife were vaudeville performers until she passed away, and he jumped up and clicked his heels in the restaurant to prove it. I went next door and bought him a new cigar.

- As we came back through Kenmore Square, I thought about watching my first Boston Marathon after a Red Sox game with Joseph Cummings, my mom's uncle, and son's name-sake, more than sixty years ago. I decided that I should run over the same ground. Very cool, although I was not.

• As I passed under Mass Avenue, I looked down and saw the three blue stripes on the road and was reminded that the Boston Marathon runners passed over this asphalt a few weeks ago. Most of those runners were going much faster than me.

That's when it hit me.

I realized that running over those blue lines was a privilege. I knew the reason that I was running. It was so simple, but the microprocessor between my ears had sped right by the answer. I run because I can.

As I headed down the home stretch on Cambridge Street and could see the finish line, the orange barricades on both sides of the road reinforced my conclusion. I had modified my goal to enjoy myself through memories, but that was secondary to my purpose.

I was *inside* the orange barriers. I wasn't a spectator; I was a man in the arena. I wasn't running to win the event. I wasn't running to set a personal best, although that would be a bonus. I was running because I wanted to be that man Theodore Roosevelt referred to in this famous quote.

It is not the critic who counts; not the man who points out how the strong man stumbles, or where the doer of deeds could have done them better. The credit belongs to the man who is actually in the arena, whose face is marred by dust and sweat and blood; who strives valiantly; who errs, who comes short again and again, because there is no effort without error and short-coming; but who does actually strive to do the deeds; who knows great enthusiasms, the great devotions; who spends himself in a worthy cause; who at the best knows in the end the triumph of high achievement, and who at the worst, if he fails, at least fails while daring greatly, so that his place shall never be with those cold and timid souls who neither know victory nor defeat.

So I failed to reach my goal on the last Sunday in June, but at least I dared greatly, salvaged the day with a stroll down memory lane, and remembered why I run. I hope all my failures turn out as well. I'll be back; I'm not leaving the arena any time soon.

The Falmouth Super Bowl

The seven-mile Falmouth Road Race has been my personal Super Bowl each August. Running it for the first time, at the time, was the achievement of a lifetime for me, considering my age and the late start I had with this running thing.

It was a huge fundraiser for the nonprofit I was dedicated to as well, raising more than $100,000 over the years as volunteers and staff ran as members of the charity program.

Seven miles with ten thousand others on the shores of Cape Cod with free frozen yogurt bars at the finish? Are you kidding me? Who else gets free frozen yogurt bars after a race? It took me about an hour and a half to complete the course the first time and stay out of the medical tent. But I was hooked.

The day after that first race, I started planning for the next year. Seriously. I tracked everything I did all year, gearing up for the event using an Excel spreadsheet to help. I tracked every run, every distance, my average heart rate, maximum heart rate, average pace, pace per mile, etc.

I try to leave no detail to chance. My socks, my shoes, my shoelaces, my hydration, my nutrition, my playlist, my knee wrap, my foam rolling, my strength training, my warm-up, my sleep, my damn toenails even get attention, and no guy pays much attention to his toenails.

This event may be the most exciting running event, but it also takes a major effort just to get to the start line.

Getting a bib: The Falmouth Experience is so popular that only a minor percentage of the runners who want to participate are able get one of the ten thousand entry bibs. There are three ways to get a number.

- First, if you live in the town of Falmouth, there is a lottery, and your name can be drawn. Entry fee: $200.

- Second, if you live anywhere else, there is a lottery, and your name can be drawn. Entry fee: $200.
- Third, if you are not a lottery winner, but you are a very nice person, you can run for a charity team. Entry fee: $200, *plus* achieve the fundraising minimum goal. Most charity partners have a minimum of $1,000.

Getting to Woods Hole: The event originally started as a run between two bars on the cape. One in Woods Hole, home of the famous Oceanographic Institute, and another in Falmouth Heights. Here are the ten steps I take each year to get to the start:

1. Since Falmouth is a little over two hours from my house, I leave home on Saturday night, about 8:00 p.m., and drive about halfway to stay at my brother's home.
2. When the alarm goes off at 4:15 a.m., I hop up, got dressed, and head to Cumberland Farms convenience store for a large decaf and the last of yesterday's bagels.
3. I pull into the parking lot at the Lawrence School in Falmouth before 6:00 a.m. and hide my wallet and grab my hat. One year, I heard the parking attendant say, "We're full. No more cars." Whew, that was close
4. The only way to get to the start line for this race is through the bus loading zone at this school. There are literally hundreds of buses that pull up, load, and depart for Woods Hole about five miles away. I get in line and take a seat in the back of the bus. Did you know that elementary school children have smaller legs than adults? It's true. Those school bus seats are so close together. By the time you get to the start line, you are friends with whoever is sitting with you.
5. So there I am, on the main street of Woods Hole each year, with more than two hundred porta-potties within one hundred yards, at 6:23 a.m. I use one immediately before it gets too crowded (remember, I've had coffee).
6. Next I find a nice bench, fold the old towel I have brought specifically for this purpose, and sit. I am going to sit for

a couple of hours overlooking Martha's Vineyard and the Atlantic Ocean.

7. At 8:30 a.m., I generally stand up, abandon the towel, and start moving around, stretching, people watching, and looking for the shortest porta-potty line for my second trip, just to make sure I am not carrying excess weight. If I find a line with less than fifty people waiting, I slowly move toward relief.

8. About 8:45 a.m., I find the "10 Minute Mile Pace" sign and settle in, turn on my prerace playlist with inspirational songs, and wait while the wheelchair racers, the elite women, the elite men go off, each with a starter's gun that gets the crowd to cheer.

9. There are now, according to the PA announcer, about ten thousand people jammed into this two-lane street ready to take off. Runners are pulsed over the start line in groups of one thousand every two minutes.

10. Since there are easily seven thousand to eight thousand people in front of me, I still have a little wait. I finally cross the electronic mat on the road that will help to time me, and it is thirteen hours after I left my home and more than five hours since I woke up.

Beaten by a girl? So picture me, with 365 days of preparation, hundreds of miles of training runs, emery-boarded toenails, and all, standing at the start line with ten thousand runners on an unusually cool August morning, twenty yards from the Atlantic Ocean, with adrenalin pumping through my veins. (It wasn't really pumping, pumping, and I think it is arteries anyway, but I've always wanted to use the phrase "pumping through my veins," and now I have.)

My fourth personal Super Bowl is about to start—and an eleven-year-old girl starts taunting me. (I know that line surprised you.) Delaney is the daughter of a friend who is also running, and I might have challenged this young lady earlier in the morning because I was still hurting over being beat by this young girl when she was ten years old the year before, running her first Falmouth Road Race.

Anyway the challenge was on. I now had the edge I personally needed to excel: the opportunity to defeat an eleven-year-old. This particular eleven-year-old, quite frankly, won the trash-talking contest before the race because my vocabulary was *severely* restricted. Vocabulary is limited when trash-talking with an eleven-year-old, if you know what I mean. Lots of words were unavailable to me.

Now before you get too judgmental about my attitude, why don't you run seven miles with a ten-year-old and see how you feel when you get beaten? It is a serious ego blow, and you don't have to be a manly man to be devastated by such a result. You also have to give the kid a lot of credit for picking on me, I mean for running that far that fast. Probably no one reading this could run that far when you were ten. Here's how the route plays out.

Getting to the finish: As challenging as getting to the start might be, finishing the race is even more of a test of will.

Mile 1: An adrenaline rush, pure and simple. Thousands of runners, maybe the same amount of spectators, orange barricades, a sound system playing the theme from *Rocky* at the top of the hill with the iconic lighthouse. Spec-tac-u-lar.

Mile 2: A no-breeze zone where you really heat up. Dense growth on both sides of the road, only a few houses (some with hoses or sprinklers to cool down the runners). And three hills that aren't too big but definitely take their toll.

Mile 3: A duplicate of mile 2. No breeze, dense growth, few houses, three hills. You do run under an old railroad bridge covered with people cheering. Or is that mile 2?

Mile 4: Brutal and beautiful. Hot, flat mile along the sand, sun beating down. Lots of spectators cheering you on. A water stop, where you take two cups: one to drink and one to pour on your head.

Mile 5: Back through neighborhoods. Hundreds if not thousands of cheering spectators, live bands every couple of blocks. A real celebration.

Mile 6: In a few words, a run around Falmouth Harbor. Boats, boatyards, restaurants.

Mile 7: The deceptive mile. There is a hill about a half mile from the finish that is so crowded, and there are so many photographers, the first-time runner sometimes thinks s/he is done. Not so fast. The hill doesn't stop, and on the other side is the downhill finish, seven miles and more than an hour for most, away from Woods Hole.

With a little help from the weather person, who delivered a cool low-humidity day, I knew I was going to set a personal best before the race even started. With a great year of training plus being motivated by taunting from an eleven-year-old, I was able to run the Falmouth Road Race in the astonishing (to me) time of one hour and twelve minutes.

Let me expand on that: everyone was astonished. Why astonished? That's seventeen minutes faster than my first time and ten minutes and thirty-two seconds faster than my previous best. The first year I ran this event, I was hoping to have at least 1 person finish behind me. On my fourth try, according to the official records, 4,073 runners finished behind me. Four-thousand seventy-three.

Oh, and one of the 4,073 runners behind me was an eleven-year-old.

Unfortunately for me, the following year, perhaps motivated by being embarrassed by a senior citizen, she finished slightly ahead of me. We haven't faced off in a race since then. She quit while she was ahead.

First Overtime: It's Not Over Until It's Over

Mile 8: Sure, it is a seven-mile race, but that's not the whole story. To get to the frozen yogurt bars and the hot dogs, you are *herded* (and that is the most accurate term) about four blocks past the finish, two blocks away from the ocean, and four blocks back to the park, where all the goodies await.

Mile 9: Did I mention that the parking lot for the shuttle buses is more than two miles from the finish? After wolfing down the hot dog and taking a bottle of water to go, I head back along the route that I just ran (cutting through a neighborhood or two to shorten the trip).

Mile 10: The last mile. I can see my car; I unlock it and sit. It is now afternoon, more than eight hours since I left this morning, and I am pretty tired. It is a good feeling to sit.

For those counting steps, I took 24,730 of them before the day was over.

Second Overtime: The Inspirational Trooper:

On the seventh time I ran this event, I ran as part of the Cystic Fibrosis Foundation team.

Unbeknownst to me (using the word *unbeknownst* in a sentence is a writer's dream), an individual who is my point of contact with a company I deal with regularly named Laura has a child with CF.

Below are the communications with Laura the week before the race. After reading the email exchanges, you will know why Elijah is an inspirational trooper.

> From: Laura
> To: Ed Doherty
> Subject: CF race
>
> Hey Ed, I know you're running this weekend for the CF Foundation. I have made a donation towards this effort—thank you for doing it! I can't remember if we've discussed this before, but my 2nd born son is adopted and he has CF. It is a terrible disease but because of fundraising efforts like this, we are hopeful that the treatments and therapies continue to improve! So much hope is there, Thank you for doing this and I hope it's a great time!—Laura
>
> From: Laura
> To: Ed Doherty
> Subject: Re: Thank You
>
> This is INCREDIBLE!!! What an amazing thing you're doing- thank you so much for running today and for bringing Elijah along. I hope it goes well

and I hope you know how much my entire family appreciates your efforts to help. Thank you!!!

From: Edward Doherty
To: Laura
Subject: Dear Elijah

Elijah, You don't know me and might not ever meet me, but I wanted to thank you for your help yesterday when I ran a 7-mile race in very hot weather along the ocean. I used your courage and spirit to keep me going when I really wanted to stop and quit. But thinking of you made me want to finish and not give up, because I know you will not give up. As you get older, remember that you can inspire almost anyone, just by being you.

Keep battling, trooper.

CHAPTER 13: TOO FAR TO GO ALONE

Smuttynose Half Part 1: Brave or Stupid?

Naturally, being competitive, 5k, 10k, and seven-mile races weren't enough for me. I had to try a real endurance race—a half-marathon. Here's how that quest evolved.

Four weeks to go: As I prepared to run the outlandish distance of 13.1 miles, I was just a little surprised at the number of friends, families, and coworkers who fell on the "he's stupid" side of the "is he brave or stupid?" question. They might be right; I might be crazy ("But it just might be a lunatic you're looking for," to quote a line from Billy Joel).

The skepticism minimally impacted my confidence level as I prepared for the event, my first half-marathon, but just to be sure, I did something about it: I got new socks. Nothing breeds confidence like new socks. I think we all have doubts about our ability, or make that our capability, of accomplishing challenges we set for ourselves. When someone else sets a goal, like the boss, we can at least complain about it. How do you complain about a goal you set for yourself? I guess you can't; you lost that right/privilege when you set it.

That's why, I believe, we often set goals for ourselves that are safe or more easily accomplished when compared to the goals that others set for us. So for me, the goofy goal of running a half-marathon might have been more about setting a challenge for myself that stretched me rather than about being crazy.

Was I a little concerned about finishing those 13.1 miles? Yes. Did it add stress to my otherwise stress-free existence? Absolutely. Did I doubt myself as I went through my training days? Wouldn't you?

I wondered what the real *why* was for me? Why was I running a distance I had never run before? Was I brave or stupid? After some reflection, with four weeks to go before the event, I really didn't know yet, but I had two good reasons for moving forward.

First, doubters have always helped drive me further. Thank goodness for doubters! My life has been highlighted (or lowlighted) by a series of people doubting me. Sure, I've had a lot of supporters as well, but someone spitting in your face creates more energy than a hug.

Chances are, if you look at your own history, you'll find some doubters there, and chances are they fueled your drive to succeed in a way your huggers could not.

Second, I knew that one of the things we could all do a little better, I think, is challenge ourselves. It's just hard to do. That's what I was doing. I was simply challenging myself to stay off the couch. I was challenging myself to see how good I could be when I was challenged.

But I have to admit, maybe I wanted to do something that would bring the doubters out? A longtime friend, who knows who he is, when he learned that I run because I can, responded with, "I don't run because I can." (Let it sink in for a minute.) Anyway those were my thoughts with four weeks to go. I was surprised that I was not hurting yet or backing out yet. And I wasn't letting the doubters get to me yet. Thanks, Billy Joel?

I have been reminded that, in general, confidence can be fleeting. When it comes to half-marathon training, confidence is fleeting. One of the T-shirts I observed at a recent race said, "30 days ago, this seemed like a good idea." That's how I felt at the start of the week. This half-marathon idea seemed okay a month or two ago, but when I was in the intense training period, I lost a little confidence. I was thinking it might be time to walk away and fake a more serious injury to save face.

One of the concepts of goal achievement, not *the* concept but a fairly well-known concept, is to tell someone about your goal after you set it. It helps you in moments of doubt. So I did. I told a lot of people that I was running a half-marathon. It helped me in moments of doubt.

Three weeks to go: With three weeks left, I trained and ran more miles than any week in my life, and I was not in an ice tub, and I could still walk. Goals and I have a long relationship. Working my ass off is second nature to me, so when you combine those two, you get—are you ready?—28 miles. Eight miles on Monday. Four miles on Wednesday. Six miles on Friday, and a whopping, and I mean whopping, ten miles on Sunday.

Not only was the week the most miles I've ever run in a week, Sunday at ten miles was the most at one time. It is a long freaking way. It took two hours, seven minutes, and forty seconds. I think we all doubt ourselves from time to time. Confidence can be fleeting. When it comes to half-marathon training, confidence is fleeting. But running twenty-eight miles in a week can do a lot for your confidence, just as setting a goal and working your ass off can do a lot for your confidence.

All week I was thinking to myself that once next Sunday hits, I am home free. That day was the twelve-mile day of my half-marathon training plan. Yep, my plan was to run by Holden Light & Power five miles away, run another mile, and then turn around and run home.

Sunday morning, 6:00 a.m. Just me and my shadow. I knew that once I had the twelve-mile day out of the way, I was home free until I got to Hampton Beach to run the race. The last two weeks before the half-marathon, I would just be keeping loose, conserving energy, hydrating, foam rolling, and worrying my ass off. Pretty simple.

At this point in the training plan for this race, a couple of surprises floated to the top of my mind.

Surprise 1: I didn't know if physical achievement is something I'd thought about much since my twenties. I have to admit when I am running on Sunday mornings, and a millennial or five passes me and smiles, I want to shout, "I've been running for eight miles. That's why I look like crap."

Surprise 2: The number of skeptics declined. The side of the boat labeled "Brave" had more residents than the other side marked "Stupid." I was still in the middle. I realize that my upcoming long run will be twelve miles, and that might be *both* a brave and stupid day. Share your goals. Work hard. Get your confidence back if it is fleeting.

Smuttynose Half Part 2: Sunday Morning Champion

Two weeks to go: I can't believe that I was shaking. I was warming up in the driveway, about to run twelve miles, and I was shaking. I was really afraid, not sure of what, but I was afraid to do it.

The sun hadn't quite broken the horizon; it was morning twilight, a little softer. I was stretching and shaking at the same time. *Oh my gosh*, I thought, *what have I gotten myself into?* Well, if it were easy, anyone could do it right? I was ready to get this thing off the ground. It was so early that there was no traffic on Main Street. No traffic, no sound, no one moving except the nut starting on a twelve-mile run.

- Mile 1, Eagle Lake: That wasn't so bad, mostly downhill. The shaking stopped once I faced up to the fact that I was doing it. As I was thinking about the return run, I knew that if I made it this far, eleven miles with only a mile to go, I would be all set. Home stretch is more about will than skill, and I've always had more of the former to make up for the latter.
- Mile 2, Railroad Bridge, just past the Public Safety building: When I ran past the local diner, the parking lot was empty. It's early. When I hit this spot on the way back, the ten-mile mark, as soon as I take one step toward home past the bridge, I would be setting a personal-distance record. I had a couple of nagging pressure points on my feet that I pretended don't exist. Thank goodness I am good at blocking things out that need to be blocked out so I can accomplish objectives. That specific ability is going to be tested today.
- Mile 3, Sunnyside Ford Dealership: Pretty much on autopilot at this point, nothing remarkable about the last mile except some gray-haired dude went whipping by me like I

was standing still, and then ran by me again in the other direction. I knew he thought he was better than me. At least I'm not wearing black midcalf socks, such a fashion faux pas!

- Mile 4, state police barracks: Okay, this was the edge of my familiar sidewalks. Beyond this mark, I'd only run a couple of times. I was a third of the way through and started thinking about the turnaround point. It has always been easier for me on the run home. In fact, however crappy I feel at the turnaround point is close to how crappy I will feel at the end.

- Mile 5, Congregational Church: If I was going to cut it short, I knew this was the point to do it. After this point, it was a brave new world. I would be running another mile out and back over territory I'd never run before, although I knew it was a cement sidewalk, always a little harder on the knees. At least there weren't any millennials showing off. Yet.

- Turnaround point, Brattle Pizza stop: I had never been so happy to turn around. It was a nice mile, with some nice homes, nice stone walls, and some gorgeous landscaping. My theory of feeling crappy would be tested soon. I was on my way home, and that is always a great feeling, whether you are running or not.

- Mile 7, Congregational Church: The first two millennials passed me. At least they were nice. Smiled and said something about the humidity. They were going so fast. I wanted to tell them that I was running twelve miles today and pacing myself but kept silent. No one cares except me. And I cared enough to keep going.

- Mile 8, state police barracks: Back on familiar turf, two-thirds of the run complete, and I hoped I could keep going. I was tired, pretty sore, pretty sweaty, and pretty. Only kidding, I'm not pretty. The millennials have woken up and now are flying all around. I was proud that I don't wear spandex in public. At least I have my dignity.

- Mile 9, Sunnyside Ford Dealership: Did I mention that I was pretty tired, pretty sore, and pretty sweaty? My socks were failing me, and I had to stop to reset them. Monday morning, I would be at Marathon Sports to get new ones. I needed to be worrying about my knees and endurance, not my socks.

- Mile 10, Railroad Bridge: Once I passed the ten-mile mark, I knew I would officially break the world record for Edward James Doherty in distance running. I still couldn't believe I was doing this, but the proof, I guess, is I was doing this. There is no way I wasn't going to finish this run. No way. If I had to crawl, I was going to go twelve miles. The restaurant parking lot is packed as I run past it. I had been running for a long time.
- Mile 11, Eagle Lake: I had run the last mile hundreds of times. Almost every route I ran included this last mile. It is all uphill, but like an old friend, so as I started the final mile, I knew I had it. My eyes were watering a bit when I thought about what I was about to accomplish. It won't be in the paper, there will be no one at the finish line cheering, there won't be a medal, but there will be something better than all of that. I will have done it. Minor achievement? Maybe. But I'd have done it, and they can't take it away.
- Mile 12, my driveway: The last time I was there was two hours and thirty-eight minutes ago, and I was shaking with fear about what lay ahead. I just ran twelve miles. They can't take that away. No matter what happens during my first half-marathon, I just ran a big-boy distance, and I used some skill, some brains, and some will. I am a Sunday-morning champion, and I feel great. Except for my hips, knees, and feet, I feel great. As I say sometimes, I really want to hop in the Jacuzzi, but since we don't have one, I take a nap instead to celebrate.

Reflection: Was it easy? Are you kidding me? Try running twelve miles. If I had to identify lessons from my achievement, it would be this:

- Everyone trying something for the first time has doubts.
- Everyone trying to achieve something new has doubts.

- Everyone trying to be better tomorrow than they are today has doubts.
- Everyone stepping out of their comfort zone has doubts.
- Everyone has doubts.

Sometimes, those doubts are strong enough to make someone shake. But if you are going to grow, you have to try things for the first time. You have to try to achieve new heights. You have to step out of your comfort zone. You have to overcome your doubts.

Smuttynose Half Part 3: Too Far to Go Alone

One week to go: Do you remember when you first got your driver's license? You couldn't believe that you had it and that the government was really going to let you drive on public thoroughfares. It took a little while to get used to the view from the driver's side, after so much time in the passenger seat or the back seat growing up.

There was a kind of lifetime achievement because your life would now be defined as before you had your license and after you got it. In those early days, it was hard to believe that you were really a driver. That's how I felt. It is hard to believe I am really a runner. How do I know for sure? The day after my twelve-mile run, my legs didn't hurt. Repeat: my legs didn't hurt. They must be in some kind of shape, and it kinda happened right under my nose.

I think that's how we get better at something: we don't realize we are getting better until we are there, and then something happens, like legs not feeling sore, that alerts us to the fact that we are better.

I felt like I was engaging in a once-in-a-lifetime experience that was testing both my mental and physical toughness. I got that. But what I was really doing was practicing and developing a higher level of discipline that should pay bigger benefits after the race, when I went back to relying on my boyish charm for success. I will always remember training for my first half-marathon.

I couldn't believe that I was actually going to do it, and the race organizers would let me run on public thoroughfares. It has taken me a little while to get used to the view from inside the orange barricades, after so many years on the sidelines.

It would be a lifetime achievement if for no other reason than my life will now be defined as before I ran it and after I finished. It's hard to believe I am really a runner. That's how I feel.

My final-week training plan consisted only of a couple of three-mile runs, a little bike work, lots of water and pickle juice (one of my three secret weapons), and of course, plenty of prayers. There are some things we all need a little extra help with, and this is one of them. People who knew me were either wishing me luck or praying for me. I was either brave or stupid, and I knew that very soon, everyone would know for sure.

The night before: I had two significant thoughts during the week as I prepared for the half-marathon. First among them was that I felt very strong. Nothing hurt. I was thinking that I have done the training. Boy, have I done the training. I was thinking that I was mentally prepared, although you can never be certain; we all have negative voices in our head that somehow escape to wreak havoc. (Great expression, "wreak havoc." Can you wreak anything else besides havoc?)

I was looking at Sunday as just another day with about 26,000 steps. twenty-six thousand is a lot of steps, and they might all be important, but I knew it was the last step that counts the most. Why? I knew that without that last step to cross the finish line, I won't have crossed the finish line. The other 25,999 steps will have been in vain. (Staying with clichés: in vain counts.) There are a lot of times where finishing or taking that last step is the difference between success and failure, glory and shame, winning and losing.

The morning of the race: I was sitting alone in my car at five thirty in the morning, waiting for the sun to rise over Hampton Beach and the Atlantic Ocean, two and a half hours before the half-marathon, and there was nowhere to run and nowhere to hide yet.

The traffic, with eight thousand people arriving in this small beach town, was supposed to be brutal, and anyone who wasn't in place by 6:00 a.m. for the 8:00 a.m. race was going to have problems.

It gave me plenty of time to think and plenty of things to think about. As I popped out of the car to get a better view of the sunrise, I was thinking that this journey taught me about three things: preparation, motivation, and mentoration.

- *Preparation*: I personally put a high priority on preparation, but planning for this event was really at a different level. I logged the time of every practice mile I ran, along with my average heart rate and peak heart rate. I used an emery board on my toenails the night before so I wouldn't have any foot issues. Me, an emery board? Of course my wife looked surprised when I asked for one.

- *Motivation*: I also personally put a high priority on motivation. After training for this event, I can honestly say that I remembered what a higher level of motivation feels like again. Once I decided to run this race, it was my goal, and nothing was going to get in my way. I thought about the half-marathon in the morning, noon, and at night. I didn't skip a single workout. Every time someone indicated, in any way, any skepticism that I couldn't do it or that I was more stupid than brave, I was more motivated to do it.

- *Mentoration*: Correct, it is a new word that you heard here first. It means being fully, completely, and passionately engaged in the teaching-learning process as the learner. For me, being mentored was not something new but not something common either.

In addition to pickle juice (in lieu of Gatorade, try it sometime), my second secret weapon on this journey was that I had a mentor, a physical therapist who agreed to help me train. Dr. Sarah Rheault, a no-BS trainer who wasn't afraid to tell me what I didn't want to hear (definition of a good trainer?), had guided my every step throughout the ten-month training regimen. Because of the brave-or-stupid issue, she also served as my mentor from her position as founder of Wachusett Physical Therapy & Wellness.

With years of personal mentoring experience, I understood the process pretty much from the other side of the table, not the one-mentored side. So my goal was to be the best learner, the best question-asker, the best inquisitive person I could be so that I could drain every ounce of wisdom, every tidbit of knowledge I could from Sarah. You are correct, I was a pain in the ass from the start, asking some smart questions but a boatload of stupid ones.

It didn't mean taking everything she said and blindly moving forward. It meant understanding all of her recommendations fully before I left the session so that I could turn her knowledge into my performance. That's really the short version of mentoration: turning someone else's wisdom into your performance.

From her point of view, she was tasked with turning this half-crazy pursuit into reality with only her words, her demonstrations, and her feedback. She had to be good—correct that, she had to be great. Could I have done it without professional help? No. Short answer.

To be honest with you, I had a lot of feelings about and during this process, and one of the best feelings was having someone to advise me on something that really stretched me. Someone I didn't want to let down. I know she didn't want to let me down either.

At six o'clock in the morning, two hours before the race, Sarah and her future husband found me sitting on the sea wall as the sun was rising over the Atlantic Ocean, and the mercury hovered around forty degrees. This was not a prearranged meeting or place; she knew me well enough to correctly guess where I would be and what I would be doing.

Mentors sometimes know more about us than we expect, because they are focused on us, not themselves. She was there to say one more time, "You've got this." In addition to Sarah and pickle juice, my third secret ingredient was that I ran as part of Kathy's Team.

For many years, I had a job working to prevent challenging birth outcomes that I frequently summed up as preventing a mother's tears, because losing a child has to be among the most devastating things that can happen to a family. I know that firsthand because it happened to my family, and I heard my own mother's tears when my ten-year-old sister Kathy was killed by a classmate driving too fast, more than fifty years ago. She was hit by the car while in a crosswalk, on the way home from Saturday confession. A long time ago, but you never forget.

As I moved to the start line, I was wearing my self-designed race shirt, using one of those iron-on decals. On the front, it said, "KATHY'S TEAM," and on the back it said, "I RUN BECAUSE I CAN." Inspiration comes in many shapes and sizes, and different amounts of inspiration are needed for different tasks. Since this half-marathon thing turned out to be one of the biggest challenges of my life, I knew I needed a higher level of inspiration than ever. That Sunday morning, I was lucky enough to take that twenty-six-thousandth step in front of the Seashell Stage at Hampton Beach with tears streaming down my face, because you never forget.

So Kathy's Team had only two members but just one T-shirt, and somehow, I finished the race. In two hours and thirty-six minutes.

I had to have help from my sister. You don't really think I could run 13.1 miles by myself, do you? That's silly; it is way too far to go alone.

CHAPTER 14: DAMN PROUD

Forty-Seven Laps at Seventy Years Old

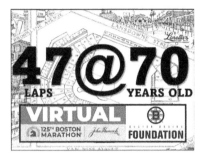

When I was a little boy, I used to go the Patriots Day game at Fenway Park that started at ten in the morning so that the fans could leave the park and head two blocks to Kenmore Square to watch the Boston Marathon Runners come through on their way to the finish line about a mile away.

When I told myself that running in that famous race, at seventy years old, would be a cool thing to do, I quickly dismissed a full-marathon race as way, way over the famous brave-stupid line I hug. But as I ran and trained and ran and trained, the thought of running in the Boston Marathon kept coming back to me.

When I told my trainer, Sarah, about the idea several years ago that I was thinking about running a full marathon, she said, "What took you?"

When I told my family, they said, "No way, too far to run."

When I told myself not to be disappointed but to think of all the pain I would be saving myself, I recovered from the disappointment. Almost. Why not?

When the Boston Marathon announced they would have a virtual element in 2021, a solution found me: I could run the Virtual Boston Marathon, the full 26.2 miles, but I could do it by running laps somewhere so that every lap, as I passed by my personal aid station, I could rest, change shoes, take a nap, use the restroom, be checked by a medical professional, etc.

So to the surprise of some, but not to others, I became an official entrant into the 125th running of the Boston Marathon, running on my own course, running for the Boston Bruins Foundation, and running on the Sunday of Columbus Day/Indigenous People Day weekend.

Notice I said *entrant*, because I knew that entering and finishing were two different things. I planned to enter and train my ass off so that I could finish, but as with anything never done before, there would still be a lot of work to do.

As a pathological planner, I designed a custom course: around the outside of Fenway Park, Ipswich Street, Van Ness Street, Jersey Street, Brookline Ave, and Lansdowne Street with a base station on the patio at Loretta's Last Call, where I planned to hold a party (if and) when I finish the forty-seven laps it will take to reach 26.2 miles. Forty-seven laps? Why not?

As part of the effort, my goal was to raise $10,000 to support the Bruins Foundation. It is an organization that was extremely generous to the nonprofit that I managed for almost fifteen years, investing thousands of dollars through sponsorships, raffles, and individual gifts for the cause of healthy moms and babies.

Not only that, but CEO Charlie Jacobs, General Manager Don Sweeney, and his wife, Christine, as well as foundation president Bob Sweeney and the head of community relations, Kerry Collins, all devoted time, treasure, and talent to the cause.

Running for the Bruins Foundation was a way of giving back to an organization that does great work led by great people.

How do you prepare for a marathon? Here was my plan:

- I had my longtime trainer, who is guiding me every step of the way.
- And I had a nutritionist, who is guiding me every meal of the way.
- And I had been alcohol-free for several years, just to maximize my conditioning.
- And I had a cardiologist who checks me out every six months.
- And I had lost a total of forty pounds since I started running.

So it must be the time to do it.

It wasn't a dream come true to try this; it was a dream about living life to the fullest. And about the brave-stupid line.

Forty-seven laps at seventy? Why not?

Singing in the Rain Is Overrated

After I announced that I was running the
Boston Marathon, it became harder for me to
back out. I had been planning to run in the event
for a while but had been very guarded about who
I shared that information with, in the event that
I lost confidence. Like any big challenge, doubts
are always hanging around the periphery.

Without going into the boring details, my
marathon training plan involved running three
times a week, two shorter runs with a long run every weekend. One
weekend, the goal was eight miles, the next week it was nine miles,
and so forth, up to about twenty miles in mid-September, and then
a tapering-off period to conserve energy and allow my body to heal
before the race.

During training, I had the opportunity to attend a conference
in Arizona.

Unsure about running a long distance in the heat, I packed
my running gear, hoping to be able to run the planned eight miles
in the desert. But with a daytime temp that I expected to be one
hundred-plus (a dry heat), I wasn't certain I could stick to my goal.
Failure to do so might back up my training another week.

With some discipline, which came from who knows where,
there I was at four thirty in the morning, next to the bell stand at the
hotel, doing my stretching. I identified the first obstacle to reaching
my goal: it wasn't the heat; it was the darkness (great metaphor?).

I noticed, as I completed my stretching and being the observant
type, that it was pitch-dark. It was pitch-dark because apparently,
streetlights have not been invented yet or at least have not come to
this part of Scottsdale.

It has also been raining for two days, and there was still a cloud
cover. (Let me rephrase: there have been two days of thunderstorms,
with 60-mph winds. More than twenty trees on the resort grounds
were down, blocking driveways, walkways, and roads. The poolside
cabanas were no longer poolside. They were in the pool.)

Nonetheless, I created about a one-mile loop around the hotel neighborhood, and I nervously started my eight-mile run with a water bottle, a towel, and my iPhone and earbuds. The first lap was a breeze, except for the darkness. No really; there was a nice breeze too. I admit I didn't avoid all the puddles, and I did take a wrong turn because I couldn't see the street signs, but it was no big deal.

At mile 2, I felt a drop and said out loud, "Uh-oh." You know the feeling? Seconds later, the skies opened. Yep, Mr. Dedication, running in the dark in the pouring rain are perfect conditions for someone straddling the brave-or-stupid line. I continued running through the driving rain and the previously referenced breeze was pushing water in my face with authority. I did not feel like singing in the rain, since my face was stinging in the rain.

When the rain stopped about a mile and a half later, my clothing was completely soaked, not to mention my squishy shoes. I wasn't going to have to worry about heat on this run. But as I pressed on, for some reason, my shirt seemed like it was ten pounds heavier as it clung to my body. It was actually really uncomfortable running with that much water and that much weight on me.

So I made one of the boldest decisions of my life—no hyperbole. I decided to run—*gulp*—without a shirt. Gasp from the audience? Gasp from me! If you've spent decades *never* taking your shirt off in public, you know what a big deal this was.

I slowly pulled my shirt off, carefully draped it on a utility box at a corner of the property, looked around, and ran free of earthly bounds; well, free of upper-body earthly bounds anyway. Remember, it was still dark, and there weren't likely to be too many nuts running after a rainstorm at 5:00 a.m., so I thought my daring exploit was not likely to cause much of a stir.

Now I know probably half the readers are not allowed to run without a top, and my intention isn't to make you jealous. Rather I share this detail because it is the most unlikely thing that could have happened to me. It was unplanned for, undreamed of, and unbelievable. I was a little shocked at my derring-do.

But I have to tell you, I felt pretty good when I glanced down at my body; not great, but pretty good. Not close to a six-pack in the ab category but satisfied that the work I was putting in had paid off and would continue to pay off.

The revelation I had as I was running (half-naked for me) in the dark, still soaking wet, about three miles into an eight-mile run, on Mockingbird Lane in Scottsdale, Arizona, was, I knew I could finish a marathon. If I could run in the rain this early and without a shirt, I could do anything.

That's not really what I thought. What I thought was, if I had the dedication to get up at 4:00 a.m. while attending a conference and run through the rain, and my conditioning had improved to the point where I could run without a shirt, then I possessed the determination and fitness to achieve my goal.

As I was in this reverie, just after daylight, a runner with a long blonde ponytail who couldn't run without a top approached me running in the opposite direction. We smiled and waved at each other, the way you'd expect two nuts running that early through puddles would do. After we passed, and I realized that I had actually been observed shirtless by another person, and that person didn't laugh or point at me (that I know of), I concluded that I was not that far from being officially cool.

For the record, I finished the eight-mile run in an hour and forty-eight minutes, at about the same pace I planned to run for in the marathon. I probably could have done a couple of more miles. I never claimed to be fast. Isn't there a story about a tortoise and a hare somewhere?

I picked up my wet shirt from the utility box and walked back to my room, feeling like I had accomplished more than I anticipated.

So not only was it a good training run and not only was I still on track in my plan, but I ended the run with the kind of confidence you can only get in the dark, in the rain, without a shirt. More fun than singing in the rain.

Don't Quit

By Anonymous

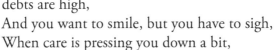

When things go wrong, as they
sometimes will,
When the road you're trudging
seems all up hill,
When the funds are low and the
debts are high,
And you want to smile, but you have to sigh,
When care is pressing you down a bit,
Rest, if you must—but don't you quit.
Life is queer with its twists and turns,
As everyone of us sometimes learns,
And many a failure turns about
When he might have won had he stuck it out;
Don't give up, though the pace seems slow—
You might succeed with another blow.
Often the goal is nearer than
It seems to a faint and faltering man,
Often the struggler has given up
When he might have captured the victor's cup.
And he learned too late, when the night slipped
down,
How close he was to the golden crown.
Success is failure turned inside out—
The silver tint of the clouds of doubt—
And you never can tell how close you are,
It may be near when it seems afar;
So stick to the fight when you're hardest hit—
It's when things seem worst that you mustn't quit.

I pulled out this poem the week before the Boston Marathon
and thought, *This is it. No room to run, no room to hide. In four days,
I will be running a freakin' marathon.*

More than a decade ago, my wife suggested that I start walking. And like every good husband, I listened to her. I walked every day for 462 days, rain or shine. I had one of those apps that track habits, and it seemed like the thing to do.

One day, I jogged about one hundred yards and was surprised I could do it. A week or so later, I tried running a mile, and I was successful. Then I set my sights on a 5k (3.1 miles), as in couch to 5k. And I did it.

Then I hurt my knee and needed physical therapy and went to see Sarah Rheault, who not only helped me recover but, in the process, became my trainer when she started her own business, Wachusett PT.

The next thing you know, with my running mentor's direction, I was running 10k (6.2 miles) races and eventually the seven-mile Falmouth Road Race. One thing led to another, and I set my sights on a half-marathon that I ran in Hampton Beach, with the direction and encouragement of my friend Rick Martino.

I cried when I crossed the finish line there because I couldn't believe I had done it, wearing a Kathy's Team T-shirt in honor of my late sister.

And then I ran another half-marathon the next year and another and another. To be honest with you, after a half-marathon in Manchester, New Hampshire, I gave up the dream of running a full marathon because I felt so crappy after the race. It took me quite a while to recover, mentally and physically, so I kind of resigned myself to the fact that I was at my limit.

Then something happened. Not sure what, but somehow I found the courage to give it one more try. I think I suspected that quitting the dream wasn't the right thing to do.

One day, I mentioned to my trainer that I was reconsidering running a marathon. Her response again was, "What took you?" Someone else thought I could do it, and that, apparently, was enough. I had my first follower, and I was off to—pardon the pun—the races.

- *Distance:* I calculated that in preparation for the marathon, I will have run 969.2 miles as part of this training plan.

That's equivalent to running from Boston to Washington, DC. And back. Or running straight through to Chicago. It is a long way.

- *Nutrition:* A year in advance, I started seeing a nutritionist, Christianna Moran, every two weeks, and the stuff I eat now, compared to before, would stagger the imagination. Yogurt-covered raisins? Beet juice? Chicken sausage? Protein powder? Exercise and nutrition. Who knew?
- *Chardonnay:* Three years ago, I started an alcohol-free plan. I planned to have a well-earned drink on Sunday.
- *Mentor:* Sarah, who is still my trainer, met with me every month for six years and created or approved every exercise and running plan during that time. The only injury I've had was when I fell flat on my face during a 5k on a rail trail. She already shared a postmarathon recovery plan and winter-strengthening plan, ready for me after October 10.
- *Weather:* I have run in wind, rain, snow, fog, darkness, and heat. All alone, all on the road. Up hills, down hills, through puddles and branches that have fallen from trees. I've also seen my share of roadkill, including skunks.
- *Hokas:* I've been through eight pairs of Hoka running shoes. Worn down the heels of five of them, will have the other three with me on Sunday.
- *Tracking:* I track everything: distance, pace by each mile, steps, and more. (By the time I started the marathon, I had already done 2,202,354 steps and been active, as defined by Fitbit, for 17,383 minutes.)

I guess my point is that when you invest enough in an effort, it becomes easier not to quit; it becomes easier to finish.

The poem above is something that I used to keep in my wallet, share with others all the time, and I still take it out and read it when I need it.

I know that the marathon is providing another chance to finish something. I was hoping and praying that I didn't get hurt, stub my toe, or tweak a muscle.

I was grateful for the support and prayers I received, and I knew that in my mind, 26.2 miles would be achieved, even if I had to crawl or be carried, because I don't quit, and I like it that way.

My advice to you?

> Success is failure turned inside out—
> The silver tint of the clouds of doubt—
> And you never can tell how close you are,
> It may be near when it seems so far.
> So stick to the fight when you're hardest hit—
> It's when things seem worst that you mustn't

quit, or when you are 26.2 miles away from the finish line.

Damn Proud

At 4:14 a.m. on Sunday morning, October 10, while driving to Boston on the Mass Pike, I received a second text from Kirsten Glavin, an NBC10 reporter, indicating she was on her way with a videographer and would meet

70-YEAR-OLD RUNNING VIRTUAL MARATHON FOR CHARITY

me for an interview before the Virtual Boston Marathon I was going to run.

My son, Joe, had managed to arrange television coverage for my attempt to run the forty-seven laps around the outside of Fenway Park as my marathon course. Must have been a slow news day? Well, not really.

There must have been something that intrigued the assignment desk at NBC, and apparently I was going to be part of their Boston Marathon coverage. As if there wasn't enough pressure, I realized there's show business to contend with too?

I might have been a little groggy when the text came in, mostly because I hadn't slept well the night before. I stopped at a rest area to respond. I had been up since 3:00 a.m. and had spent the last few days in a very anxious state of mind, as I thought about the monumental task of running 26.2 miles. After that text exchange, I was very wide awake, with my anxiety doubling and the pressure building.

The reason for such an early start for this event was because the Red Sox had made the playoffs and that they were to host a home game on Sunday, scheduled to start in less than twelve hours.

I thought about asking Major League Baseball to delay the game a couple of hours so I could finish *my* event but decided against it. An afternoon game meant that I had to run a marathon, have an after-party, and get everyone out of the area before the parking rates rose to $60-plus for the game, and the meters were blocked off. (It was close: my brother and I almost had our cars towed and had to settle for $90 tickets.)

I knew if I started about 5:15 a.m., I could get twenty miles in by 9:30 a.m., when folks would start showing up to watch the last few miles. So there I was, on an abandoned street, where a half dozen nightclubs had closed just a few hours earlier, with a microphone in my face, trying to explain what I was doing.

When Kirsten pointed the mic at me, and the videographer Steve aimed his camera, I breathed a big sigh of relief and dove in.

I knew from experience that once the game started, the pre-game jitters generally went away. When the lights went on, and the microphone was put in front of me, the game started, and the jitters left quickly.

I finished the interview, followed my regular stretching routine, hit the timer on my Fitbit, and took off in the dark on the longest run of my life. A run that, if successful, would enable me to forever say (quite casually), "Yes, I have run a marathon," and that's not something everyone can claim.

On the other hand, if I failed, while that might be better TV, I would be disappointing the friends and family and donors and those who came to cheer me on at the finish. That's the type of pressure that leads to clichés like pressure causes some to break, and others to break records.

In reality, while that is true, I would be disappointing myself the most. When I started the run, I realized that I was going to finish it and hoped that I had done the work, enough work, to make 26.2 miles happen.

I had about forty-five donors to the Boston Bruins Foundation, and I wrote those names on strips of tape on my forearms, and as I passed the Ted Williams statue on Van Ness Street, I read a name, thought about our relationship, and dedicated the upcoming lap to them in appreciation of their friendship and generosity.

It helped, because twenty-six miles is too far to run alone, and I felt like I was with that person as I remembered our experiences together.

On the Wednesday before the marathon, as I was visiting my ninety-one-year-old mother, she reached out and handed me a small object wrapped in a tissue. She told me it was to keep in my pocket during the run. When I unwrapped the small crucifix, I teared up.

Although I could have run in the actual Boston Marathon as part of the Boston Bruins Foundation Team, my family and I were concerned that such a tough course might take a toll on a seventy-year-old guy, who only had about ten years of running experience and had never run a marathon. We settled on a virtual event that would consist of short laps so I could rest and refresh any time I wanted.

Because Loretta's, our favorite Boston eating and drinking place, was behind Fenway Park, I put two and two together and reserved the patio area of the restaurant as our base of operations, with the route being .56 miles around the park.

Much to my surprise, the station had assigned the reporter and videographer team to stay with me for most of the morning. That meant follow-up interviews, running shots at different points around the park, and shaking pebbles out of my shoes. Originally, they planned to stay for the whole six hours, we learned shortly after I started, but a shooting in Stoughton called them away. Both Kirsten and Steve were great to us. Just the five of us, including a brother and my son, on a darkened street before 6:00 a.m., all of us hoping I had the heart to make it the six hours it would take me.

About two hours after I started or, as we runners say, about ten miles later, daylight washed over the neighborhood. The videographer had been following me around, getting action shots as I lumbered down behind the Green Monster or in front of the ticket office or through the dueling construction sites that dominated part of the route.

The Fenway Park security guards, some of whom recognized me from previous training runs, waved, and I joked that I was going to run a lap around the warning track.

The Red Sox Clubhouse manager, Tom, a friend who had given me a bottle of champagne from the 2018 World Series, popped out of the park to encourage me, and it worked.

The laps and miles went by. The route started over patched and repatched blacktop between two constructions sites, then to a long and fairly new sidewalk by the statues, then onto Jersey Street and the ticket office, and finally, a nice gradual downhill behind the left field wall on Lansdowne Street.

Time went by. Ten, twenty, thirty laps. With a brother and sister who joined my son to staff the aid station, and with Dr. Markenson coming with anything I might need, or I mean, he might need to help me; the morning was moving right along.

I monitored my heart rate and reported in to the good doctor, grabbed a Clif energy gel every hour, drank plenty of water, and stopped to chat with my family and/or the reporters for most of the laps during the first four hours. I was not running for time; I was running for distance. I didn't care how long it took, as long as I made it.

My feet were hurting first, then my knee. Not enough to quit, just enough to remind me of my age. My first goal was to make it to fifteen miles. A high school friend, Joe, had told me that it was a psychological tipping point, and once I hit that mark, I knew I would be on the homestretch.

About 10:00 a.m., or about twenty-two miles into this thing, friends started arriving for the after-party, with two of them, Carrie and Kerry, ready to run some laps with me. Now I had peer pressure working for me.

First, Kerry ran with me with a customized playlist to keep me motivated, and then I ran with both. They were amazed that I could still talk, breathe, and run after so long, but it was no big deal to me. They also prevented me from getting hit by at least one car. It was like having a police escort with sneakers instead of motorcycles.

Fortunately, I also had a trainer and a nutritionist who knew what they were doing; I am good at following directions, so I knew I had the conditioning. It was only a question of *whether* I really had the heart.

At mile 22, I started running laps with T-shirts I had made in appreciation of donors, sponsors, clients, and organizations I volunteer with, a total of twelve in all.

For the final push to that magical 26.2-mile finish line, I took my son, who uses a wheelchair, and pushed him partway up Lansdowne Street, and turned around. The after-party guests had commandeered a roll of toilet paper from Loretta's and stretched it across the street as a finish line, and Joe and I broke through with tears streaming down my face and proof that I had the heart to do this.

So to answer your questions. The training part of this is not something I enjoyed. Lots of lonely miles, which made the last few so enjoyable. Did I have doubts? Absolutely, right up to the microphone. Would I do it again? Not this way. I would wait for the Red Sox to have a crappy team and for the construction to be finished around the park.

What was the best part? There were two that I will always remember.

First, the number of people who said or wrote to me that they were inspired by my effort will have a lasting impression on me. That is an impact that lasts beyond the six hours and twelve minutes of the run. While they were thanking me, it was I who owed them thanks for making my effort make a difference.

Second, I think deep down inside, from the time we are pre-kindergarten, we want others to be proud of us. We might never talk about it, and over the course of our lives, we probably don't hear it that much. I heard the phrase "Proud of you" more in the seventy-two hours after the event than at any other time in my life. And at the end of the day, I'm proud of me too.

The slogan of my fraternity, Phi Sigma Kappa, is "Damn Proud," and I *am* damn proud.

CHAPTER 15: ELIMINATING CONFUSION

Ripping a New One

I personally do not own a pair of torn, distressed, or ripped jeans or whatever your personal preference is for naming them. In fact, I have no jeans at all, preferring the khaki-casual look. I am not a cowboy.

Once, on a trip to Nashville, I saw so many ripped jeans with so many different-sized holes, locations, and tears that it got me thinking, *Why wouldn't everyone in the world want to be an expert on this social and fashion phenomenon?*

And of course, when it comes to fashion, who wouldn't like to know my thoughts? Right?

If you currently wear ripped jeans or, like me, have always wondered why people do, then read on, because in a few short paragraphs, I will share my extensive research on ripped jeans and some of my observations about the style.

Ancient History

In case you didn't know, a couple of guys named Levi and Strauss were early American fashion magnates and created what we refer to today as blue jeans. Raise your hand if you knew that? Very good, class.

Historically, dating from the Levi and Strauss era, jeans were for workingmen and were actually dyed blue so everyone would know that the wearers were workingmen. Kind of a class distinction, not unlike today's hard hat.

Torn jeans happened in those days because of repeated use or an accident and remain torn or ripped because the primarily poor folks wearing them couldn't afford to replace them. But it wasn't cool then to wear ripped jeans; it was embarrassing.

Recent History

The whole modern ripped or torn jeans look started as part of the punk rock movement (see my brother's Wikipedia page. Chris

Doherty and his band, Gang Green, were early pioneers of this musical genre.)

The style was borrowed by the grunge movement a decade or two later and surfaces every now and then, seemingly more now than then.

Originally, the twentieth century incarnation was one of those signs of defiance and rebellion that young people engage in (just repeating what I've read). Like rock and roll and butterfly tattoos.

That's all you need to know about the history.

Ripping for Style

Our next lesson is on ripping jeans. Some sources indicate there are established ways to reach ripped-jean fashion heights. You can rip at home, on your own. Clever concept.

They can be ripped by things that rip things: knives, ex-girlfriends, handsaws.

You can obviously buy them ripped. And in answer to your question, sometimes they are preripped by hand (very expensive because ripping jeans is obviously a talent).

Or they can be—are you sitting down?—ripped by lasers. That's right, you can wear laser-ripped jeans. Who knew?

Ripped Jeans FAQs

Why did my mother get mad when I was a kid and ripped my jeans?
Okay, so she had limited fashion sense. Why couldn't I wear anything that was torn to school? This was the first known suppression of my fashion sense by a parent. If I ripped something, she sewed it, or it didn't go to school.

How many cuts or rips are cool?
The more cuts, the better? Is there a level of tearing of the jeans that makes them mesh jeans, like mesh stockings? Can you wear mesh stockings under mesh jeans? Asking for a friend.

Are ripped jeans like snowflakes?

Absolutely. No two are the same. If I had a pair of ripped jeans, and I saw someone else with the tears in the same place, I'd rip another hole on the spot. (Clever use of the words *rip* and *hole* in a sentence, don't you think?)

Do you wear ripped jeans in the winter?

If so, you're going to have to explain that one. Isn't that like turning the air-conditioning on in the winter? Wouldn't you call ripped winter jeans air-conditioned jeans?

Are ripped shirts and tops next?

They do exist? What will they think of next?

How about ripped dresses?

Maybe too hard to see the tears among the folds?

Okay, torn hats, shoes, or underwear?

Maybe not, but after thinking about it, why not?

They put holes in jackets too?

A complete line of air-conditioned winter wear. Something is wrong here.

Are shorts cool?

Well, they are cooler than full-length jeans, because they are shorts; unless those jeans are ripped extensively, making them air-conditioned pants. Where do you think the best place to rip shorts might be?

Why are all the cuts in the front?

I don't even see much action on the back or the side. I guess no one wants a butt cut. Forget the question.

Are there age restrictions for ripped jeans?

I'm not sure that an eight-year-old or an eighty-year-old could look as cool in them as an eighteen-, twenty-eight-, or thirty-eight-year-old.

My number 1 question: are vertical rips or horizontal rips cooler?

I stared at a lot of legs for this project and horizontal rips way outnumber verticals. I wonder why?

New Fashion Statement?

As a result of the extensive research I've conducted, I am still planning to launch my own line of clothing that follows in the tradition of ripped jeans: stained shirts.

That's right, you will soon be able to buy dress shirts and tops that have been prestained with soup, coffee, and salad dressing.

What was formerly a garment taken out of circulation with a stain will soon be considered cool, just like ripped jeans. And, like ripped jeans, my clothing line will have both horizontal and vertical stains, in a variety of hues.

My kind of fashion since I've been wearing the style for years.

Wicked Pissah

The words and phrases below are *not* meant to be representative of *all* New Englanders because I haven't lived all over New England, although I've worked all over New England.

Massachusetts, and especially Boston, is where I learned the slanguage, and I feel pretty confident in the accuracy of the material that follows.

With that being said, here are some phrases that make a difference.

Bang a uey: Not sure why it is "bang' a uey," but the words cannot be separated. By that I mean you can't "make a uey" or "bang a U-turn." It must be "bang a uey" for authenticity. Most drivers believe that the No U-turn signs are merely suggestions.

Whole bellies: There are two types of fried clams. There are those clam strips that contain leftover pieces of clam formed into a shape, and then there are whole belly clams that have flavor, mouth feel, and occasionally some sand. That's real summer eatin', although you may have to take out a loan to buy a quart of clams down the cape in the summah.

Bubblahs: The generic term *drinking fountain* may work in most of the country, but here, those fountains are bubblahs. The same warning applies to all children: don't put your mouth on the spigot.

Brown bread: Many people have never had the pleasure of eating bread out of a can. Brown bread has the same exterior markings or impressions as jellied cranberry sauce out of the can, but it is larger and browner. Saturday night suppah includes brown bread, baked beans, and hot dogs.

Carriage: When you go to the grocery store, or mahket, you might use a shopping cart, but the majority of us here use a shopping carriage to hold our brown bread, lobstah, and pastah. Some places have signs in the parking lot that say Carriage Return for people with manners who return the carriages.

Clickah: We know that a synonym is remote control, but clickah is how we were raised and is the most accurate description. Note: even soundless remote controls are clickahs. (Note: clickah is also a synonym for automobile turn signal.)

Elastic: Everyone knows what elastic means, but here a rubber band is commonly referred to as an elastic. Not sure why. Elastics are saved and stored on a designated doorknob. Again, not sure why.

Fluffernutter: Since marshmallow fluff was invented here, along with Thanksgiving and constitutional democracy, putting fluff and peanut butter together gives you a fluffernutter sandwich, the ideal lunch for an elementary school child since no refrigeration is required. Not exactly sure what food group marshmallow fluff belongs to. Any suggestions?

Frappe: It is not "frapp-A," it is frapp, rhymes with—never mind (the *e* is silent?). Milkshakes are only lowly milk and flavored syrup, but a frappe is made with ice cream instead of milk, and it is thick, cold, creamy, and delicious, not to mention way overpriced almost everywhere.

Frost heave: So a crack in the road gets filled with water, then freezes and creates a bump that then collapses into a pothole. So a frost heave is a prepothole.

Grinder: You may know it as submarine sandwich, but up here it is a grinder. Can you imagine if Subway was called Grinderway? Just in case you wondered, the phrase submarine sandwich was originated here, but when they are called grinders, they taste better. If this term is new to you, then you may not know that grinder trucks preceded food trucks by decades.

Jimmies: When I was a kid, my nickname was Jimmy, and I felt a sense of pride when I learned that the tiny colorful candies sprinkled across ice cream or birthday cakes were called jimmies. You can have chocolate jimmies or rainbow jimmies, according to family preference, but a jimmy is a jimmy.

Johnny: A johnny is a hospital gown, especially in Boston. It's believed the term came from the gown's open back, designed to provide easy access to the toilet, a.k.a. the john. I have never met anyone who smiled when wearing a johnny, have you?

Leaf peeper: Leaf peepers are tourists who visit New England in the fall to look at trees and the colorful leaves that appear. We all feel grateful that we don't have to stay in a hotel or bed and breakfast to see colorful trees; we just look out the window. If you are a leaf peeper, thanks for boosting the economy every year.

Mud season: So the snow melts a little bit, sinks into the ground, ruminates, and produces mud and more mud. The kind of mud that ruins shoes and gets tracked into the house and results in punishment for the perpetrator, regardless of age. Mud season is the original reason for removing shoes when entering a house, and of course, the mudroom was invented to isolate the mud to noncarpeted areas of the home.

Packie: Massachusetts once had the most restrictive alcohol-sales laws in the nation. Blue laws prevented sale on Sundays, kept alcohol sales away from church neighborhoods, and so forth. Liquor, beer, and wine were only available at a package store, a "packie," apparently because the things purchased were in a package or a brown paper bag. A common phrase is "a quick run to the packie." Everyone knows what that means.

Pissah: From the Latin *pi-sa*, meaning to "urinate." Somehow pissah became the opposite of sh——tty and no one knows how or why. We all know when something is pissah, though, whether it is a move, a car, a football player, or a whole belly clam.

Prince Spaghetti Day: For decades, a little kid, Anthony, in the television commercial for Prince Spaghetti was called home by his mother from an iconic North End brownstone on Wednesday because it was Prince Spaghetti Day. Most of us grew up eating pastah on Wednesday, and some still do.

Regular coffee: If you walk into any place (except maybe Starbucks) and order a regular coffee, it will automatically come with cream and sugar. That's what regular means. If you order regular coffee and are greeted with an inquisitive look, you know that you are being served by an outsider.

Rotary: A circular intersection is called a rotary. Some may call it a roundabout or a traffic circle, but not the traffic reporters sharing that "the Falmouth Rotary is backed up over the bridge."

Tennis shoes: They may also be referred to as sneakers, but most of us grew up with tennis shoes even if we never played tennis. Because "Keds are for kids" was an advertising slogan in the old days, some still refer to athletic shoes as Keds. But they are tennis shoes.

Scrod: If it is firm whitefish, regardless of whether it is cod, halibut, haddock, or pollack, it can appear on a menu as scrod. The Parker House hotel in Boston claims to have created the term (along with Parker House rolls and Boston cream pie) so that its menus would not need to be updated depending on the catch of the day.

Tag sale: Doesn't matter whether it is in a garage, driveway, or sidewalk, it is a tag sale. Summer Saturdays boom with tag sales.

Tonic: This term for a carbonated beverage, you may know as soda, is still used in the Boston area. More than once in my travels across the country, I stumped a server with a request using the word *tonic*.

Wicked: This is probably the most famous slang term attributed to the area. It kinda sorta means "really" or "very" and can be used as an adjective with hundreds of nouns.

Wicked pissah: Combining two of the more famous vocabulary words creates the highest praise a New Englander or Bostonian can apply to anything. There were years that the New England Patriots were wicked pissah, and other years when the weather was wicked pissah, and I am hoping that this book is also wicked pissah.

Driving Me Crazy

I have never met anyone who doesn't talk to other drivers who, of course, can't hear them. Some people talk to them all the time, and some only when weird maneuvers are made. Massachusetts has a reputation for, shall we say, bad drivers?

Some of these drivers rise to a special category and have their own Wikipedia definition. See below.

If you live in Massachusetts or New England, you already know what a Masshole is. If you don't, your first guess will be pretty close.

The Oxford Dictionary added *Masshole* to its roster in 2015 and defines it as a "contemptuous term for Massachusetts inhabitants," though most of us know it with a specific meaning. Reserved for aggressive or clueless drivers who cause many of the transport pains in the state, the term applies to drivers who cut others off, turn without a signal, and stop abruptly for no apparent reason.

Driving Me Crazy

Here is a partial list of the things that drive me crazy when I'm driving. I think you might also find some things that also might drive you crazy

Trucks: Trucks drive me crazy. No matter what anyone tells you, trucks own the road, and passenger cars are an inconvenience to them. I am not besmirching (finally got to use that word in a sentence) truck drivers. I am just expressing the reality that size matters, and trucks can dominate if they choose. With Walmart offering $100,000 in driver salaries and sign-on bonuses offered by most trucking companies, trucks will maintain their dominance for the foreseeable future, and the quality of drivers isn't necessarily going to improve. I am an expert on trucks on a highway. I can tell when a driver is too tired or under the influence because a couple of his wheels spend time in the breakdown lane. We've all seen the occasional rogue driver who breaks the law by getting into the passing lane and scares the crap out of a Prius. And of course, nothing is quite as exciting as being behind a truck going 66 mph passing a truck going 65 mph, according to my brother Chris, is almost a blockade. The thing with trucks that gets me most anxious is when I am behind a car that is beside a truck. And stays there. The most dangerous spot on the road is beside a truck. The sun is blocked, your vision of the rest of the highway is blocked, and you are not visible in the truck driver's rearview mirror. You are trapped. I am amazed that some drivers like to be trapped. As mentioned, I have an occasional word to say to other drivers who cannot hear me, and I am experienced at hand gestures or, as someone recently called it, half the peace symbol. One of the most frequent things I say in the car to nobody listening is pass the truck. When I was young hockey player, I used to say pass the puck, so I guess I have been a passing advocate for years.

Gas prices: I have one of those apps on my phone that enables me to pay for gas at a regional chain of convenience/gas locations. Saves me a dime a gallon and makes me feel cool every time I use it. When I started driving, just after automatic transmissions were invented, gas was 16¢ a gallon, and you got a free drinking glass with a fill up. Still have a set of Boston Celtics glassware from back in the day. Boy, does that sound like another planet or what?

Washer fluid overspray: Is there any official washer fluid etiquette? Random spray from another vehicle drives me crazy. Does anyone else think it is rude to put on your washer fluid at sixty-five miles per hour and have the overspray hit the six cars behind you? The result is that those cars then have to spray their windshields and have the overspray hit the six cars behind them, who then have to—and on and on. My recommendation is that you wait until there is no one behind you and spray away, front and back if you have them. It is the courteous thing to do.

Dashboard clocks: Daylight savings time drives me crazy in the car. Automobile manufacturers make changing the clock in your car kind of like a detective game. Since you only do it twice per year, you never remember how. You might look it up or push buttons here and there. It generally takes me about a week after the time changes to figure out the clock. You know how back in the day, companies got together and developed a standard format for eight-track tapes, and today there is a standard format for CDs and DVDs? Can they come up with a standard format for car clocks to handle daylight savings time? Currently, my touchscreen clock automatically changes, but the dashboard clock doesn't. For a week, I enjoy both times. Let's hope the legislation passes to eliminate DST, or there is a car clock standard created. Right now, I'm good through October.

Cupholders: I once bought a car because I really liked the cupholders. True story. I've been ashamed to admit this to others for decades, although my wife has always known. A 1985 Chrysler. Regretted the decision before I got home but drove that sucker for five years, or sixty months, as the bank remembers it. It was a crazy decision. Cupholders are rarely perfect. They are either too big, and the cup sloshes around, or they are too small, and you cannot fit a large iced coffee in them. They are either too far away so you have to reach, or they are too close to the between-seats console that might hang over one. You may not be fussy about cupholders, but with the number of miles I drive—and I drive many of them with a decaf coffee and a bottle of water to keep me company—the cupholder is a critical element of transportation.

Merging etiquette: Let me get this straight. Someone trying to enter a highway is supposed to be able to see behind themselves going 50 or 60 mph and enter the far-right lane. But the Masshole who is already in the far-right lane doesn't have to slow down to let them in or speed up to get by them; s/he just keeps their own speed and honks at the driver attempting to merge? Or conversely, the car in front of you entering the highway believes that 30 mph is the best speed to merge into a stream of traffic going 75 mph? Okay, as long as both are right, I'll stay silent. There oughta be a better law.

Road striping: Okay, I'm old, and my eyesight might not be what it used to be. I get it. In spite of the fact that I am color-blind and can only legally see out of one eye, I still see a lot.

But when I am on, as the Eagles said, "a dark desert highway" or even the on ramp to I-495 after dark, a little paint on the road would help, a lot. How much does it cost to stripe a road or a highway? Unstriped roads drive me crazy. Driving in the rain at night on a road without lines is never fun and probably dangerous. Cities and towns, save money somewhere else, please? I read somewhere that traffic accidents are up. Does anyone know the criteria for striping a road? Is it a one and done, and it lasts a lifetime? Is it at the discretion of the town or State Highway Department? Is the paint on a cargo ship off the port of Los Angeles? Is there a downside to striping a road clearly?

Everything that is wrong is going to be blamed on the pandemic: Red Sox losing streaks, long lines at the ice cream stand, and a shortage of watermelon at the grocery store. Accidents will be blamed on COVID-19, I'm sure.

In my opinion, I think one reason that accidents are up is because people like me, and you, need lines on the road. In fact, metaphorically speaking, we are all better off having lines on the edge of the road we are traveling.

Massholes: These people are an important part of the tapestry of driving in the state. These are people who, on a two-lane road in a small town, get right up on your you-know-what and, at the first opportunity, try to pass you so that they can be one car ahead of you at the next stoplight. These are the people who, on a two-lane road, get right up on your you-know-what and stay there, maybe even with their high beams on. Try hitting the hazard button on your dash to watch them back off. These are the people who are turning left, and instead of inching over to the left so you and other cars can pass them, they plant their butt in the middle of the road and stop all traffic behind them. These are the people who pull out into the traffic lane when turning left and sit there waiting for the traffic in the other direction to let them in. These are the people who, when the light turns green, make a fast left-hand turn instead of yielding the right of way. These are the same people who turn left after the left green arrow has changed to red because they are in a hurry, and you were sleeping at the switch. And of course, these are the people who drive 65 mph in the passing lane, because after all, that is the speed limit. These are also the people who are knowledgeable about the shortest interval ever measured by science: the time between the light turning green and the Masshole behind you hitting the horn for you to move.

Bye, Bye, Ms. American Mall

Lots of things have changed since COVID-19 was or was not started in a lab on the other side of the Pacific. One of the biggest changes I have observed has been how we spend our money.

The new "mall" is our own computer screen or smartphone. They have taken the place of the physical-shopping experience.

- Instead of driving to the mall, we fire up the laptop.
- Instead of searching for a parking space, we search for a product.
- Instead of wandering to the next store, we change our search criteria.
- Instead of fumbling for cash or a credit card, we autofill our information when it is asked for with PayPal or Apple Pay.
- Instead of walking out of the store with a logoed bag, we move on to the next thing.
- Instead of unloading the car when we arrive home, we unload the mailbox or the front porch when UPS or USPS or FedEx delivers our purchases.

Instead of discarding the bag our things came in, we cut up cardboard boxes for the recycling process.

If I described the things that you do now, it is not a coincidence that it is a list of things that I do now. Recently, I had a reason to physically visit a mall and was a little surprised at what I found or didn't find. Disclaimer: I am not a professional shopper, and I have spent very little time in shopping malls compared to other members of my family, if you know what I mean.

In the event you are like me and eventually decide to physically go to a mall, you might be in for a surprise, because it might remind you of a ghost town.

About twenty-five minutes from our home, there is a large regional mall with three anchor stores and about one hundred other retail businesses, plus a dozen or so food court offerings. I've been going to this location for about fifteen years, although not very often and not as much as before the pandemic. I'd head there for birthday and holiday shopping, occasionally for a book or a Hallmark gift or card.

Recently, I had the need to visit the Genius Bar (modest name?) at the Apple Store. I walked into a ghost town. Two-thirds of the stores were closed and empty, the Hallmark store among them. Some percentage still had merchandise in the windows, but they were closed on a Saturday. Closed on a Saturday! Ten of the twelve food court locations were shuttered. (Thank goodness the Dunkin' was still open.)

That extra parking deck to handle the overflow holiday crowds? Closed. The information desk at the busy crossroads inside the mall? Replaced with a phone-screen replacement kiosk. The busiest location in the ghost town, I mean mall? The Apple Store.

Change is inevitable, and while walking around, I thought about how the life cycle of the regional mall had entered a new stage—the ghost town stage.

I am old enough to remember the beginning of the mall concept. I had memories come back to me as I wandered through the ghost town that used to be a vibrant center of retail activity in Central Massachusetts and wondered why the genre had deteriorated so quickly.

Obviously, the growth of online shopping didn't help the mall.

Equally as obvious is the pandemic didn't help the mall.

But as I started to think about what I was observing and why, I realized that some businesses were actually thriving, but the only stores that were busy or open were those locations that offered something that couldn't be bought online or was better purchased when touched.

Locations where you wanted to be physically present to obtain the goods or services. Those were the survivors. Who knew that was going to happen?

You can't get some things online. Like a haircut, help with a cell phone, a Dunkin' Donut, or a neck massage. But for almost everything else, a mall is a distant second place to a computer.

Change is inevitable, and as I wandered around, amazed at the transformation of the mall genre, I thought about the stages before the ghost town stage.

Stage 1, new and suburban: Malls were developed to replace downtown businesses in a clean new environment, with more (and free) parking than the small-town merchant areas. Shopping became easier and better at a mall.

Stage 2, growth, one-stop shopping: Malls grew and became indoor places with every kind of business under the sun. They were efficient in a one-stop shopping kind of way. Shopping took less time at a mall.

Stage 3, sale, sale, sale: They eventually entered the stage where 20 percent, 30 percent, 40 percent, 50 percent, 60 percent, and 70 percent off signs dominated the windows. Shopping became less expensive at a mall, and then outlet malls drove home the point.

Stage 4, entertainment: They eventually jumped the shark, as they say, with the Mall of America in Minneapolis that has a full-size amusement park, including a roller coaster inside to go with their 520 retail locations. There was an entertainment factor ranging from the aforementioned roller coaster to vibration lounge chairs to a Madame Tussauds wax museum in a Nashville mall. Shopping was more fun at a mall.

Stage 5, lose the roof: Open-air malls, like the original South Shore Plaza, became the new thing. Why people liked to move their car three times while shopping, and get wet when it rains, I'll never know.

Stage 6, repurpose: Make it something else. Before it was demolished, there was a mall in Worcester that was a—are you ready?—college campus.

Stage 7, ghost town: Plenty of parking, few stores, a couple of food court locations, one of the three anchor stores closed and the other two more or less empty, and on and on. Malls are dying a slow death.

- The reasons why are obvious.
- Shopping can be easier and better online.
- Shopping can take less time online.
- Shopping can be less expensive online.
- Shopping can be more fun online.

Change is inevitable; nothing lasts forever. Forgotten American success stories include:

- Buggy Whips: They are hardly used anymore.
- Howard Johnson's Restaurants (invented the clam strip): The last one just closed.
- Pay phones: Quick, tell me the last time you used one. Do you remember how much it cost?
- Pontiac automobiles: "Huh?" a young reader asks.
- Mimeograph machines: The smell cannot be duplicated and is forever etched into the nasal memories of a generation of elementary school students.
- Eight-track tapes: I still miss them.

Change is inevitable; nothing lasts forever. What's next? Of course if you knew, it would probably make you rich. It could be:

- Gas stations: California has claimed dibs on eliminating this institution.
- AM radio: Come on, why is it still around?
- Supermarkets: Food delivery is way, way up and as the population ages.
- Desktop computers: Try to find one at a Best Buy or a Staples—all laptops.

- Bookstores: Many are already gone. Remember Walden Books at every mall?
- Board games: We have a digital table with Scrabble, Monopoly, Score Four, checkers, chess, and forty other games. Don't be so sure.

The point is that nothing lasts forever, and the phrase "ghost town" was created to label a place that was once thriving and now is inhabited only by ghosts.

Businesses, occupations, cities, automobiles, industries, communities, nothing is guaranteed to last. Change is inevitable, and ignoring signs or resisting change or denying trends has never been part of any success formula. Just take a walk through the mall near you for a wake-up call for the proof.

Bye, bye, Ms. American Mall. Can't wait to see what's next for you.

CHAPTER 16: INSPIRATION
AND PERSPIRATION

(John and) David versus Goliath

The famous biblical story of David and Goliath has come to take on a more secular meaning through the ages and is referenced when something big and something small clash.

A fearless underdog going against a giant. Instead of running away, David had heart and fought back.

America loves an underdog, and so does Worcester, Massachusetts (the second largest city in New England behind Boston), where another version of David and Goliath is playing out with David (represented by the Worcester Bravehearts baseball team), under the lights at Fitton Field on the campus of the College of the Holy Cross, and Goliath (represented by the Worcester Red Sox) at Polar Park.

Worcester Baseball Background

Worcester actually had a Major League Baseball team from 1880 to 1882. The name, quite original, was the Worcester Worcesters. True story.

To raise the capital to support their entry into the National League, the team sold shares for $35 (with the price including a season ticket), sponsored a walking race that attracted three thousand people, arranged for discount packages of train fare and baseball tickets for fans from outside the city, and held benefit concerts and dramatic performances.

The next citywide team of note, or at least of my note, were the Worcester Tornadoes from 2005 to 2012. They were members of the Canadian American Association of Professional Baseball, an independent baseball league which was not affiliated with Major League Baseball. My son, Joe, and I started going to games right after moving to Massachusetts in 2006. Close to home. Good accessibility for wheelchairs. Oh, and did I mention inexpensive?

When the Tornadoes folded after the 2012 season, or should I say imploded after the 2012 season, leaving a bitter taste in the mouths of vendors they owed money to and the city itself, the lazy (inexpensive) summer nights at the park were no more. That is until the Creedon family stepped up and entered a team in the New England Futures League to start in 2014.

This team is in a summer league for college players, similar to the famous Cape League, where hundreds of Major Leaguers have passed through on their way to the big time. Some players are local and attend local colleges, while others stay with host families for the summer.

Since I had an ongoing business relationship with Creedon & Company for many years, prior to the baseball team's inception, I knew that customer satisfaction was a core principle of the company, so I was looking forward to the new team.

It didn't surprise me that John Creedon Jr., the president, had the team start by having the fans select the team nickname, and Bravehearts was the winning choice. Aside: You should also know that if you get a Bravehearts tattoo, you get season tickets for life, and so far, seventeen fans have taken the plunge, or the needle as the case may be (I am *not* one of them).

Their history of customer focus in other businesses morphed into fan friendly, and championship after championship followed with the team winning four in their first five seasons.

With the famous Dave Peterson as the general manager, the team became the most successful in the league using any metric. Nicknamed "Peterman," Dave is *the* most enthusiastic person I know, and one of the reasons I know is that my son interned for him many years ago.

With those type of relationships with the team's leadership, and our love of baseball, of course we went to games. Close to home. Good accessibility for wheelchairs. Oh, and did I mention inexpensive? But there was something different about the Bravehearts. They didn't just talk fan friendly; I think they tried to reinvent it.

On game day, everyone parks free, players in uniform come into the stands to sign autographs, kids run from foul pole to foul pole once per game, accessibility is a top priority with golf carts helping folks to the gate, and they sell all-you-can-eat tickets with hot dogs, angus burgers, popcorn, and soft drinks included.

Oh yeah, they also host a Bark in the Park, where you can get your dog a $3 ticket, and that money is donated to dog-related charities. You get the picture. Focused on the fan experience.

That's just game stuff. As part of the community:

- They have a reading program that reaches ten thousand school children.
- They have a Pen Pal Program in conjunction with Easter Seals, where the players are the pen pals and meet their pal before the season is over.
- They have another Pen Pal Program with senior citizens.
- They have a Junior Bravehearts program, where they provide uniforms.
- They sponsor a girls' softball team.
- They have more than three hundred kids attend Bravehearts summer camp.
- They host charity events where players wear game shirts with a nonprofit logo and design, which are then auctioned off or sold.
- They even play some games at 11:00 a.m. so school groups can attend as a field trip.

No wonder the Better Business Bureau awarded them a Business of the Year award.

Pawtucket Red Sox: Things were rolling along for the Bravehearts until the Rhode Island legislature voted not to build a new ballpark for the new owners of the Pawtucket Red Sox, a Triple-A Minor League team affiliated with *those* Red Sox.

So the owners of the Rhode Island team turned their eyes to the second largest city in New England, and eventually, Worcester agreed to build a multimillion-dollar state-of-the-art facility at taxpayer expense, betting on the economic development sure to follow.

So much for the Bravehearts, right?

- How could they possibly compete with the Red Sox name only forty-seven miles from Boston?
- How could they market the team in the face of overwhelming publicity for the new kid in town WooSox?
- Who would go and see unknown rising college kids play instead of future Red Sox stars?
- How could they hold onto corporate sponsors with the more glamourous team, venue, and affiliation beckoning?
- How could Worcester support two baseball teams?

Overwhelming odds like this generally mean fold. Probably a large part of the population expected the team to either go inactive or move to another city.

I mean, who'd have the heart to go into a battle with odds so stacked against you that even friends might think you were a little stupid to try?

There has always been a thin line between bravery and stupidity, and the Worcester Bravehearts had to make a choice: fold and move along, or do something else.

They chose something else. They hoped it was on the brave side of the line, and being the curious type, one day I sat down with John and Dave and talked about their battle with Goliath. Because the reality of today is that whatever they are doing is working.

Several years later, the team is still kicking and still drawing fans.

Of course, the fan-friendly focus, the programming, and the promotions are helping to drive attendance, but that is never enough.

My curiosity was pushing me to dig below the surface and find out how the Bravehearts live on, in spite of millions of dollars invested in an effort that really should have pushed them out of the baseball business in Worcester.

What I found out is their success in battle is based on their attitude about two things.

People: You might have been hoping for something more glamorous, but no, a major reason the team is still alive and kicking and, in fact, showing an attendance increase is their attitude toward people, part of the company philosophy and business model.

If you were to go to work for the Bravehearts, at orientation, you'd learn the mantra when interacting with the public is simple: How do I make this person smile? The team goal is for fans to have *fun* at a game. What a unique concept, eh? Isn't that why people get tickets to anything? To have fun?

It would be a great world if every business and every employee in every public-facing business had that as a personal mission statement. (Note: the smiley face was invented in Worcester.)

But in order to have a staff that lives that attitude, they have to be treated right.

Unlike many sports teams, I learned that the Bravehearts pay their interns, not universally an industry standard, and they lead by example. Here's an example: they do not use a cleaning service after games; the staff, including the general manager and the owners, clean the park, including the restrooms.

Imagine being a summer intern for the Bravehearts and cleaning a restroom alongside the general manager? Leading by example has no substitute.

Persistence: At this point in my journey to figure out their success, I knew a lot about the how but not much about the why. I understood how they kept going, but I was less clear on why they kept going.

That turned out to be fairly simple: persistent people press on. So you ask, they are still here because they decided to be? Yes.

They decided that what they had already accomplished was too important to throw away. They decided that they had the skills, talent, and willingness within the organization to climb over or around the obstacles. They decided that being an underdog might be fun. And they decided that persistence and determination are omnipotent.

Of course, there is no guarantee that the Bravehearts will be around forever. Putting people first seems like a solid bet in any business, and nothing in the world can take the place of persistence.

But isn't it kind of magical that nine years ago, the fans of Worcester named the team the Bravehearts without knowing that the nickname applied to the team on the field that would be managed and led by John and David who would prove they had brave hearts too?

Play ball.

Proud to Be an American

The Damar Hamlin story has impacted America in many ways. Most know the story of the twenty-four-year-old defensive player for the Buffalo Bills, who was resuscitated on the field after suffering cardiac arrest.

Just a few days later, he woke up from a medically induced coma in a Cincinnati hospital bed and greeted his teammates back in Buffalo via Zoom. The last time they had seen him, they were on the field as a trainer saved his life with CPR, and he was being loaded into an ambulance.

As the week after his revival played out, more and more about America was revealed, at least to my eyes and ears. I heard a news story related to the situation, that made me get up and write. What did I hear? Let me start with some background about why the follow-up to the story makes me proud to be an American.

The incident happened in Cincinnati. My family lived there for about eleven years, from sixth grade through college for my son. I have been to the stadium where the incident took place, dozens of times. I'm sure there were one hundred people at the game that I knew, maybe two hundred people, including ushers, who may have received a towel from us when we moved back to Massachusetts.

I have actually been on that field, very close to where the incident took place. This one hit close to home, even though it was 848 miles away.

My family was also watching the game together. We are all Patriots fans, of course, but having lived in Cincinnati with so many friends there makes the Bengals our second favorite team.

What follows are six reasons that this incident made me proud to be an American.

But first, in a nonpolitical way (if possible), I'd like to share that I have been somewhat disappointed in America in recent years, and it is mostly because a lot of what we read and hear is about how we are so divided.

"United" States of America may apply to geography, but not to what the media reports about us. The old expression "I don't watch the news. It's too depressing" has some validity. I do watch the news, but what depresses me almost as much as the bad news is how the media highlights how we don't get along and how we don't work together, and we don't care about each other.

It seems that hate gets viewers and sells papers, and love gets pushed to the background at six and eleven. That's not the America I know. The America I know cares and tries to make a difference and takes care of each other and responds to a crisis.

One football player being injured hardly qualifies as an American crisis, but it does qualify as an event where we can peek through a different window to reaffirm why I personally am proud to be an American.

1. *Outside the hospital:* Cincinnatians joined Buffalo fans outside the hospital after the game in a candlelight vigil. When I saw this, I was proud to have been part of that community for more than a decade. I just thought it was a classy, noble, and very American thing to do. Instead of highlighting a fistfight between partisans with different team jerseys, the vigil showed that Cincinnati, and America, cared. I was proud to be an American.

2. *Team leadership:* The coaches for the two teams, Sean McDermott for the Bills and Zac Taylor for the Bengals, decided at midfield before the ambulance left, they weren't going to play the game, even if ordered to.

    One or both coaches decided that *not* playing was in the best interests of the individuals they were responsible for. There are too many times we hear about leaders *not* standing up for their team or *not* having their best interests at heart.

    Too many times, we hear about moments of crisis where leadership fails, whether in the House of Representatives or cryptocurrency exchanges. In my own mind, as I was watching,

I thought to myself, *If I were the coach of Damar's team, I would forfeit before I would put my team back out there.*

That night on television, instead of highlighting one of the dirtbags who abuses employees, the night showed leaders who cared. I was proud to be an American and live in a place where leaders were taking care of their team in front of the whole world.

3. *The Chasing M's Foundation:* Having worked in the dona-tion-raising industry for many years, I was impressed that a twenty-four-year-old second-year player had started a founda-tion to raise $2,500 to provide holiday toys to local children in his hometown.

I also knew that the first dollars the foundation raised prob-ably came from his own pocket. That's how fundraisers start. The foundation reached and exceeded its goal, as more than $8 million had been donated to the nonprofit by Americans who wanted to do something to help but couldn't do it with their expertise, so they used their wallets.

Instead of highlighting someone who siphoned off donations from a nonprofit, the week showed off the spirit and generosity of our country, and I was proud to be an American and one of the small donors involved.

4. *The prayers:* The first call when something bad happens is to pray for the victims. Each week in our country of hundreds of millions of people, many things happen that are bad, and there are victims.

But usually, the call to prayer is a one-and-done. Not this week. The family consistently updated the country and always, always, always asked America to pray for their son, and I think America did.

Those of a certain perspective know that it worked. Instead of letting the call to prayer evaporate, the week kept the power of prayer alive and showcased a side of America to be proud of, a country that owes part of its heritage to religious freedom and where, in recent years, public displays of religion have been challenged. The call wasn't for Christians to pray; it was for America to pray. Proud to be an American.

5. *Corporate America:* Okay, so it wasn't the entirety of corporate America, and only one company, but the story that I heard that prompted me to get up at four thirty in the morning and start typing was this: Damar Hamlin jerseys were flying off the shelves (physical and interest shelves) so fast that the company fanatics announced they were donating all proceeds of the jersey sales to the Damar Hamlin foundation instead of profiting from the situation.

Instead of a cash grab, this one corporation decided to rise above the scramble and do something. My experience is that more corporations than not do the same thing every day for many causes, and I am proud to be an American and live in a country where this kind of thing happens.

6. *Denny Kellington:* The assistant trainer who administered first aid to Damar when he was lying on the field. His name will likely not be remembered, except in Buffalo, but his deed will always be famous and a source of pride to him.

When Damar finally woke up in the hospital, he asked the doctors who won the game, and one of them replied, "You did, Damar, you've won the game of life."

That was very true, and there was another winner last week; however, in my opinion, that winner was America, and that's why I'm proud to be an American.

Some Things Are Hard to Forget

How often have you had a once-in-a-lifetime experience, and you knew it was at that level while it was happening?

That happened to my son, Joe. Even though it was planned to be a once-in-a-lifetime event, it turned out even better than expected because of kindness  and loyalty and became an evening in South Carolina that will be hard to forget. This story is on the long side because it was twenty-five years in the making.

If you are a country music fan, you are probably going to love this story. If you are not a country music fan but like to hear stories about nice people, you will also love this story. If you don't like people, *and* you don't like country music, please leave the room now.

They say country music fans and the artists have a different connection than in other types of music. I agree. They are special. Hopefully, this is a story that you won't forget because I won't.

Part 1: Did I Shave My Legs for This?

His name was Billy Ray Cyrus, today more famous as Miley Cyrus's dad, but back then when "Achy Breaky Heart" was released, he rocketed to fame. My ten-year-old son attended his first live concert in Memphis that year, featuring Billy Ray, and was hooked on country music.

A couple of years later, we traveled to Nashville for something called Fan Fair at the Nashville Fairgrounds, and it was heaven for a country music fan. Two stages, nonstop music, and an exhibition hall where each recording artist had a booth and held meet-and-greet sessions with fans who waited in line, sometimes for hours.

In a dimly lit warehouse, up the hill from the Nashville speedway track, my son met country artist Deana Carter for the first time.

Her initial album and songs included the classic "Strawberry Wine" and "Did I Shave My Legs for This?"

The next year, with Joe as a member of her fan club, we traveled to the country music festival, went to her hometown of Goodlettsville, Tennessee, and attended her first fan club party at the roller rink where she skated as a kid.

That day, we waited anxiously at a table for her to come around for a meet and greet. When she did, my son's face lit up like never before. He had bought a T-shirt with her picture on it, and he had her autograph the shirt. She asked us to skate with her, and she pushed his chair around the rink a couple of times. Some things you don't forget.

Over the next few years, Joe followed her career, bought and memorized all her albums, and didn't miss connecting with her at her annual fan club event on our trips to Nashville. Each time they met, Joe and Deana chatted for a bit, she signed the T-shirt, and we enjoyed the show.

Time slipped away, she moved to LA, raised a son, and did some acting. We kept going to Nashville, but she did not perform during the festival. Until ten years later.

We were excited when we learned that she would be performing on one of the many stages downtown in front of the Nashville Predators NHL hockey rink. We got there early and found a spot by the side of the stage, hoping for a glimpse and a wave but not really having any expectations that she would be able to come over.

After about an hour of waiting in place, we saw her unload her guitar case and move to the back of the stage as the next artist up.

Then she looked over and moved quickly toward us. What she said as she reached us made my eyes water. As she closed in, she said, "Hi, Joe," with a big smile on her face and gave him a hug. Ten years. Hi, Joe. Some things you don't forget. Joe and Deana chatted for a bit, she signed the T-shirt again, and we enjoyed the show.

Several years later, we traveled to Maine when we learned she was performing at a fundraiser at a local high school. We met her before the show in the cafeteria next to the auditorium. Joe and Deana chatted for a bit, she signed the T-shirt once more, and we enjoyed the show.

In 2019, she performed at Charles Esten's charity show in Nashville before the CMA Fest.

She spotted us when she arrived and quickly said we'd connect after the show as she made her way backstage. After everyone performed, we nervously sat around for a half hour, wondering if she had forgotten about us, and then Jim, her husband, came out and took us backstage to the green room.

For thirty minutes, fan and star hung out in a real once-in-a-lifetime event. Joe and Deana chatted, she signed the T-shirt again for the fifteenth of sixteen times and made my son feel like the most important person in the world. Again. Some things you don't forget.

During the pandemic, most Wednesday nights, Deana did a Facebook Live show and interacted with fans, including my son. He asked questions, suggested songs, and had something to look forward to every week during the lockdown. She regularly gave him a shout-out as a superfan, and smiles on anyone's face during the lockdown were precious. Some things you don't forget.

Part 2: Wake Me Up

Although we moved back to Massachusetts in 2006, we kept going to Nashville every year but really needed more country music. Let me rephrase that: my son needed more country music.

It started in a small barbecue joint in Franklin, Tennessee, in 2015, on one of our trips when we saw a rising artist Jilly Martin, who just happened to be from Chelmsford, Massachusetts.

We started going to her shows when we came back home, and soon she connected with Ryan Brooks Kelly and formed the band Martin and Kelly. My son followed their career and schedule, and if they were playing within two hours of our home, we were there. Some shows started at 7:00 p.m., but others started at 10:00 p.m. and went on to 1:30 a.m. After a ninety-minute drive home, we often went to sleep after 3:00 a.m.

Since that first show in 2015, we'd seen Martin and Kelly play more than two hundred times in six states, in dozens of venues. They countrified Avicii's song "Wake Me Up" and sometimes dedicated it to me because they knew I had to take a nap to attend the late shows. They usually did a specific song for my son during most shows.

Martin and Kelly have performed up and down the Eastern Seaboard and all around the country and, of course, in Nashville, but no one has seen as many shows as my son. No one is even close. Since they also do acoustic appearances without a band, we've joked that Joe has been to more shows than their bass player, and it is true.

Needless to say, my son knows every word to every original song Martin and Kelly and Deana Carter have released. He knows all the words to all the covers they play as well. (For two years, as a fund-raiser for the March of Dimes, Martin and Kelly played at Loretta's Last Call and helped raise over $10,000 for the cause.)

Part 3: Merry Christmas, Joe

Time goes by for all of us, and this year, the twenty-fifth anniversary of Deana Carter's debut album and the start of her career was celebrated by Capitol Records, and she went on tour, including a gig as a presenter on the recently nationally televised CMA Music Awards.

Since Joe follows her on Facebook, he always knows where she is performing. He also follows Martin and Kelly, and one day, we were startled to find out that Martin and Kelly were opening for Deana Carter in Sumter, South Carolina, on Friday night, less than a week away.

The obvious question was: How could we miss such a show? It was only 852 miles away. I was sure that we could make it there in eleven or twelve hours: a two-hour drive to Boston airport, some air-port time, a two-hour flight to Charlotte, and a two-hour drive from Charlotte to Sumter. Some might think that is too much trouble and too much money, but it was a once-in-a-lifetime chance to see two favorite acts on the same stage on the same night, and it would be a Christmas present for my son that would be hard to forget.

As a former professional traveler, I know a thing or two about booking travel, so I arranged a couple of discount tickets on American Airlines with a free rental car and redeemed some points for two free nights at the Holiday Inn Express in Sumter. Easy. We left on Thursday, watched the Patriots defeat the Falcons from our hotel room in South Carolina that night, and at 5:00 p.m. on Friday, headed for downtown and the Sumter Opera House.

We took our seats about an hour before the show, in the front row, and waited patiently. Martin and Kelly came out. We clapped, hardly believing that we were actually there. They sang their signature songs, and Joe sang along and (illegally) recorded them.

First Highlight Of The Night:

Jilly pointed at Joe from the stage, and in the this-one's-for-you mode, they performed one of his favorites for him, to huge applause from the sold-out crowd of 5,500. The night was off to a great start.

About thirty minutes into Martin and Kelly's set, the opera house manager tapped me on the shoulder and said that Deana and her husband wanted to see us in the green room. We hurried back, and sure enough, in about ten minutes, she was hugging Joe and telling us how happy she was to see us and couldn't believe we traveled all that way. She had spoken with Martin and Kelly earlier, so she knew the connection we had with them.

Second Highlight Of The Night:

We hung out in the green room for about twenty minutes. Martin and Kelly joined after their set, and stories were swapped, and laughs were everywhere as talk about the years gone by and Joe's fan loyalty took center stage.

At one point, Deana said that her longest relationship of her life was with Joe.

When we left the green room, we thought the highlight of the night had happened, but we were wrong. Very wrong.

Highlight Number 3:

Back in our seats, singing along and still (illegally) taping song after song, Deana paused and told the audience the story of a fan who had traveled from Boston to see the show, had been a fan for twenty-five years, and how much she appreciated him.

Before she finished, audience members were shouting "Joe, Joe," and he waved at them with tears in his eyes. She dedicated her next song to Joe, "Count Me In," and blew him a kiss from the stage after the song. Very hard to forget.

The show went on, and when it ended, Deana and her husband waved at Joe again, and we left. On our way out, people called out, "Hi, Joe." A real celebrity.

I could tell you this was a story about planning or coincidence or adventure, and while that might be true, this was really a story about dedication. To artists, to fans, to music, and to caring. Caring and dedication are what make once-in-a-lifetime events happen. Some things you don't forget.

Heavy Lifting

Lifting weights has always scared me a little bit. They are so heavy! Someone who is into lifting weights has to love grunting, and that's not really my thing.

Lifters have to like the smell of chalk finding their nose. They have to be dedicated and daring and dynamic, I get it, but I would rather be that way without the callouses, or I would rather watch someone throw a football with those characteristics.

I know someone dedicated to the sport, and without warning, she inspired me twice, a couple of years apart, and here are the details.

We use the phrase "heavy lifting" to refer to a workload or the toughest part of a job or project. A friend of ours is a real weight lifter and uses that term to describe herself, not as a metaphor.

We went to the Baystate Games at UMass Boston to watch the Massachusetts State Championship competition in Olympic-style weight lifting. Yes, I know I travel in diverse circles. I had no idea what to expect, and neither would you, probably.

In a hockey rink with boards covering the ice. Two platforms, side by side, red and blue, male, and female. Lots of judges who were positioned *American Idol* or *America's Got Talent*-style. Lots of weights. Lots of spandex. Lots of muscles. Lots of clanging.

I learned pretty early in my first experience with weight lifting competitions that how you drop the barbell after an attempt is an important part of the style. The cool kids dramatically drop it to maximize the clang effect. I know I personally would be better at clanging than lifting.

Being my first competition, I didn't know what to expect, but I caught on quickly. In technical terms—and I'll go slow here—the complete process for lifting a barbell loaded with weights in a competition is: Approach, pause, grunt, lift, clang. Approach, pause, grunt, lift, clang.

For about an hour, we watched young lifters and older lifters (euphemistically called masters) approach the bar, pause in very deep thought, grunt from the gut, lift to the skies or in that general direction, and try to look cool while dropping the weights to finish with a clang. Some made the lifts, some didn't. Some grunted once, some grunted twice. Some got high fives, some slumped away. All of them clanged.

At this stage of your weight lifting education, it doesn't really matter if you know the difference between a clean and jerk and a snatch; they are both elements of the competition that are incredibly hard to do right and incredibly hard to do with a lot of weight, regardless of whether you are lifting kilos or pounds (plus, I'm not sure I remember which is which).

We were watching the first dozen participants on two platforms alternate lifts, with weights of one hundred pounds or more. I was thinking the whole time about the dedication and hard work and sore muscles it must take to be a top-tier weight lifter.

All these folks down on the rink had to practice, overcome disappointment, and try again. In fact, the whole sport was based on individuals trying to do a personal best.

A Hush Fell Over the Arena

As our friend was announced and approached the bar, the entire arena hushed, and most everyone stopped what they were doing. All eyes were on the red platform.

While the guy on the other platform was struggling to lift one hundred pounds over his head, our friend's weight attempt was announced over the PA system (do they still call it a PA system?), in kilos of course, at a weight I converted with my app and realized it was more than two hundred pounds!

My mouth fell open; the weight was way more than that of any other competitor we'd seen on either platform so far. The announcement of the weight also hushed those who were not already hushed.

Our friend approached the bar, paused, grunted, lifted, and clanged. Missed on the first lift but had a nicely dramatic *clang* to end it. The second lift was successful at two hundred-plus pounds.

Are you kidding me? Some of you may wonder why this experience was worth sharing and writing about because a lot of people can lift two hundred pounds. A couple of reasons.

The Inspiration

First, our friend goes by the name Tiffany, and she was twenty-five years old and weighed in at 121 pounds that day, or whatever that is in kilos, and she lifted more than any male competitor we observed. By a lot.

Now maybe we missed the real big lifters; we didn't stay. They may have been coming later. And maybe she didn't do as well as she wanted to with all her lifts that day, but here's what she didn't see from the platform.

She didn't see how the whole arena stopped, frozen in time when she approached the bar. She didn't feel the whole arena hoping she could do it. She didn't realize that everyone in the building was hoping they were looking at a future Olympic champion when the bar peaked over her head.

She couldn't know how many people thought she was crazy for trying and how many left the building that day thinking about what they were afraid of trying. She didn't see or feel how inspirational her attempt was to those watching.

So even though our friend didn't break her personal best, and even though she was disappointed that she didn't "snatch this" or "clean and jerk that," it didn't matter to me.

She didn't get what she wanted but gave me something I wanted. I simply went to support but left with even more respect for her than I had when I walked in, plus I took away a little of that inspiration.

Champions

Champions don't say, "I'm going to inspire that person." They let their actions do most of the talking and supplement their actions with some appropriate words. Or in the case of a weight lifter, appropriate grunts.

Many times, champions aren't even aware of who or what they are inspiring. She had no idea of the impact her lift had on me. If you push the metaphor to the edge of the driveway, don't champions, in all walks, approach, pause, grunt, lift, clang? Approach the challenge, pause to gather themselves or their resources, inwardly grunt as they struggle with the hardest part of the challenge, and then go for it (and collapse with a nice glass of chardonnay or an ice cream cone or a jelly doughnut regardless of the outcome. The clang.).

Champions don't realize sometimes that how they inspire us is not just the attempt, but it's that we figure out quickly that they have a high standard for dedication and hard work. These are the same characteristics—maybe minus the sore muscles—it takes to be a top-tier anything. The practicing, overcoming disappointment, and trying again are more or less core to champion-level performance.

When you stop to think about it, the whole sport of weight lifting is based on individuals trying to do their personal best, and that is where greatness begins in any field. It is based on individuals who aspire to be the best.

Aspire is one of my all-time favorite words.

I may never attend another weight lifting competition. But sometimes, when I am a little bit frustrated at my inability to get done what needs to get done, a picture of a 121-pound champion, lifting 220 pounds over her head, pops into my mind.

And if you see Tiffany Beaupre on NBC walking into the Olympic stadium in Paris in 2024, or Los Angeles in 2028, we'll both know she, like all those who made it there, did so with dedication, hard work, and sore muscles while trying for a personal best, every day. They aspired.

CHAPTER 17: LOOKING IN THE MIRROR

Reasons or Results

Sports are filled with inspirational stories. A lot of people played sports when they were younger and remember or applied the lessons learned.

A lot more people watch sports in person or on television and get emotionally attached to their teams and actually feel the pressure when one of their favorite players is shooting a free throw with the game on the line, or at bat in the ninth inning trailing by a run, or with eighty yards to go and less than a minute left.

This story is about an Olympic champion from 1912 who had that same type of pressure on him, but at the last minute, something happened that took all of his determination and skill to overcome a very unfair circumstance. History proclaims his results instead of his reasons.

Reasons or results? You know that life isn't fair, right? Much of the frustration in the world, whether in politics, business, social interactions, or traffic, is due to people *not* accepting that fact.

Should life be fair? Probably. Is it? Sometimes, but it is a matter of degree. You have probably never won the lottery, played Major League Baseball, won a Nobel Prize, or written a book. Is that fair?

On the other hand, you were speeding last week and didn't get a ticket. You found the partner of your dreams and might not deserve him or her. You were invited to a big game by a friend at the last minute. You found a $20 bill in the pocket of an old coat. The list goes on and on.

Sometimes life is fair; sometimes it is not. You don't need any advice about the subject when life is fair. You do a pretty good job of reacting to fairness.

What do you do when life isn't fair? Do you focus on reasons or results?

Or do you use the life-isn't-fair excuse to excuse your results? In certain cases, you'd be correct.

But being right doesn't really help much when life isn't fair. But in my experience, life isn't fair doesn't automatically doom you to failure.

- Is it fair to have to stop at a red light when you are late for a meeting? No.
- Is it fair to be behind someone with a large order at a Dunkin' drive-through? No.
- Is it fair to have a flight delayed on your trip back home? No.
- Is it fair to be passed over for a promotion you deserve? No.
- Is it fair to have your computer crash at a critical time? No.

The list is endless of the unfair things that happen, and some happen every day.

Now let's make a list of all the accomplishments that have been achieved while whining and pouting about how life is unfair.

I'm waiting.

Okay, let's make a list of all the good things that have happened while angry and complaining about how life is unfair.

I'm still waiting.

The point is, if you dwell on the unfairness of life, you are just dwelling and not living.

If you've never heard of Jim Thorpe, get ready to learn about someone who overcame a truly bizarre instance of "unfairness" and went on to become a champion.

From Wikipedia:

James Francis Thorpe (Sac and Fox (Sauk): Wa-Tho-Huk, translated as "Bright Path";[4] May 22 or 28,[2] 1887–March 28, 1953)[5] was an American athlete and Olympic gold medalist.

A member of the Sac and Fox Nation, Thorpe was the first Native American to win a gold medal for the United States in the Olympics.

Considered one of the most versatile athletes of modern sports, he won two Olympic gold medals in the 1912 Summer Olympics (one in classic pentathlon and the other in decathlon).

Amazing athlete: To say Jim Thorpe was a great athlete would be an understatement. He played Major League Baseball in the National League for the New York Giants. He played in the National Football League for the Canton Bulldogs. (Canton is the site of the Professional Football Hall of Fame and had a team in the NFL.) He was also a pretty good basketball player.

1912 Olympics: But he is most famous for participating in fifteen different events during the 1912 Summer Olympic Games, the pentathlon (five events) and the decathlon (ten events). He won eight of the fifteen and earned a gold medal in each event.

The pentathlon was created based on the skills needed by a battlefield courier: fencing, shooting, swimming, 200 meters, and horseback riding and was included in the 1912 Olympic Games for the first time.

The decathlon's ten events included the pole vault, high jump, long jump, javelin, shot put, discus, 110-meter hurdles, and the 100-meter, 400-meter, and 1,500-meter races. (Caitlyn Jenner became famous as Bruce Jenner for winning the decathlon at the 1976 Olympic Games for the historians in the crowd.)

Last-minute crisis: Just prior to the start of the 1,500-meter race, he reached into his bag to pull out his shoes, and they were missing. This was the last event, and the winner of the race would win the gold medal for the decathlon.

There are different theories about what happened to his shoes and why they were missing or who took them or what happened, but Jim Thorpe had a matter of minutes to get to the starting line and didn't have shoes.

He frantically went to his teammates and asked if they had any extra shoes.

The stories vary, but one version says that someone had a single shoe, but it was too small, but he squeezed his foot into it anyway.

Legend also says that he found another shoe in a trash bin, but it was too big, and he had to put on a couple of extra socks to make it fit.

Then he went out and competed against the greatest athletes in the world and won the race. Wearing the same shoes, he won the gold medal in the pentathlon the same day.

Was it fair for Jim Thorpe to have his shoes disappear minutes before an Olympic event?

No. And if my shoes are stolen before a race, I probably won't win it (Come to think of it, I probably won't win a race with my own shoes.)

The story, however, is a reminder that you don't have to give in to the excuses that can hold you back. So what if life hasn't been fair? What are you going to do about it today? (It's always today, isn't it?)

Whatever you started with or without this morning—stolen shoes, ill health, failed relationships, or something else—that doesn't have to stop you from running your race.

You will experience more success in life if you can get over the excuses and get on with moving ahead.

You can focus on reasons, or you can have results, but you generally cannot have both.

Image and Results

One of my bread-and-butter mentoring themes over the years has been my belief that more often than not, the  formula for success depends 50 percent on image and 50 percent on results.

Few people would argue with the concept of image and results being important, but most would have their own idea of the percentages that should be ascribed to each one.

Then of course, there is the example of the Oscar-winning actor slapping the comedian for offending his wife. There are lots of questions about this one. Did the comedian know? Was the wife really offended?

What good does a slap do? (What good has a slap ever done, anywhere, by anyone to anyone else, except athletes getting butt-slapped on the field.)

In the Oscar-slapping situation, both image and results are impacted. The actor's image suffered greatly, with labels of inappropriate violence, etc. On the other hand, the comedian's tour showed impressive results with an exponential increase in ticket demand. (In Boston, tickets went from $45 to more than $800 per seat in the secondary market.)

My experience is that most people, including me, focus a little too much on either image or results and wonder why they were not more successful in a specific endeavor without attributing the level of success to the level of balance between the two.

I think that is because too much emphasis on image (you phony!) or too much focus on results (you cut-throat) doesn't work well and impacts both image and results negatively.

Since we started this with an actor reference, consider the occupation and the fifty-fifty rule. An actor needs a certain image to fit the part but also needs to produce results like a great portrayal. But think about everything that hinges on the right combination of image and results.

Think of all the things that have to balance image and results.

- Clothing needs to be warm in the winter but also needs to look _____.
- Makeup needs to hide (?) but also needs to look_____.
- Cars need good mileage but also need to look _____.
- Homes need to be weatherproof but also need to look _____.

The list could go on and on, and no matter what thing you put in the sentence, there will always be two needs in it. It needs to perform, and it needs to look_____ when it does.

The same applies to companies and individuals.

I have a longtime aversion to wearing spandex leggings. In this context, while they may produce the desired results, too many people wear spandex who really should know better because it doesn't help their image.

The analogy that I've used for years to illustrate the difference between image and results is a bacon-and-egg breakfast. (I know, I have a lot of food analogies but no allergies.)

If you took two perfectly prepared bacon-and-egg breakfasts with four crisp slices of thick cut bacon, two large eggs, over easy, buttered wheat toast, and home-made home-fried potatoes and put the ingredients for one of the breakfasts into a blender, whipped it up, and poured it on a plate, both breakfasts:

1. Would cost the same for the ingredients
2. Would have the same nutritional value
3. Would take the same time to consume
4. Would fit on the same plate
5. Would have the same caloric content

Only the image would be different.

- An employee in a dirty ripped shirt could provide excellent service in any occupation, but image wise, there is usually a problem with that look.
- Paper plates project a different image than fine plate ware but can have identical impact on a meal.
- A Honda automobile may in fact be better constructed than a Cadillac, but the image isn't quite there.

The point is that the reason I personally attribute 50 percent of success to image is that image can have a much bigger impact on decision-making than results and, in many cases, impacts judgment far more.

People may be hired and promoted based on their image, but achievement is based on results. A wine we try is based on its image but continuing to drink it is based on taste.

Not that I actually remember, but dating selections may be based on image in a big way, but lasting relationships are based on results.

So what's the best way to balance image and results? I like to think of it this way: Results are what you do; image is how you do it. Want to improve your image? Focus on how. Want to improve your results? Focus on what. Want to stand out? Focus on image and results in equal measure, and you are more likely to be labeled a performer because you get things done and look appropriate doing it.

Since results are relatively objective and can be validated or documented, the hardest part is identifying the image part of performance.

The best way to do that is to give someone you trust permission to share insights about your image. Not always fun, not always positive, but always valuable.

An Umbrella Matrix

It doesn't matter whether it is shopping, exercising, eating, leading, reading, seating, driving, diving, singing, clinging, paying, borrowing, loaning, smelling, selling, wheeling, dealing, stopping, or popping, the when of taking action has an enormous impact on the outcome.

To illustrate, I like to use the simple act of buying an umbrella when you need one.

You only have three choices, and there are only three times you can buy one.

You can buy an umbrella before it rains.

You can buy an umbrella while it is raining.

You can buy an umbrella after it rains.

The same simple act or activity has very different consequences that are worth understanding.

Let's take a look at each one in a little bit of detail.

BEFORE IT RAINS

What if you are looking for an umbrella the day before the weatherman predicts you will need one. (Editor's note: meteorologist is the only occupation where being wrong is 100 percent blamable on the computer model or the Great Lakes.)

Availability? Unlimited: No lines, umbrellas everywhere: Macy's, Kohl's, Walgreens, CVS, and more. Walk in, decide on the color and style, grab what you want, and get safely and dry to your car. Sweet. No one will look at you funny, and you will probably have a smirk on your face because you acted.

Expense? On sale: There is no guarantee, but if an umbrella is ever going to be on sale, it will be a dry day, when the merchant wants to deplete the supply of those damn umbrellas. Now of course if the merchant watched the same TV weather as you did, they might be full price, but probably not.

Dryness? Totally dry: Logic tells you that if you buy the umbrella before it rains, you'll have it handy when it rains, and voilà! You'll be dry. (I used to know what voila meant. Can anyone help me?)

Anxiety? Low: No hurry, no lines, no water on your hair. What could be more relaxing?

Reputation? Good planner: "Oh, look, s/he planned ahead and has an umbrella. Obviously, a good planner."

Leadership? Commended: Maybe not additional accolades, but surely any criticism of your leadership has to be put on hold. You already have your umbrella? Wow! Remember, *lead* means being in front, showing the way, etc., etc.

Efficiency? High: No hurry, no lines, very little time spent.

Choice? High: The selection will be maximized since no one else has bought an umbrella or is looking for one. What could be better?

Quality? Possible: Depending on where you go, you can buy the most expensive or least expensive umbrella you want; your call. You want a cashmere umbrella? Look for one before it rains.

WHILE IT IS RAINING

What does this look like when it is raining? It is very different and not as much fun.

Availability? Depleted: There is no guarantee that there will be any umbrellas left at your first stop, and you may have to make additional stops to find one. Each stop gets you a little bit wetter.

Expense? Not on sale: Anyone who discounts umbrellas while it is raining is not part of the capitalist system and has probably never heard of the concept of supply and demand and will never attend a Taylor Swift concert as a result.

Dryness? Partially wet: You may enjoy being partially wet or not. The alternative is to search for a store in a covered mall or with underground parking. Good luck.

Anxiety? High: There is a double-anxiety factor when buying an umbrella in the rain. First, you might be anxious about getting wet on your way into the store, and then you might be anxious about the store selling out of umbrellas. Ouch.

Leadership? Questioned: It is hard to look graceful or like a leader running in the rain. Of course, if it is a romantic walk in the rain, that's different. But running in the rain into Walgreens without an umbrella? Not a good look for a leader.

Efficiency? Lowest: Both before it rains and after it rains, you can sort of take your time, but when it is raining, you lose all sense of focus and priority. Nothing matters except getting that damn umbrella, no matter how many stops it takes.

Choice? Risky: During the rain, you get what you get. There is no chance of resupplying with a more appropriate color or design. You are concerned only with function and not style, so whether there is a poodle on the umbrella or Superman logo on it, doesn't matter.

Quality? Secondary: So you run into the store, getting wet on the way. You find the cheapest piece of fabric with the flimsiest frame holding it into umbrella shape. Are you going to leave it there and get wet again going back to the car? I don't think so. You are out of luck and need to take what you can get.

AFTER IT RAINS

Okay, so it rained, you were wet, and now you have woken up and are planning for the next rain event. Good for you. Here's what to expect.

Availability? Limited: If you are looking for an umbrella after it rains, there may not be one readily available, depending on the rain and the number of other people who didn't plan ahead. It may take you more time to find the one you want.

Expense? May be on sale: Immediately after the rain, it is unlikely that umbrellas will be on sale, unless the ones with purple polka dots didn't sell well. It may cost you more out of pocket to find the one you want or even one you don't want.

Dryness? Very wet: The purpose of obtaining an umbrella was to be dry during the storm, but buying an umbrella after the fact is right there with missing the boat and locking the barn door.

Anxiety? Too late: You can't get the feeling back of those anxious moments when you knew you were about to be drenched but had no choice but to run in the rain to the car or the store or the school. Anxiety takes a toll on anyone.

Leadership? Ignored: Let's face it, you don't look very good to those who look up to you when you go through a storm getting wet. It is hard to look up in the rain anyway. It may cost you some credibility if you don't protect yourself in a storm.

Efficiency? Low: It is hard to make a case that your behavior was efficient. I believe that an earlier metaphor involved locking the barn door. Since I don't have a barn and have never been on a horse, I don't use that one, but you understand.

Choice? Variable: As referenced, you may have your choice of purple polka dots or football graphic or Mickey Mouse on the umbrella or more. This is for sure: your choices will be limited after the umbrella stand has been picked over.

Quality? Limited: Is the best quality the last one selected in pickup sports or for a committee or for a political office? Getting to choose late always means quality is a crapshoot.

The soon-to-be world-famous matrix is filled in above. Comparing the options, it would appear that one of the choices makes the most sense. Not only that, but it also makes the most sense 100 percent of the time.

The next time you get wet, remember, *when* you do something can have significantly different.

Everyday Greatness

What is greatness anyway?

Do a great steak and a great kid and a great wine and a great brother and a great car and a great company and a great game and a great volunteer and a great shower and a great day and a great computer and a great event and a great shirt and a great show and a great zoo and a great race and a great book and a great movie

and a great concert and a great beer and a great school and a great doctor and a great friend and a great flight and a great golf course and a great hairdresser and a great deal and a great trip and a great teammate and a great boss and a great office and a great fisherman and a great meeting and great shoes all have something in common?

If we want to be a great _____, what do we need to do? Greatness, to me, has three factors.

Greatness Means A Higher Standard.

However you contribute, and to whatever or whoever you contribute, it means setting a higher standard for you. In all the examples above that are modified by the word *great*, that word clearly means not average at a minimum and unbelievable at a maximum.

Sometimes we settle for less than great because we are too busy or too stressed or too tired or too lazy. We know when we move to a higher standard, because we can't avoid knowing we've moved to a higher standard, because we are proud. Higher standards mean more pride, and that feels good.

So the first criterion for greatness is not settling today for what was okay yesterday.

It could be the cleanliness of the trunk of your car or how you treat your significant other. It could be your effort or your output.

If you want to be great, raise your own bar. Greatness means deciding that good enough is not enough.

"Great" Means "Better."

Greatness means facing reality and reacting to it in a positive manner.

It means looking at the hard cold facts of your situation, and some of those facts may be revealed by a mirror.

Face it, none of us lead a perfect life with a perfect job and a perfect boss and a perfect family. That is not a revelation. No one is perfectly motivated, disciplined, and dedicated. At least no one I've met.

What leads to greatness is honestly looking at your situation and deciding to take action to react to your environment and, in many cases, to proact to your environment.

It could be that no one is calling you back (boo-hoo).

It could be that you just lost your best volunteer or client because she moved (oh my).

It could be that your car needs major repair work (oh ——).

It could be that your significant other doesn't appreciate you enough (likely?).

Greatness is not achieved because of the lack of obstacles; it is achieved by overcoming obstacles.

Greatness is rarely achieved by people placed in perfect situations with no problems or issues. Lots of people give up; lots of people quit. There is rarely greatness in those behaviors.

Don't think you won't have obstacles in the upcoming year—you will. Get ready now to have a mindset to overcome them. Face the hard cold facts and act. Good enough is not enough to overcome obstacles; it is good enough, at best, to maintain the status quo, and even that isn't a certainty.

"Great" Means "Action."

Greatness means working hard at something without supervision.

Can you think of a better compliment you could give someone other than you work hard when no one is watching?

Chances are, you've never said those words because the people who work hard without supervision are the kinds of people who don't need anyone to compliment them.

How could you possibly achieve greatness by only working hard when someone was watching? It doesn't make sense and doesn't happen often. Good enough is not enough.

"Great" Means "Work."

If you combine the three criteria, being great means working hard at something when no one is watching as you've faced up to the hard cold facts of your situation and decided to act in a positive manner because you've set a higher standard for yourself.

I think that is something we all can do, if we decide good enough is not enough, and we are striving for everyday greatness.

Effort, Progress, Results

There is an unwritten or
unspoken mindset about evalu- **Effort. Progress. Results.**
ating performance that almost
everyone follows but very few ever articulate. I think it is an unwritten rule because people are usually not even aware that they are evaluating performance using effort-progress-results method.

And if those judging aren't aware of this model, it is likely that those being judged are equally unaware.

The mindset occurs in the business world, in family life, in politics, and in other aspects of life where evaluation is important.

The phrase "leaders and evaluators" is used because much of the time, judgment doesn't come from a leader but from a peer, a significant other, a child, a neighbor, a client, a customer, or a government official or agency.

Always Looking at Two Things

Leaders and evaluators judge performance on two things, but those two things regularly change for the same task or activity.

The two things at the start of an assignment, project, or position, and most of the time and in most situations, judgments are primarily, if unofficially, effort and progress.

But after a while, the two things change because effort is less important to the leader or evaluator, and judgment morphs to analyzing progress and results.

The two things change again after another while, when progress matters less than results, so the judging takes place on results and results.

Effort and progress. Progress and results. Results and results. That is almost the natural continuum in which evaluation of performance takes place.

The Effort and Progress Stage

This concept is fairly easy to understand and generally done with good awareness. Someone just starting out, whether that is as student teacher, an airline pilot, a bus driver, or a new team member is evaluated based on how much effort is put into the job or the learning and if progress toward the ultimate goal of competence or excellence is happening. Lots of patience is usually a characteristic of this judgment phase.

When I ran restaurants, at certain times, new service team members would wear a button that said "I'M TRAINING AND I'M TRYING," which is asking the guest to have patience and recognize the effort and the things being done right (the progress).

Remember, I am not claiming this is the correct model 100 percent of the time, only that it happens more often than not and, in many cases, is a good way to look at someone learning or doing a task for the first time or in a new situation.

Next Up: Progress and Results

After an indeterminate amount of time that varies with the task and the individual, leaders or evaluators drop from their judgment the effort part of the equation but are still focused on evaluating two things: progress and results.

Results replace effort. There are only so many fumbles or interceptions that a coach can tolerate from a quarterback or strikeouts from a slugger or errors in a report. The natural next stage is progress and results. Moving in the right direction and hitting the target replaces trying hard as the intuitive evaluation criteria.

Trying, especially if getting paid for performance, counts less, and progress is still important, but getting some results is an increasingly important part of the judgment.

Results and Results

Yes, these are two things, not one. There inevitably comes a point where leaders are not only not concerned with effort, but their reliance on progress as a determinant of performance declines as well, and they are still interested in two things, and they are results and results.

Results and results covers not only *what* was accomplished but *how* it was achieved. We all know there are ways to get results that are not considered good ways.

Leaders and evaluators feel that you've had time to learn, you've made progress, now it is time to deliver the results the way they should be delivered.

Leaders and evaluators do this, in my experience, subconsciously. You may have experienced a leader or an evaluator who had a very short effort-progress stage or a very long progress-results phase. Subconscious judgment, like implicit bias, is hidden beneath the surface and not really predictable.

As a Leader (or Evaluator)

It may sound strange, but there can be value in understanding that this may be how you think and actually recognizing when you flip from effort and progress to progress and results and/or from progress and results to results and results.

In my experience, you become less frustrated with your team when you are aware of this natural trend or less frustrated with your local restaurant or Dunkin' Donuts.

From time to time, based on the situation, I have shared with team members that this is how I evaluate their performance. It puts people on notice that there is a learning period, where progress matters, and then there is a period where effort doesn't matter because results are needed, and that is followed by a performance period where the effort and progress aren't in the picture because results are needed.

I don't think I am inventing a messaging system. I believe I am simply sharing what really goes on in many, if not most, situations.

As a Follower

The key concepts for a follower to recognize are:
That the patience shown to you at the beginning doesn't last forever.
That expectations of making some sort of noticeable progress are immediate.
That expectations of results and results are just around the corner.

As Yourself

Not sure if you remember that we also judge ourselves. I think we follow the same continuum. When we start something—for example, running long distances—we judge ourselves based on our effort (did I do the training miles?) and the progress (is my distance improving?).

We then switch our self-evaluation to progress (am I getting better?) and results (am I getting to the finish line in a reasonable amount of time?).

Finally, we judge ourselves based on results (what was my time or distance?) and results (how did I accomplish it?).

Translated to this discussion, we tend to stay planted in the effort-and-progress phase longer than we should ("I meant to, I was going to, I tried to"). But we jump quickly to results and results when evaluating others; for example, when a steak isn't cooked to our specifications at a restaurant.

Effort-progress, progress-results, results-results.

Awareness of these three phases, whether as a leader, an evaluator, or a follower, can help facilitate clarity of expectations. And when expectations are clear, performance is better, whether for a nuclear power plant operator or a dish machine operator. And after all, what makes us focus more than clear expectations?

EPILOGUE

A World-Class Mother

When loved ones pass away, it is never easy, no matter how old or the reason. When my ninety-two-year-old mom finished up her time here on earth, even though we always knew it wasn't too far away, it was still unexpected.

Her legacy includes seven surviving children and a lifetime of service and dedication.

I recently had the experience of a lifetime that capped a lifetime, and I had the unique opportunity to honor a final wish for my mom, a world-class mother. But let's start at the beginning.

My mom was raised by Uncle and Auntie when her parents couldn't afford to take care of her. Joseph and Louise Cummings were the personification of love, and our son is named after Uncle.

My mom and dad were married in 1950, and sure enough, the next year, I arrived in the world with little fanfare. As a first lieutenant in the United States Army, my dad was in Germany as part of the force occupying that country during the Nuremberg war trials.

After a year or so of single parenting, my mom and I joined Edward Ambrose Doherty in Germany and were there long enough for my sister Joanne to be born there.

That accounts for two of the eight Doherty children, with Kathy, Brian, Sheila, Susan, Paul, and Chris to follow. For more than seventy years, answering to Ma and Mom, she persevered as a parent, through good times and bad. I answered to the name Jimmy as a kid and always to my mom.

For almost forty years, she did double duty as Nana with six grandchildren: Joe, Kaleigh, Curtis, Shannon, Ryanne, and Grace. Along the way, my dad and her split, and instead of going back to her maiden name, she changed her last name to Cummings in honor of Uncle and Auntie.

For more than ninety-two years, she lived life on her terms. In recent years, she still lived in her own apartment, with daily wellness, social, cleaning, shopping visits from one or more of the five children who lived close enough to connect, until her condition took a turn for the worse, and she wrapped things up in hospice at South Shore Hospital.

As the oldest, I was assigned the task of delivering the eulogy at her wake, an assignment and challenge that I did not relish and had let-this-pass-from-me thoughts. But I knew that I needed to deliver for my brothers and sisters, not to mention my mom, who expected me to rise to the occasion.

I only had a few days—no directives from my late mom and no experience. So I did what I try to do in those pressure situations: I prayed and hoped that I could deliver a eulogy with two criteria: with mom watching, I wanted her to be proud, and I didn't want to be a buzzkill at her service.

I know, I know, by its very nature, a wake is a buzzkill. But I decided that I wanted people to smile during the eulogy.

On behalf of my brothers and sisters, who contributed to what follows, meet the legacy of my world-class mother.

This ends with how one of her final wishes was fulfilled, which brought some closure to my mind, my heart, and my spirit.

Catherine Cummings: A World-Class Mother

We'd like to share some things you may not know about our world-class mother so that you may leave here with insight into her legacy.

She was a world-class philosopher: Our mother could be profound on purpose but accidentally as well. One of her quotes was, "You lead a very, very interesting life, and it's all your fault."

She was a world-class host: She had a full house but one time took in a sister's friend who had no place to live. At Thanksgiving, we had friends or students or friends of friends—that kind of house.

She was a world-class duct-taper: She used duct tape to fix almost everything and wasn't limited to the traditional gray but also was fond of black tape and an occasional roll of blue. When she transitioned to a walker, we had to duct tape the edges of carpets in her apartment so her walker wouldn't catch. I think she liked the look. We used black.

She was a world-class early bird: If you were picking her up, she'd be waiting thirty minutes in advance. And if you were late by more than five minutes, you could be sure to hear, "Where have you been?" There was, of course, no good explanation.

She was a world-class seamstress: She made a lot of our clothes when growing up. She could sew anything.

She was a world-class coordinator: Getting a houseful of kids up for school at different times was complicated. Three different schools, one and a half baths. At Howard Street, we mostly slept on the second floor, and there were sets of steam pipes that ran through the first floor: one pipe with steam going up, and one with steam going down. To wake us up for school, she'd bang on the pipes under the appropriate room, alerting us that it was time to rise and shine.

She was a world-class stocking stuffer: She had stockings for kids, grandkids, and others on her mantle at Christmas. After moving from Howard Street, she never had a fireplace but always had a mantle for the Christmas stockings. She worked on them all year, and once Thanksgiving was over, she hung them in birth order.

She was a world-class gardener: Her rock garden in Braintree was a source of pride for her and attracted a lot of attention from the drivers on Howard Street. More than one fender bender took place out front as people slowed down to admire it and weren't paying attention.

She was a world-class Red Sox fan: As you know, she was an early riser and couldn't stay up for most of the games, so she'd watch *Red Sox Classics*, with games from the past twenty-five years, at 5:00 a.m. most mornings.

She was a world-class Patriots fan: She would have one of us call her to wake her up for a night game. She actually rode a bus to Buffalo for a Patriots game. Buffalo!

She was a world-class school sports fan: She attended a lot of events for the kids, from gymnastics to hockey to soccer.

She was a world-class hockey mom: Speaking of hockey, she froze her ass off at Ridge Arena for her sons in the '60s and '70s.

She was a world-class dog lover: She loved her dog Bella, who was the center of her world, and kept her youthful for years but loved all the family dogs.

She was a world-class punk rock fan: Only kidding. A typo.

She was a world-class furniture mover: Even at ninety-plus years old, we'd show up at her apartment, and she'd have moved something she shouldn't have. She used a walker and moved furniture. I know.

She was a world-class teacher: Some of her messages were:

- Good things come to those who wait.
- You're going to work the rest of your life. Pick something you like.
- Always say what you mean, but you don't have to be mean when you say it.
- Be honest. It is easier to remember the truth than a lie.

She was a world-class caregiver: At the emergency room at South Shore Hospital, because she was there so often with one of the kids, they knew her by name. She'd take stitches out at home. She also gave you a damp facecloth to suck on when you were hurt. Not sure why it helped, but it did.

She was a world-class nana: She loved her grandchildren and self-selected to be known as Nana, after flirting with Grandma.

She was a world-class Energizer Bunny: She said, "I wish there was an operation to take some of the 'go' out of me and give it to some lazy bastard lying on a couch."

She was a world-class mother: In closing, her spirit still lives on because she lived a very interesting life, and a lot of it was her fault, but a lot of it was our fault as well.

Rest in peace. Jimmy, Joanne, Brian, Sheila, Susan, Paul, Chris, and Kathy.

The Rest of the Story

A close connected friend was at our house on Christmas Eve Day, and I approached him about assisting with one of my mom's last wishes: to have some of her ashes spread on the field at Fenway Park.

So at the appointed date and time, I connected with my close connected friend, and we walked out to left field; I had the chance to go inside the Green Monster, Left Field Wall. We made small talk and talked about the Red Sox. I realized that neither one of us had done this before, and we were making it up as we went along.

I looked over the field, out to where two of my mom's favorites roamed for the Red Sox, Ted Williams, and Carl Yastrzemski. I walked out on the grass, unscrewed the cap on the small urn, and let her ashes drift down between the blades of grass—my mom was now forever a part of Fenway Park—as tears proudly streamed from my eyes.

It was done. I expressed my gratitude, and that of my siblings, for a favor we can never repay.

I had two assignments from my brothers and sisters after our mom passed: deliver the eulogy and honor your wishes and spread some of your ashes on the field at Fenway Park. I delivered, Mom, and I hope you are proud of me. Thanks for living an interesting life.

ABOUT THE AUTHOR

Ed Doherty is a Massachusetts native who has lived and worked all over the United States in his roles as a restaurant executive, leadership development expert, and volunteer. Best known for developing talented individuals into top performers, Ed's varied experience includes roles as vice president for a national company's $58-million region based in Los Angeles and San Francisco, years as the chief human resource officer of an eleven-thousand-employee company based in Memphis, and serving as president of a $22-million franchised restaurant group in Cincinnati. His volunteer experience spans decades with the March of Dimes, Phi Sigma Kappa Fraternity, his community, and his church.

Today Ed heads up Ambrose Landen LLC, a consulting firm that specializes in strategic planning, leadership development, and employee engagement in both the nonprofit and for-profit sectors.

One client hired him because in her words, "Everyone who works with him gets better."

Printed in the USA
CPSIA information can be obtained
at www.ICGtesting.com
LVHW091257230224
772520LV00001B/126